Regulatory Risk and the Cost of Capital

Determinants and Implications for Rate Regulation

Burkhard Pedell

Regulatory Risk and the Cost of Capital

Determinants and Implications for Rate Regulation

With 18 Figures and 13 Tables

Springer

Professor Dr. Burkhard Pedell
University of Stuttgart
Betriebswirtschaftliches Institut
Abteilung V – Lehrstuhl Controlling
Keplerstraße 17
70174 Stuttgart
Germany
burkhard.pedell@bwi.uni-stuttgart

ISBN-10 3-540-30801-6 Springer Berlin Heidelberg New York
ISBN-13 978-3-540-30801-0 Springer Berlin Heidelberg New York

Cataloging-in-Publication Data
Library of Congress Control Number: 2005938554

Springer is a part of Springer Science+Business Media

springeronline.com

Printed in Germany

Hardcover-Design: Erich Kirchner, Heidelberg

SPIN 11596783 88/3153-5 4 3 2 1 0 – Printed on acid-free paper

Foreword

One of the central objectives of the European Union is the liberalization of markets and, in particular, of utility sectors such as the telecommunications, postal services, and energy sectors. National regulatory systems and authorities are installed in order to control the transition process from monopolistic to liberalized markets. In this process, the determination of prices assumes a prominent role. As in the relevant network industries capital costs account for the largest share of total costs, this book addresses a central issue of (de-)regulation.

At the same time, a change in the concepts of cost accounting from a traditional, operation-based view, to a more market-based view can be observed in Germany. These trends form the background for the analysis contained in this book. Burkhard Pedell develops a comprehensive concept for the study of regulatory risk and its implications for cost-orientated rate regulation that is founded in state-of-the-art economic research. The concept includes the major variables of regulation that are relevant to the risk (adjusted cost of capital) of rate-regulated firms and investigates the interdependences between them.

Central problems such as the circularity between regulation and investors' expectations, the commitment of the regulator, the employed depreciation methods and their connection to the interest rate, the determination of the regulatory rate base and the capital market-based assessment of the cost of capital are discussed. Answers to all these problems are given building on modern economic theory and the findings of empirical research. Two prominent results concern the depreciation method and the regulatory rate base: It is shown that, in many situations, depreciation should not be based on historical costs but on used replacement costs. Convincing arguments emphasize that, in a system of rate regulation, the book value of assets, and not market value of capital, should be used in the regulatory rate base.

In this book, the problems associated with the assessment of risk (adjusted cost of capital) for rate-regulated firms are comprehensively discussed. It develops a theoretically and empirically well-founded concept for the determination of cost-orientated prices in such firms. The results presented in this book advance existing research and are well-suited to supporting the process of deregulation. Therefore, they will prove useful both to regulators in European and other countries as well as regulated firms.

Munich, January 2006 *Prof. Dr. Dr. h.c. Hans-Ulrich Küpper*

Acknowledgments

This book was accepted as a post-doctoral thesis by the Munich School of Management of the Ludwig Maximilian University of Munich, and benefited considerably from the support and encouragement given by a great number of individuals.

First of all I am very grateful to my post-doctoral supervisor Prof. Dr. Dr. h.c. Hans-Ulrich Küpper for his unfailing commitment to the project, for providing concrete help when difficulties arose, and for creating a very positive working atmosphere at his institute. Prof. Dr. Dr. h.c. Wolfang Ballwieser agreed at short notice to write the second review and made very helpful and detailed suggestions that have significantly improved this version of the book. The Munich School of Management provided me with the degree of trust and cooperation essential for long-term project work and made helpful suggestions during the project's early stages.

The participants of the post-doctoral workshop organized by Accounting Commission of the German Association of University Professors of Management gave me helpful feedback concerning my initial ideas while shedding light on the problems and hopes associated with a post-doctoral project during the course of a friendly and open discussion. Similarly, the discussion between the participants of the 27th annual meeting of the European Accounting Association in Prague helped me straighten out my line of argument in chapter 5.

Prof. Dr. Dr. h.c. Paul Kleindorfer and Prof. Dr. Howard Kunreuther received me with great hospitality as a post-doctoral fellow at the Risk Management and Decision Processes Center of the Wharton School at the University of Pennsylvania. Howard Kunreuther, together with Dr. Erwann Michel-Kerjan, directed my interest towards the interesting topic of governmental intervention in the context of terrorism insurance. Particular thanks go to Paul Kleindorfer who spent a lot of time discussing regulatory issues and helped me broaden and deepen my understanding of the fascinating subject of regulation enormously as well as focus my own work. He paved the way for many interesting discussions in the U.S. and vividly showed me through his own example that hard work should and can be great fun. The scientific and financial support of the Deutsche Forschungsgemeinschaft and the Fulbright Commission in relation to the post-doctoral fellowship at the Wharton School is gratefully acknowledged.

Many people provided me with helpful insights into the different issues discussed in the book, including Dr. Rainer Kiefer, Dr. Bente Villadsen, Jörg Wiese and Prof. Dr. Dres. h.c. Robert Wilson, to name just a few. My colleagues at the Institute for Production Management and Management Accounting in Munich proved extremely cooperative; while working on this book, Dr. Rouven Bergmann and Prof. Dr. Gunther Friedl in particular were always willing to share ideas and discuss problems, and became good friends.

Katharina Wetzel-Vandai, together with her team at Springer, handled the publishing process with admirable circumspection and patience.

Finally, while work should always be fun, it is never complete without a fulfilling private life. I would therefore also like to express my gratitude to my family and closest friends for the immense and unconditional support shown to me while writing this book.

Stuttgart, January 2006 *Prof. Dr. Burkhard Pedell*

Contents

1 Introduction

Investments in infrastructure are of paramount importance for the functioning of an economy. However, it cannot be taken for granted that an efficient level of infrastructure investment is attained. If utilities are owned by private investors and if at the same time their rates are regulated by the government or by governmental agencies, the regulatory regime is of crucial relevance for investment incentives and, accordingly, for the level of investment. Therefore, extraordinary care has to be exercised when designing as well as when changing a regulatory scheme; this holds true in particular during processes of market liberalization and deregulation.

The California energy crisis is a vivid example of how inconsistencies in the regulatory regime can lead to a shortage of energy supply and seriously endanger the financial viability of utilities.[1] There are indicators that the Scandinavian Norpool risks to face similar difficulties,[2] and also for the UK shortages already have been predicted.[3] Continental Europe has seen a decrease of investment over the last years, but so far no shortages of energy supply are expected.[4] In Germany, investment in electricity generation and distribution has continuously declined since 1984 except for a short period after the reunification.[5]

However, the extraordinarily hot and dry summer of 2003 in Europe has shown that the reserve margin in power supply in continental Europe decreases towards zero when hydro-electric and wind power plants fail and nuclear power plants cannot run to full capacity due to the heating of rivers that provide cooling water. In some countries, e.g. Italy, electricity had to be cut off completely on a few days. The blackout in the northeastern U.S. and Canada on August 14, 2003, left some 50 million people without power, and underlined the vulnerability of the North American power grid. It did not come as a surprise to experts, as investment in the grid did not

---

1 The reasons leading to the California electricity crisis are discussed in more detail in section 4.4.

2 Cf. Frankfurter Allgemeine Zeitung no. 38, February 14, 2003, p. 12.

3 Cf. Shuttleworth/MacKerron (2002, 26ff.).

4 Cf. UCTE (2002) and VDN (2002).

5 Cf. Karl (2003, 43).

keep pace with demand growth over the last ten years.[6] This very large blackout was followed by a series of blackouts in Europe during the summer of 2003. On August 28, 2003, a blackout during the evening rush hour paralyzed the London underground for more than half an hour.[7] Some three million people in Denmark and Sweden were left without electricity for several hours, after 20 percent of the electricity generation capacity had failed due to a series of technical defects.[8] On September 28, 2003, the last blackout in this series hit Italy, which is heavily dependent on power imports from other European countries. When thunderstorms caused damages to high-voltage lines and widely disconnected the Italian grid from the European network, parts of the Italian power supply collapsed for the better part of a day.[9]

The importance of adequate investment in infrastructure is emphasized by all these experiences. This view is shared by the European Commission, which estimates the investment needs for power generation capacity in the European Union, including acceding countries as well as Switzerland and Norway, to be 250 billion Euros until the year 2020, and aims to promote investment in the grid and generation capacity by a draft law presented on December 3, 2003.[10] The U.S. Energy Policy Act of 2005, signed into law on August 8, 2005, among other things, aims to promote investment in generation and transmission capacity by means of massive tax incentives.[11] Clearly, security of supply is not an absolute end in itself, but has to be traded off against the cost of providing this security when determining the adequate level of investment.[12]

---

[6] The Economist, August 21, 2003, interviewed several energy experts and came to the conclusion: "Sadly, the signs are that America's grid was ripe for blackout."

[7] Cf. Frankfurter Allgemeine Zeitung no. 201, August 30, 2003, p. 12. However, this blackout was not due to lack of investment in generation capacity or in the grid, as argued in spontaneous reactions, but was due to a faultily installed system of emergency power.

[8] Cf. Financial Times Deutschland, September 24, 2003; Frankfurter Allgemeine Zeitung no. 232, October 7, 2003, p. T1.

[9] Cf. Frankfurter Allgemeine Zeitung no. 227, September 30, 2003, p. 13.

[10] Cf. Frankfurter Allgemeine Zeitung no 279, December 1st, 2003, p. 11.

[11] Cf. Frankfurter Allgemeine Zeitung no. 175, July 30, 2005, p. 11.

[12] This point is also stressed by MacKerron/Lieb-Doczy (2003). Para. 1 of the German Bundestarifordnung Elektrizität (BTOELt) obliges electricity companies to ensure provision of electricity as secure as possible *and* at prices as low as possible. Clearly, these two conflicting objectives cannot be maximized simultaneously.

Investments of regulated utilities are usually characterized by a high portion of sunk costs; especially investments in energy, water, communication and transport infrastructure are highly irreversible. The high degree of irreversibility makes these investments potentially risky. At the same time, most infrastructure investment is characterized by economies of scale. Combined with irreversibility, this creates monopolistic bottlenecks[13] that call for some form of permanent governmental intervention in order to prevent the abuse of market power.[14] Examples of monopolistic bottlenecks are distribution networks for electricity, natural gas and water as well as the local loop in the fixed line telecommunications network, the so-called last mile.[15] If the way of regulation is taken by the government in order to discipline market power, retail pricing for consumers and access pricing for competitors to monopolistic bottlenecks are issues of central interest.

The outlined examples show that it is of the utmost importance to keep investment incentives alive by allowing investors an adequate rate of return including appropriate compensation for risk. With insufficient rates, private investors are reluctant to bear the investment risk, which would result in a correspondingly higher system reliability risk to be borne by consumers. The issue is even more important if, as in the case of electricity in the U.S. and in Europe, in the coming years large parts of the existing infrastructure will call for renovation or replacement. Incentives for new investment by investor-owned utilities only exist if it can be expected that investments will be profitable over their entire lifetime on average. Ultimately, this requirement cannot be ignored by any form of rate regulation; as a consequence rate regulation has to be orientated towards the long-run cost of the regulated firm.[16] As most regulated industries, such as telecommunications, transport and energy, are extremely capital-intensive, immense emphasis has to be placed on the determination of the cost of capital, made up of interest and depreciation, when setting the level of regulated rates.

The Bundeskartellamt, the German Federal Cartel Office, on February 19, 2003, ordered the Thüringer Energie AG (TEAG), an affiliate of the E.ON group, to immediately lower the rates charged to competitors for access to its grid. The decision was justified by the Cartel Office in particular

---

13 Monopolistic bottlenecks are characterized in more detail in section 2.1.1.

14 Possible objectives of rate regulation are discussed in section 2.2.

15 However, the local loop in telecommunications is exposed to increasing competition by substitutive technologies; see section 2.1.2.

16 Riechmann/Schulz (1996, 386) share the view that, ultimately, every form of rate regulation should be cost-orientated.

on the grounds that TEAG had inflated its access rates by using an excessively high cost of equity. The Cartel Office for the first time made use of the option to verify the cost calculations of a firm. According to the Cartel Office the lowering of rates will cut revenues of TEAG by approximately ten percent. Meanwhile numerous law-suits against electric utilities because of supposedly excessive rates are pending in court.[17] The decision of the Cartel Office was overruled by the Oberlandesgericht Düsseldorf [Higher Regional Court] on February 11, 2004, on the very grounds that the Cartel Office only has competences for monitoring abusive pricing policies, but not for auditing individual cost elements and calculation procedures.[18]

The Regulierungsbehörde für Telekommunikation und Post (RegTP),[19] the federal German Regulatory Authority for Telecommunications and Posts, lowered the interconnection rates that competitors have to pay to Deutsche Telekom AG (DTAG) by approximately 9.5 percent with effect from December 1st, 2003.[20] According to press reports, this will bring about a loss of sales volume for DTAG ranging in the dimension of a low triple-digit Million € amount.[21] These cases underline the fundamental importance of assessing the appropriate risk-adjusted rate of return for rate-regulated utilities as well as the dimension of the impact of regulatory rate setting on the revenue situation of regulated utilities. It is therefore all the more important that the regulator exercises special diligence when assessing the risk-adjusted cost of capital.

In the special case of rate-regulated firms, the risk heavily depends on the very design of the regulatory regime. Existing research in this field builds on one of two different approaches to regulatory risk. The first ap-

---

[17] For this decision, see Bundeskartellamt (2003, in particular 22ff.); see also Financial Times Deutschland, February 19, 2003.

[18] See the press release of the Oberlandesgericht Düsseldorf on February 12, 2004, available at www.olg-duesseldorf.nrw.de.

[19] In July 2005, when its responsibility was extended to include the regulation of electricity and gas, RegTP was renamed Bundesnetzagentur. In the following, the name RegTP is used, as all references are before that time.

[20] Rate regulation in the German telecommunications sector is regulated by the Telekommunikationsgesetz (TKG) [Telecommunications Act], by the Telekommunikations-Entgeltregulierungsverordnung (TEntgV) [Ordinance on rate regulation in the telecommunications sector], as well as by additional Verwaltungsvorschriften im Bereich Kostenrechnung [Administrative regulations of cost accounting] published in Amtsblatt 5/2001 (p. 647f.) of the RegTP. For the development of the German telecommunications sector over time, see Witte (2002).

[21] Cf. Frankfurter Allgemeine Zeitung no. 278, 29.11.2003, p. 15.

proach involves investigating how systematic risk, i.e. the covariance with a market portfolio as measured by the beta factor, is affected by regulation as compared to a non-regulated firm. According to the familiar buffering hypothesis,[22] established by Peltzman (1976), rate regulation acts as a buffer that protects a regulated firm against external shocks, and, consequently, reduces the risks a regulated firm is exposed to. In some cases, even the extreme view is supported that rate regulation eliminates all risks of the regulated firm. For instance, the German Federal Cartel Office, in its decision against TEAG, argues that TEAG is not exposed to any risk due to regulation, and, consequently, the risk-less interest rate should be used as the cost of capital.[23] Less extreme positions argue that risks are not completely eliminated by rate regulation, but that they are at least unequivocally reduced. For instance, the German Monopoly Commission, in a recent special report on the development of competition in telecommunications and postal services, argues with respect to the divisional cost of capital of DTAG that, in principle, risk is higher in non-regulated businesses as compared to regulated businesses. However, rate regulation takes away pricing flexibility from the firm, which might even increase the vulnerability to external shocks.

The second approach addresses asymmetric regulatory risks.[24] These are caused by regulatory measures that make the cash flow distribution of the regulated firm (more) asymmetric, in particular by regulatory measures that cut off the upper (and/or lower) tail of the distribution. Both approaches deliver an abundance of individual findings; however, a comprehensive concept of regulatory risk has yet to evolve.

Against this background, the following analysis aims at developing such a comprehensive concept of regulatory risk and integrating the existing theoretical and empirical patchwork. The focus of this investigation is (1) on explaining how the design of the regulatory system and process influences the risk of a rate-regulated firm, and (2) on analyzing how rate regulation and, in particular, regulatory risk affect the appropriate methods for the determination of the regulatory rate base and for the assessment of the adequate allowed rate of return. To this end, the major design variables of rate regulation are identified and systematized into three clusters: variables determining the scope of regulation, regulatory system variables, and regulatory accounting variables. The impact of these variables on the risk that a regulated firm is exposed to is thoroughly analyzed.

---

22 The buffering hypothesis is discussed in detail in section 3.3.2.

23 See Bundeskartellamt (2003, 23); this view is shared by the expert opinion of Zimmermann (2003, 49).

24 Asymmetric regulatory risk is discussed in detail in section 3.3.3.

Regarding the determination of the regulatory rate base, at the center of the debate is the question of whether the market value of capital or the book value of assets should be employed. While from a financial theory perspective it is clear that investors expect to earn an appropriate return on the market values of capital, international regulatory practice requires the book value of assets to be used. There is a deficit in the academic debate when it comes to detecting and analyzing explanations for this conflict and showing how it can be reconciled; this investigation contributes towards closing this gap. Furthermore, specific methodical issues concerning cost of capital assessment for rate-regulated firms are elaborated, i.e. the circularity of rate regulation, the sharing of risks between capital owners and rate payers, the length of the regulatory review period, the regulation of the capital structure as well as the conversion of a post-tax to a pre-tax WACC (weighted average cost of capital).

The results of the analysis can be used to explain observed differences in the cost of capital of regulated firms across industries, countries and time, as well as to set an appropriate rate of return in regulatory hearings, most notably when the regulatory regime undergoes major changes or when benchmarks of firms subject to a different regulatory regime are used. Furthermore, they can be used to improve the design and the implementation of regulatory systems.

The investigation is organized as follows (see Figure 1.1): In Chapter 2, fundamental elements of cost-orientated rate regulation are explained, i.e. models, objectives, the process, cost concepts and types of rate regulation. Furthermore, the role of the cost of capital is compared across different types of rate regulation, as well as with its role in non-regulated firms. Chapter 3 and chapter 4 analyze the impact of regulation on the risk of the regulated firm, with the cause and effect chain turned upside down. Starting from a descriptive framework of rate regulation and an analysis of the fundamental circularity and time-inconsistency problems, firstly the effects of rate regulation on risk (section 3.3) and secondly the direct and indirect transmission mechanisms (section 3.4) are investigated in detail. Thirdly, a regulatory control panel is developed that comprises individual design variables of rate regulation that, ultimately, are the causes of regulatory risk (chapter 4). Chapter 5 and chapter 6 show how rate regulation is reflected in the appropriate methods for the determination of the regulatory rate base and for the assessment of the adequate allowed rate of return. Chapter 7 is by way of conclusion.

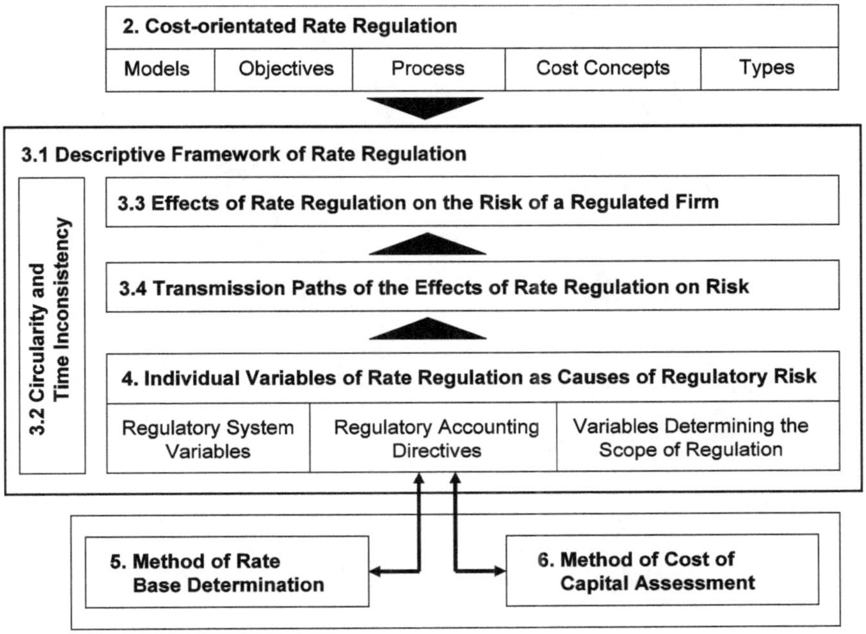

Figure 1.1. Organization of the analysis

2 Basic Elements for a Comprehensive Concept of Regulatory Risk – Models, Objectives, Process, Cost Concepts and Types of Rate Regulation

2.1 Characterization of the Two Basic Models of Rate Regulation

Regulation of rates, in principle, can be based on two different models: the monopolistic model and the competitive model.[25]

2.1.1 Monopolistic Model of Rate Regulation

The monopolistic model assumes subadditivity of costs due to economies of scale or economies of scope. This means that there is a natural monopoly, i.e. one firm is able to serve the complete market more efficiently than several firms. If all investment were reversible, according to the theory of contestable markets, this firm would be disciplined by potential competitors in its price setting behavior. However, if investment is irreversible,[26] relevant costs of the established firm that has already sunk its investments are lower than those of potential competitors, which means that market entry barriers are erected. Only the combination of subadditivity *and* sunkness of costs establishes a stable monopoly position, as depicted in Figure 2.1. In this case, the main objective of rate regulation is ensuring provision of regulated services at low prices while, at the same time, profitability of the regulated firm and incentives for replacement and new investment in the regulated business must be guaranteed if the services are to be provided by the private sector.

---

25 Cf. Carne/Currie/Siner (1999, 4ff.).

26 The application of a perfect contestability standard that assumes reversibility of investment to irreversible investment does not seem appropriate; see section 4.2.1. For the causes and effects of irreversibility of investment, see in more detail Pedell (2000, 69ff.).

	irreversibility / sunk costs	reversibility / no sunk costs
economies of scale/ natural monopoly	monopolistic bottleneck	monopolist disciplined by potential competitors
no economies of scale / no natural monopoly	competition of several active competitors	competition of several active competitors

Figure 2.1. Characteristics of monopolistic bottlenecks[27]

The balancing of interests between regulated utility and consumers is at the core of the discussion about objectives of monopoly regulation. It is aimed at preventing the abuse of monopoly power, while maintaining the benefits of economies of scale. If a universal service obligation without (or with restricted) scope for price discrimination is imposed on the monopolist, competitors have the chance for cream skimming, i.e. they compete for the consumers whose costs are below the uniform price set by the regulator. For this reason, the government can decide to protect regulated monopolists against competition, e.g. by demarcation contracts that grant them regional monopolies without competition in exchange for a universal service obligation, as had been the case in the German energy sector until the liberalization in 1998. A similar scheme had been established by the so-called regulatory compact in the U.S. energy sector.[28]

2.1.2 Competitive Model of Rate Regulation

In contrast, rate regulation in the competitive model principally aims at simulating competition or actually admitting and stimulating competition. Complete or partial opening up of hitherto protected monopolies for competition is what is usually understood as deregulation.[29] In this case, the regulator has to make sure that rates are set at least at such a level that current acquisition costs of assets as well as operating expenditures and return on investment are covered. Otherwise, new competitors have no chance to

27 Cf. Knieps (2001, 33).

28 For a more detailed discussion of universal service obligations, see section 4.3.1.

29 In the majority of cases, deregulation brings about only modifications, not a complete removal of regulatory interventions. For the difficulties associated with the concept of deregulation, see Crew/Kleindorfer (2001, 2ff.).

enter the market. This is done to avoid predatory pricing of the incumbent monopolist. Conversely, the established firm loses market share to an unreasonable extent if the regulator sets it rates way above the competitive level. The risk of competitive distortion is especially large if the incumbent firm is unilaterally subject to rate regulation and new competitors have pricing flexibility, i.e. if there is an asymmetric scheme of rate regulation.

In most network industries, the incumbent firm(s) has (have) monopolistic bottlenecks that are characterized by economies of scale and irreversibility of investment, as depicted in Figure 2.1. Examples are the last mile in telecommunications (local loop)[30] as well as local distribution networks for electricity, natural gas and water. Duplication of these monopolistic bottlenecks would not be efficient from the perspective of the overall economy. In order to induce fair competition in the rest of the network, non-discriminating access to these essential facilities has to be granted by rate regulation. As soon as competition is working, rate regulation should be confined to monopolistic bottlenecks.[31]

In most instances, high access prices will advantage a vertically integrated incumbent regulated utility, as this makes it more difficult for new entrants to compete in the retail market.[32] Therefore, it is not surprising that the level of rates and, in particular, the adequate allowed rate of return are contentious between regulator and regulated utility, particularly in the case of access pricing. If competition is admitted in the retail market, too high a level of retail rates may even represent a risk for the incumbent regulated utility, as it becomes more vulnerable to competition.

2.2 Systematization of the Objectives and Principles of Rate Regulation

Fundamentally the aim of rate regulation is the prevention of abuse of market power in monopolistic bottleneck areas. When setting concrete

---

30 However, copper wire house connections in telecommunications are increasingly exposed to substitution competition by wireless technologies (wireless local loop), by internet telephony (voiceoverIP) as well as by data transfer technologies over the power cable (powerline) and the TV cable.

31 See Knieps (2001, 101ff.), who argues that regulation should be phased out as soon as competition is working.

32 If the incumbent utility is not active in the retail market, the case is less clear cut, as the revenue increasing direct effect of higher access prices has to be traded off against the indirect effect on volume.

rates, the regulator can be guided by different objectives[33] that can be classified into efficiency and equity objectives (see Figure 2.2). Efficiency refers to the utilization of existing investments (static efficiency), to the incentives for new investment (dynamic efficiency) as well as to the institutional implementation of regulation itself (institutional efficiency).

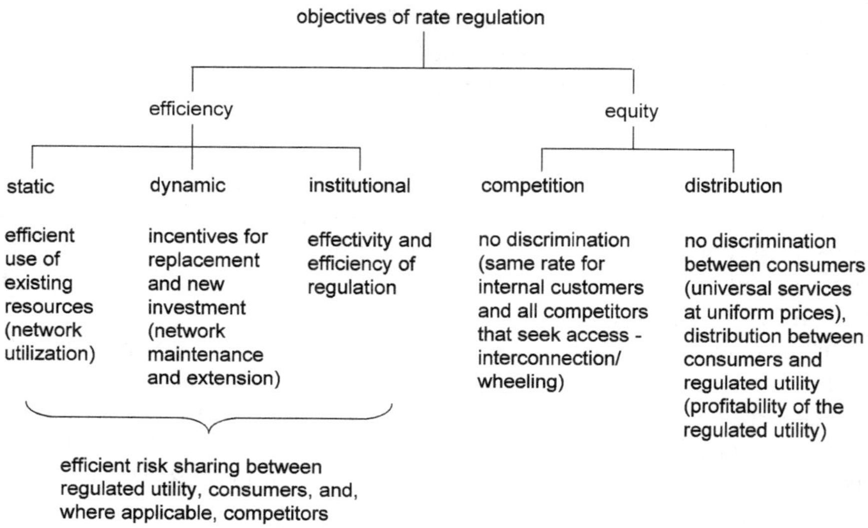

Figure 2.2. Objectives of rate regulation

As is well known, there is a potential conflict between static and dynamic efficiency. As soon as a regulated utility has irreversibly invested in specific assets, the regulator has an incentive to lower the utility's rates to the level of short-run decision relevant costs in order to improve efficiency from a static perspective. This improves the capacity utilization rate of the network infrastructure already in place, as the regulated utility has no incentive to reduce the provision of services from existing investments. However, incentives for investing in maintenance and extension of the network are extinguished.[34] In order to keep them alive, it is of paramount importance that capital owners of the regulated utility can expect to earn an appropriate return on their investments. If there is uncertainty about the adequate risk-adjusted rate of return, and if the regulator attaches most im-

[33] For the objectives of rate regulation, see also Bromwich/Vass (2002, 1678).

[34] This is of direct relevance for the discussion of time-consistency of rate regulation in section 3.2.

portance to dynamic efficiency, the cost of capital should be set rather too high than too low.[35] The promotion of competition is directed towards improving compliance with the static and dynamic efficiency criteria. Aside from these fundamental efficiency dimensions, institutional efficiency of regulation itself can be explicitly distinguished, even if, in principle, it is already covered by static and dynamic efficiency.

Equity refers to the prerequisites for fair competition[36] or to distributional issues. As discussed in the previous section, fair competition requires non-discriminating access to monopolistic bottleneck facilities. Distributional equity refers to the distribution between the regulated utility and consumers, i.e. the level of rates, as well as between different consumer groups, i.e. the structure of rates. Distribution between consumer groups is affected, for instance, if the regulator imposes a universal service obligation without price discrimination on a regulated utility, as is the case for fixed line connections in Germany that have to be provided at a uniform monthly fixed rate by DTAG. The requirement that the regulated utility be profitable can not only be justified on the grounds of dynamic efficiency as referred to above, but also on the grounds of distributional equity between consumers and the capital owners of the regulated utility. In most countries, the regulator does not have the complete discretionary freedom to determine the distribution between consumers and capital owners, but is bound by law to respect the property rights of capital owners. In Germany, for instance, protection of property rights is explicitly codified in the Basic Constitutional Law.

The different dimensions of equity can be complementary to or conflicting with the efficiency dimensions, depending, among other things, on the underlying model of rate regulation. Non-discriminating access to monopolistic bottleneck facilities clearly is only relevant in the competitive model, and works towards efficient utilization of existing networks, while possibly lowering incentives for investments in maintenance and extension of these networks. Universal service obligations with uniform rates inhibit the setting of Ramsey prices, which requires price discrimination according to price elasticity of demand.[37]

---

35 Cf. CAA (2001, 33).

36 This does not refer to the monopolistic bottleneck that, by its very definition, is not a competitive area, but to the upstream and downstream supply chain levels that are dependent on the service of the monopolistic bottleneck.

37 As a consequence, the resulting solution will even fall short of the second best solution of static efficiency that in theory is established by Ramsey prices. The first best solution would set prices to marginal cost. However, these prices are not sufficient to cover total cost in the case of economies of scale. Ramsey

The objectives of rate regulation allow a number of underlying *principles* to be deduced. Incentives for new investment are only present when equity providers expect their investment to be profitable over its whole economic lifetime. All types of rate regulation must take this latter requirement into account, and consequently rate regulation should be *orientated* towards the *long-run costs* of the regulated company.[38] For the purposes of rate regulation, *verifiability* of costs by the regulator is of the utmost importance.[39]

2.3 Characterization of the Cost-Orientated Rate Setting Process

Under a cost-orientated rate regulation regime, the regulator ideally proceeds in the following three steps[40] as illustrated in Figure 2.3: Firstly, the *regulatory rate base* is determined, which, in principle, comprises all investments that have been made to provide the regulated service.[41] Secondly, the adequate *allowed rate of return* on this rate base is assessed based on the risk-adjusted cost of capital. Thirdly, *regulated rates* are set in such a way that the allowed rate of return can be expected to be just about realizable. While the first two steps determine the upper limit of the total expected revenues, the last step establishes a structure of regulated rates. Differentiation of rates with respect to consumers, regions and hours as well as the allocation of joint and common costs to several regulated services are major issues that require demand aspects to be taken into consideration.[42]

---

prices minimize the welfare loss subject to coverage of total costs of the regulated utility by regulated rates. For a formal discussion of Ramsey prices, see Crew/Kleindorfer (1986, 17ff.).

38 Riechmann/Schulz (1996, 386) share the opinion that, ultimately, every form of rate regulation has to be cost-orientated; see also Ehrmann/Mellewigt (1997). Picot/Burr (1997, 265ff.) rank the significance of cost accounting for regulation somewhat lower, playing an important, but not the central role. For the rationale of a cost-orientated regulatory standard, see Bonbright/Danielsen/Kamerschen (1988, 109ff.).

39 Cf. Küpper (2002, 34).

40 Cf. Brigham/Tapley (1986, 16.5f.); Kahn (1988, 25/Iff.).

41 The determination of the regulatory rate base, potentially contentious issues associated with it as well as interdependences with the adequate allowed rate of return are discussed in chapter 5 and in Pedell (2003a).

42 For instance, Ramsey prices are set according to demand elasticity.

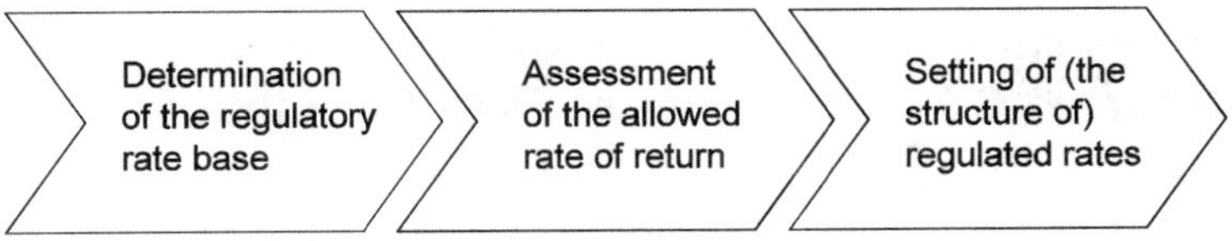

Figure 2.3. Cost-orientated rate setting process

These three steps represent a logical process; however they are not unilaterally dependent but interdependent. The determination of the regulatory rate base has an impact on the risk-adjusted cost of capital. For instance, the risk of the regulated utility depends on whether the regulatory rate base is determined on the basis of the actual, path-dependent quantity structure, or a hypothetical, improved quantity structure, and on whether the regulator reserves the right to disallow single investments that he deems not useful to be included in the rate base. Likewise, differentiation of rates can have a significant impact on the risk of the regulated utility, e.g. if competition is admitted, and if it depends on the scope of rate differentiation, how flexibly the regulated utility can react to market developments and, in particular, to movements of its new competitors.

As most regulated industries, such as telecommunications, transport, and energy, are extraordinarily capital-intensive, immense emphasis is placed on the determination of the cost of capital, made up of interest and depreciation, when setting the level of regulated rates. Orienting regulation to full costs implies that the average rate of the cost of capital should be used.[43] If it is to be feared that, as a result, investment decisions may be distorted to an unacceptable extent, the regulator may set different costs of capital for existing and new investments, thereby allowing differing levels of return to be earned.[44]

---

43 However, when making investment decisions regulated utilities will use marginal cost of capital just as non-regulated firms do. The cost of capital will be different in the case of each investment project and, in most instances, deviate from the (average) rate of return allowed by the regulator; cf. Brigham/Tapley (1986, 16.22).

44 The U.S. Federal Communications Commission for instance argues that different risks for existing and new services should be accounted for by using different levels of risk-adjusted cost of capital. At the same time, however, it admits that such a procedure might increase administration efforts to an unreasonable extent; cf. FCC (2003, 420, para. 683-684).

2.4 Comparison of the Role of the Cost of Capital in Different Cost Concepts of Rate Regulation

The objectives of rate regulation are reflected in the cost concepts employed by the regulator. Figure 2.4 gives an overview of regulatory cost concepts[45] and the role of the cost of capital in these concepts. If regulation is exclusively aimed at optimizing the utilization of existing assets, regulated rates theoretically must be based on short run marginal cost (SRMC). However, in the case of natural monopolies with economies of scale, the resulting rates are then not sufficient to cover total costs, and in particular, cost of capital is not included in SRMC. Therefore, this approach sooner or later inevitably results in the bankruptcy of the regulated utility.[46]

If rate regulation is aimed at ensuring the profitability of the regulated utility and the keeping alive of investment incentives, a long-term investment perspective must be adopted. Here, regulated rates are based on costs between long run incremental costs (LRIC) and stand-alone costs (SAC). LRIC are the costs that could be avoided if a certain amount of additional demand did not have to be served and if all inputs were completely flexible,[47] whereas SAC are the costs that would arise if a certain service was provided completely uncoupled from the other services supplied by a regulated utility. Clearly, SAC are at least as high as LRIC. In the case of gas transmission, for example, LRIC for a certain transmission capacity are those costs that are additionally incurred for a gas pipeline whose total capacity is incrementally enlarged by the capacity in question. SAC are the costs that are incurred for building an isolated gas pipeline for the transmission capacity in question. LRIC and SAC differ in the extent to which joint costs, or joint savings of costs due to economies of scale, are included. Returning to the example of gas transmission, the consumer of a certain transmission capacity partakes to the full extent in the economies of scale of gas pipeline construction and operation, when LRIC are employed, whereas he is completely excluded from participating in economies of scale when SAC are used.

---

45 Regulatory cost concepts are presented in detail by D'Almeida et al. (2000); utilityregulation.com (2003); see also Küpper (2002, 17ff.).

46 Hence the reason why Baumol/Sidak (1994, 34) call this approach a 'recipe for bankruptcy'.

47 Cf. Bromwich/Vass (2002, 1684).

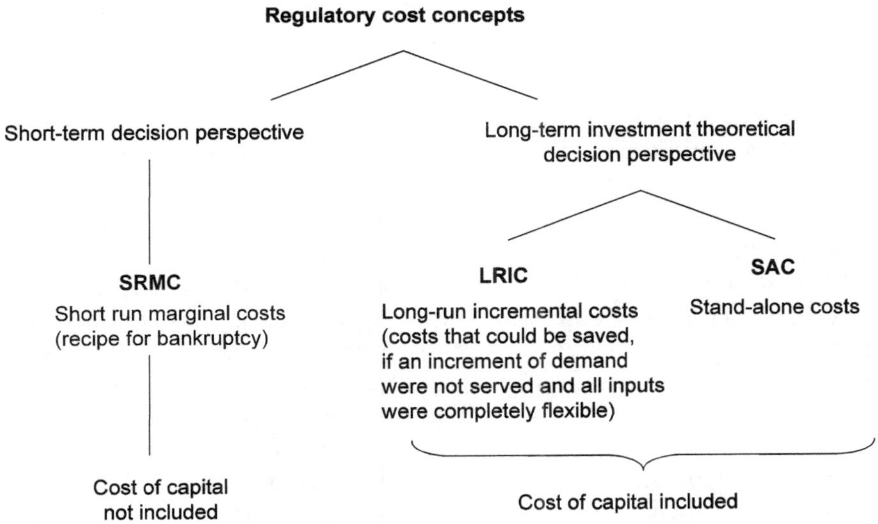

Figure 2.4. Regulatory cost concepts and cost of capital

By definition, only costs between LRIC and SAC are free from cross-subsidization, and these therefore should be employed for rate setting purposes.[48] It is not possible to choose a value between LRIC and SAC without any discretion. § 3 para. 2 of the German TEntgV specifies that long-run incremental costs for the provision of a service plus an adequate allowance for activity quantity neutral overhead costs, each including an adequate return on the capital employed, are to be used for rate setting in the German telecommunications sector.

48 Cf. Baumal/Sidak (1994, 61ff.). This so-called constrained market pricing approach can be interpreted as a third best approach to setting rates, with marginal cost prices being the first best, and Ramsey prices being the second best approach. The test involving the estimation of whether costs lie between LRIC and SAC is referred to as the 'burden test'; cf. Crew/Kleindorfer (2002, 10). For an extension to intertemporal pricing in connection with regulatory depreciation schemes, see Gunn (2003).

2.5 Comparison of the Role of the Cost of Capital Under Different Types of Rate Regulation

Rate-of-return regulation and price cap regulation are the poles of a spectrum of possible types of rate regulation.[49] In a regime of *rate-of-return regulation*, the regulator sets rates so that a certain target rate of return on capital employed is expected. Usually, this allowed rate of return is set equal to the cost of capital. In a first best world with perfect competition, where all non-regulated firms earn just about their cost of capital, this is clearly an appropriate approach. However, in a second best world without perfect competition, where non-regulated firms can earn on average above normal returns, i.e. returns above cost of capital, the very setting of the allowed rate of return of a regulated utility equal to its cost of capital might cause distortions of investment decisions.[50] Likewise the creation of incentives for technological progress might require a rate of return above cost of capital.[51] One major problem of rate-of-return regulation are the evidently poor incentives for efficient investment and operation. Therefore, in many instances, more incentive-orientated schemes such as price caps are used.

Price cap regulation[52] was developed and implemented first in the UK telecommunications regulation by the then Director of the Office of Telecommunications (Oftel) Stephen C. Littlechild. In a *price cap* scheme, the regulator puts a ceiling on rates, usually by referring to a weighted basket of regulated services. Essentially, the idea is that the regulated utility should be entitled to retain efficiency gains that drive costs below capped rates, and therefore have an incentive to increase efficiency. Price caps can be combined with price escalation clauses, e.g. by linking the cap to the Retail Price Index (RPI), and with targets for efficiency increases that involve the tightening of the cap over the regulatory review period by the so-called X-factor. These efficiency gains targets do not remain with the regulated utility but feed through directly to consumers. Indexation to the Retail Price Index and efficiency targets together yield the well-known (RPI-X)-formula. Price caps are usually set for a regulatory review period of two to five years and are thereafter revised by the regulator.[53]

---

[49] For a detailed overview of types of regulatory systems, see Vogelsang (2002).

[50] Cf. Kahn (1988, vol. I, 44).

[51] See the discussion about investment incentives in regulated industries and real options in section 3.4.2 and section 4.3.1.

[52] For the price cap approach and its use in the German telecommunications sector, see Picot/Burr (1996, 187ff.) and (1997, 269f.).

[53] In the German telecommunications sector, two years are common practice.

In principle, the actual costs of a regulated utility, including the cost of capital, do not have any influence on regulated rates during the regulatory review period unless the regulatory review process is reopened ahead of schedule.[54] However, when setting the initial level for a price cap as well as when revising efficiency targets, the regulator needs cost (of capital) information. If he fails to take into consideration the profitability of the regulated company when setting the price cap, he risks suppressing incentives for investment in maintenance and extension of the network. In reality, therefore, the difference between rate-of-return regulation and price cap regulation is simply a matter of degree,[55] and cost of capital *de facto* plays a central role in any system of rate regulation.

2.6 Comparison of the Role of the Cost of Capital and the Rate of Return in Regulated and Non-Regulated Firms

Table 2.1 compares the role of cost of capital and rate of return for regulated and non-regulated firms. While cost of capital in non-regulated firms is used as a hurdle rate to check for the profitability of investments, profitability of investments is assumed for rate-regulated utilities.[56] Rate of return of non-regulated firms is an uncertain quantity that capital owners have expectations of. The actual rate of return of rate-regulated firms is determined more or less by regulation, depending on the design of the regulatory scheme. In the hypothetical benchmark case of a perfect and continuous rate-of-return regulation, the actual rate of return always equals the allowed rate of return. In reality, the actual rate of return is subject to fluctuation even in systems of rate-of-return regulation, taking into account the inevitable adjustment lags for rates alone. In some instances, fluctuations can even be larger than without regulation, as a regulated utility does not have the flexibility to adjust its prices immediately and independently to changed conditions.[57]

---

54 Regulatory systems differ with respect to whether a premature reopening also can also be requested by a regulated utility or can only be initiated by the regulator.

55 See section 2.2, where it is argued that, in the longrun, every form of rate regulation has to be cost-orientated.

56 Brigham/Tapley (1986, 16.17) compare the capital budgeting process of rate-regulated and non-regulated companies; see also Grout (1995, 389).

57 See also the discussion of the buffering effect of rate regulation in section 3.3.2.

Table 2.1. Comparison of the role of cost of capital and rate of return in regulated and non-regulated firms

Criterion	Not rate-regulated	Rate-regulated
Profitability of investments	Profitability is checked	Profitability is assumed
Certainty of the actual rate of return	Expected rate of return that is uncertain	Rate of return more or less determined by rate regulation
Possible deviations between expected and realized rate of return	Upward and downward deviations of the realized rate of return	In some instances only downward deviations of the realized rate of return due to asymmetric regulatory behavior
Relation between (normal) rate of return and cost of capital	Rate of return equals cost of capital in perfect competition; rate of return above cost of capital in the case of competitive advantages	Normal rate of return has to be above cost of capital in some instances
Reference to the market	Market forces bring rate of return to its equilibrium, i.e. in the long-run to the level of cost of capital	Cost of capital assessment aims at simulating competition
Connection between cost of capital and prices / rates	Achievable prices determine rate of return	Cost of capital determines rates
Consequences of cost of capital assessment	Cost of capital assessment only affects realization of marginal investment projects	(Nearly) all rates are affected by the cost of capital assessed and employed by the regulator; more serious consequences of faults

The actual rate of return of non-regulated firms can usually deviate upwards or downwards from the expected rate of return. Rate-regulated utilities are exposed to a high degree of asymmetric risks.[58] E.g. due to political influencing, the regulator can claw back above normal returns without compensating in the reverse case for below normal returns. In this case, the normal rate of return has to exceed cost of capital in order to ensure a sufficient average rate of return on capital employed. The rate of return of non-regulated firms can lie more or less above cost of capital depending on

[58] For a detailed discussion of asymmetric regulatory risk, see section 3.3.3.

the degree of perfection of competition. In the long run, market forces bring down rates of return to the level of cost of capital. Rate regulation aims at mimicking this market result. Under rate regulation, cost of capital determines the setting of rates, whereas without rate regulation achievable prices determine the rate of return.

A particularly important difference in the role of cost of capital for regulated utilities as compared to non-regulated firms lies in the consequences of cost of capital assessment. Firms that are free to make their investment decisions and that do not suffer from capital budget restrictions will realize all investment projects whose net present value is positive, with cost of capital used as the discount rate and faulty assessment of (marginal) cost of capital only affecting the realization of marginal investment projects. This also holds true for the capital budgeting process of rate-regulated firms. However, in the case of rate-regulated firms, the cost of capital assessed by the regulator becomes relevant for investment decisions. The (in most instances, average) cost of capital employed by the regulator affects all rates and consequently the realized rate of return on all investment projects, and, as a result, faulty cost of capital assessment by the regulator has more serious consequences for investment behavior.[59] This is aggravated by the fact that rate regulation usually applies uniform cost of capital to all investment projects.[60]

2.7 Characterization of Regulatory Risk

Before analyzing in chapter 3 the impact of rate regulation on the risk of a regulated firm, the underlying concept of regulatory risk is characterized. As briefly outlined in chapter 1, existing research builds on one of two approaches to regulatory risk. The first approach investigates the issue of how systematic risk, i.e. the covariance with a market portfolio as measured by the beta factor, is affected by regulation as compared to a non-regulated firm. The second approach, in contrast, concerns the asymmetric regulatory risk caused by regulatory measures that result in the cash flow distribution of the regulated firm becoming (more) asymmetric, in particular as a result of regulatory measures that cut off the upper tail of the dis-

---

59 With respect to investments that are already completely sunk, only capacity utilization decisions, i.e. output level decisions by the regulated firm are directly affected by the rates that are set by the regulator.

60 Clearly, when valuations of entire firms are required, as is the case for example, when mergers or acquisitions are being considered, the cost of capital assessment has more than marginal consequences for non-regulated firms as well.

tribution, e.g. by not allowing all investments to form part of the regulatory rate base.[61]

In the following the understanding of regulatory risk employed throughout the investigation is characterized. Risk is usually defined in one of two ways, either as a negative deviation from a reference value or, in a broader sense, as the impact on the probability distribution of possible outcomes. In this analysis, it is the broader definition of risk that is used.

It is common practice to make a distinction between business risk and capital structure risk.[62] Business risk (also called cash flow risk) is a firm-level risk and captures the impact on the probability distribution of the cash flows of the entire firm. Capital structure risk refers to the risk incurred by the equity owners of a firm earning its residual income once the claims of debt owners have been met. The business risk of an entire firm is reflected in the risk that equity owners are exposed to and is determined by its capital structure. Both cash flow risk and capital structure risk are addressed in this investigation. The central theme, however, is cash flow risk. Also analyzed is the way in which the regulator influences the financing of the regulated firm, either by directly dictating capital structure or indirectly by changing financing incentives via rate setting or accompanying measures.[63] Furthermore, methodical issues regarding the capital structure used by the regulator for weighting the cost of equity and the cost of debt are discussed.[64]

Strictly speaking, the concept of regulatory risk employed in this investigation goes beyond pure cash flow risk and capital structure risk, as rate regulation repercussions on investment and financing behavior and on the flexibility of the regulated firm are included in the analysis. However, these repercussions are ultimately also reflected in the cash flows.

Finally, as far as the impact of regulation not on the overall risk but more specifically on the cost of capital is concerned, risk is confined to systematic risk as measured by the beta factor.[65]

---

61 For asymmetric regulatory risk due to disallowances see in detail section 4.2.3.

62 See, for example, Hax (1998, 199f.).

63 See section 3.4.2 and section 4.3.1.

64 See section 6.3.

65 See section 3.3.2.

3 Impact of Rate Regulation on the Risk of a Regulated Firm

Chapter 3 and chapter 4 contain an analysis of how the design of the regulatory system and process affects risk (adjusted cost of capital) of a rate-regulated firm. In section 3.1, a descriptive framework of rate regulation is developed. The fundamental problems of circularity and time-inconsistency are investigated in section 3.2. Based on this fundament, the cause and effect chain of the impact of rate regulation on risk is analyzed in the opposite direction of causality, from the possible effects in section 3.3, over the transmission paths in section 3.4, to the individual design variables of the regulatory control panel as causes in chapter 4. The theoretical analysis is supported by references to existing empirical research.

3.1 Development of a Framework of Rate Regulation for the Analysis of Regulatory Risk

The analysis of regulatory risk is systematized by the framework of rate regulation developed in Figure 3.1 that can serve as a basis for both theoretical and empirical analysis. The regulated firm and the regulatory commission are the two main actors in this framework. The regulated firm gives the commission *information* about its cost and demand. As discussed above, every regime of price regulation, in the long run, has to take into account to a certain degree the cost of the regulated firm in order to avoid investment distortions or situations of financial distress when regulating prices of the firm. Cost information is based on the accounting system of the firm. In the context of regulation, the main functions of the accounting system are the calculation of the operating expenses, as well as the determination of the rate base for calculating depreciation and imputed interest. To this end, the regulator sets an allowed rate of return that is supposed to equal the utility's cost of capital, usually assessed by using market data.[66]

[66] In addition, accounting data of competitors can be used as a benchmark, as is done under the comparable earnings standard; see Pedell (2004b, 86ff.).

The expected rate of return may differ from the allowed rate of return for numerous reasons, e.g. if not all investments are included in the rate base.[67] In addition, the commission usually uses market data for the assessment of cost of capital assessment.

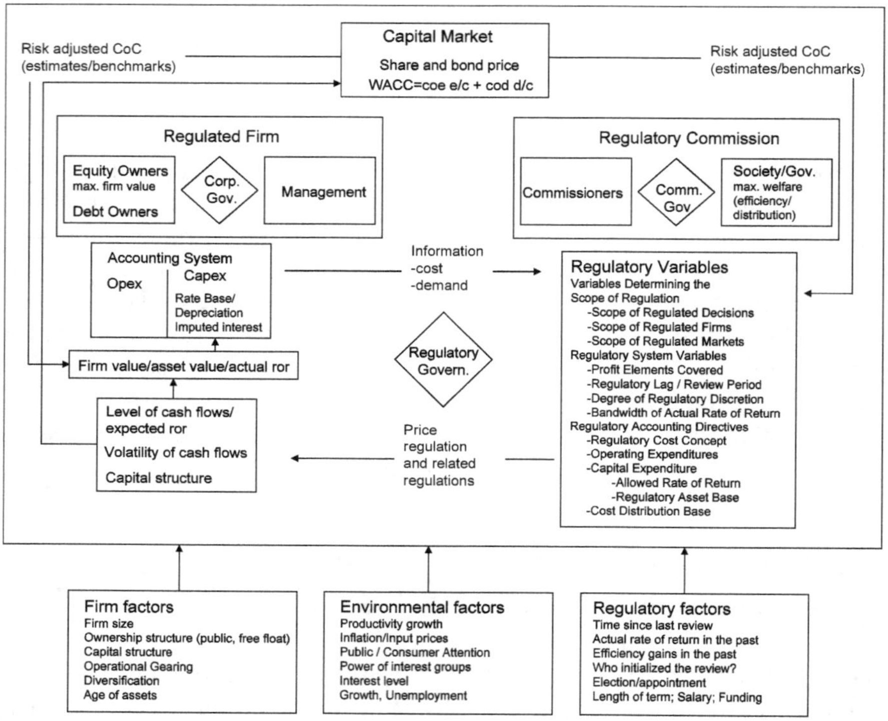

Figure 3.1. Descriptive framework of rate regulation

A regulatory regime consists of a multitude of *variables*, partly determined by the legislator, that can be grouped into variables determining the scope of regulated markets, firms and decisions, variables concerning the basic design of the regulatory system and processes, as well as accounting directives. These variables influence the level and the volatility of the cash flows of the firm as well as its capital structure. The capital market processes this information and values the firm, and, accordingly, determines its cost of capital. The individual variables are discussed in detail in chapter 4.

Since information asymmetries exist, above all regarding the cost for the different products or services of the regulated firm, *regulatory governance*,

[67] Cf. Myers (1972, 75f.); see also section 3.3.3.

i.e. the governance between the regulatory commission, which is supposed to maximize social welfare, and the regulated firm maximizing its value, becomes an important issue. Regulatory measures such as unbundling and accounting separation (to prevent cross-subsidization between regulated and unregulated products or services of the firm), external cost benchmarks and incentive regulation aim at handling this issue. Neither the regulated firm nor the regulatory commission are a monolithic economic unit, but consist of different decision makers that pursue their own differing goals. The major players in the regulated firm are the equity and debt owners and the management. Prominent conflicts of goals and information asymmetries between capital owners and the management as well as between equity owners and debt owners have to be handled as part of the *corporate governance.*[68] The issue of *regulatory commission governance* usually receives less attention. The commissioners engaged by the society or by the government to maximize the overall social welfare may also pursue their own goals.[69] For example, a regulatory commissioner may aim at using his experience gained in regulatory proceedings and his insider knowledge by taking up a well paid position in a regulated utility after his term and therefore may act more leniently during his term. Moreover, according to the theory of regulatory capture[70], the close collaboration of decisions makers of the regulatory commission and of the regulated firm in regulatory proceedings over a longer period creates the risk that the regulatory commission adopts the perspective of the regulated firm and favors the interests of the regulated firm over the interests of rate payers.

The interaction of the regulatory commission and the regulated firm is influenced by numerous factors that can be subdivided into *regulatory, firm, and environmental factors*. For instance, the objective function of a regulatory commissioner is different, depending on whether a regulatory review takes place at the beginning or at the end of his term, and whether or not another term is possible.[71] A related factor is the accountability of the regulator.[72] In an investigation of the return on equity of U.S. electric utilities, Hagerman and Ratchford (1978) find that the actual allowed rate

---

68 For the impact of deregulation on corporate governance structures, see Kole/Lehn (1999); Lehn (2002); Geddes/Vinod (2002). For the use of relative performance evaluation in regulated firms and its feedback on the optimal level of regulated rates, see Hofmann (2002).

69 Cf. Picot/Burr (1996, 176f.).

70 See Posner (1974) and (1975). Bonbrigth/Danielsen/Kamerschen (1988, 26ff.) give an overview of theories of regulation.

71 Cf. Ergas et al. (2001, 9).

72 Cf. Ergas et al. (2001, 15).

of return is positively related to the length of the regulatory commissioners' term.

As for firm factors, size and ownership structure are for example factors that influence the outcome of the regulatory process. The findings of Hagerman and Ratchford (1978) confirm that the size of a utility exerts a positive influence on the allowed rate of return. Holburn and Spiller (2002) use panel data of more than 700 rate reviews for U.S. electric utilities in the 1980s and find that utilities tend to postpone rate reviews in states with consumer advocates and elected regulatory commissioners, as in these states the allowed return on equity tends to be lower. Crew and Kleindorfer (1985) and Crew, Kleindorfer and Schlenger (1987) investigate U.S. water utilities, and find evidence that large companies benefit from economies of scale in regulatory proceedings. If the government is among the shareholders of the regulated utility, it seems less likely that investors are only allowed a rate of return below the cost of capital by the regulator or that they are expropriated by other means.[73]

Environmental factors that are likely to impact the outcome of the regulatory process include inflation, growth, productivity, technological progress and the development of input prices. Nwaeze (1997) collects price data of 87 U.S. electric utilities from 1969 to 1990, and finds a negative relationship between lagged growth indicators on the return on equity, as well as a positive relationship for lagged industry average return on equity and lagged bond yields. The discussion of factors is not extended here, but references to empirical evidence on their impact are made throughout chapter 3 and chapter 4.

The descriptive framework does not show explicitly the underlying interactions and dynamics. The level and volatility of cash flows and the capital structure not only depend on regulatory directives, but also on the reaction of the firm to regulation (as well as the reaction of competitors). On the other hand, it depends on the design of the regulatory system, whether and to what degree the firm has freedom to react to regulation and to exert a certain control over its own cash flows and cost of capital, e.g. by investment, financing, pricing and procurement decisions. The behavior of the regulated firm and the regulatory commission depends on past experience. This interdependence over time is indicated by some of the regulatory factors (actual rate of return in the past, efficiency gains in the past). Uncertainty may be especially high if there is no experience at all with

[73] See the discussion of the possibilities to mitigate the risk of regulatory discretion in section 3.2.

regulation.[74] As indicated above, the framework does not explicitly show all involved parties. Competitors may play an important role, if competition is admitted for the regulated product or service or if downstream or upstream competition feeds back on its market. Competitors also may interfere in regulatory hearings to influence the outcome to their advantage, just as other interest groups. The degree of independence of the regulatory commission depends on the design implemented by the legislator who could change the design at relatively short notice.[75]

3.2 Analysis of Circularity and (Time) Inconsistency as Fundamental Problems of Rate Regulation

The rate regulation process is subject to a *dual circularity*, as shown by Figure 3.2. The outer circularity is well-recognized and runs from regulated rates over expected future cash flows, value of the rate base and finally interest and depreciation back to regulated rates. The regulatory commission sets prices (or price caps) for the regulated firm and, to this end, uses cost data.[76] The most important cost elements of utilities, usually, are imputed interest and depreciation. The prices set by the regulator have an influence on expected future cash flows, which, in turn, have an influence on the value of the rate base. If market value serves as a basis for imputed interest and depreciation, the price setting process clearly becomes circular.[77] The single most important reason why most regulators use the book value of the regulated firm's assets in the rate base is to break up this circularity.[78]

---

74 For an analysis of the problems associated with circularity and dynamic inconsistency, see section 3.2.

75 All the involved parties may fall back upon the knowledge of experts, e.g. in accounting, finance, economics and engineering, testifying in regulatory hearings. Joskow (1972) investigates 20 rate cases of electric utilities in the state of N.Y. between 1960 and 1970, and finds a positive relationship between cost of capital testimony and the rate of return allowed by the commission. However, conflicting cost of capital testimony by intervenors had a negative effect.

76 The use of cost data is more or less explicit depending on the regulatory system, but, ultimately, every regulatory system has to be cost-orientated to a certain degree.

77 This circularity is formally shown by Grout and Zalewska (2001).

78 For a detailed discussion on the question of whether the market values of capital or the book values of assets should be used in the regulatory rate base, see chapter 5, in particular, section 5.2.

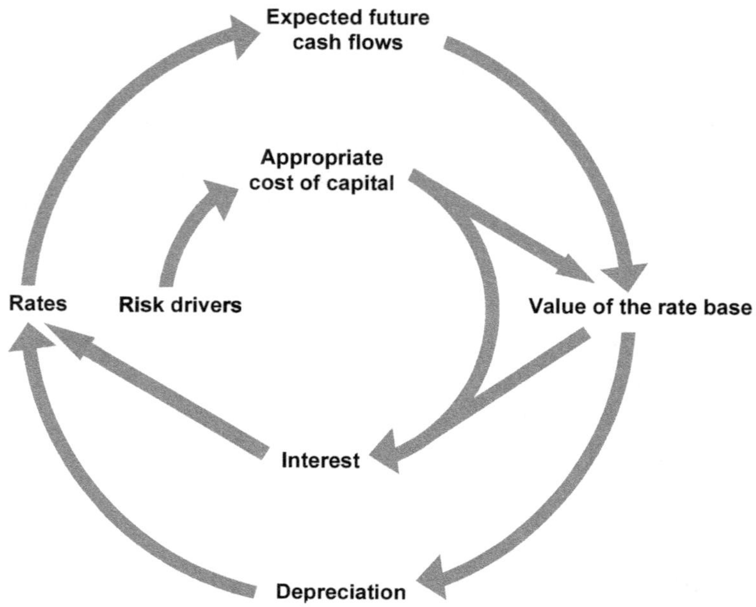

Figure 3.2. Dual circularity of rate regulation

It is noteworthy, that the cash perspective and the accounting perspective are intermingled in this circularity. However, while imputed costs, such as depreciation and interest on equity, have no direct cash flow-relevance in the case of non-regulated firms, they directly influence the cash flows of a rate-regulated company if used for calculating rates by the regulator. Clearly, numerous frictions occur between the cash flow level and the accounting level,[79] and, in reality, this is not a one-to-one relationship, even in the case of rather strictly cost-based rate regulation.

The inner circularity captures the issue of regulatory risk that, in most instances, is ignored in the discussion of circularity problems.[80] Through its directives, the regulatory commission not only sets prices but also has a significant influence on risk and risk-adjusted cost of capital. The commission exerts this influence directly via the expected distribution of cash

[79] For a discussion of the relation of the two perspectives, see Küpper (1995); Edwards/Kay/Mayer (1997); Küpper (1985) bases cost accounting on investment theory.

[80] One of the few exceptions is the survey article of Robichek (1978, 699): "To require that the rates be set after giving due consideration to "risk" is circular when such "risk" is determined to a large extent by the rate-making process."

flows and the capital structure of the regulated firm, as well as indirectly by determining the regulated firm's freedom of action and flexibility of reaction to moves of competitors (if competition is admitted) and external shocks. The resulting risk-adjusted cost of capital is one of the determinants of asset value, and it is used in the calculation of interest. These interdependences establish a risk-driven circularity with the rate-setting process. The regulatory commission has to take into account an appropriate risk-adjusted cost of capital when calculating prices, and, at the same time, its directives are one of the major risk drivers or even *the* most important risk driver for the regulated firm.

In the hypothetical benchmark case of a perfect rate-of-return regulation that would guarantee the regulated firm a pre-specified rate of return on all investment at any moment in time, both circularities would become irrelevant: the inner circularity, as regulation in this case would absorb all risks[81], the outer circulation, as prices would be entirely determined by the pre-specified rate of return. If this rate of return equaled the cost of capital, the regulated firm would permanently exhibit a market-to-book ratio of one,[82] in other words, the equity of the regulated utility is *de facto* converted to a bond.[83] This assumes that the firm either provides only one service or, if it provides more than one service, that the value of the different services is additive.[84] Furthermore, this would require perfect information of the regulatory commission about the investments of the regulated firm as well as its ability to credibly commit itself to such a regulatory regime. Clearly, none of these conditions ever can be met in reality. Therefore, the empirical evidence that market-to-book ratios are subject to large fluctuations is not surprising. Carleton, Chambers and Lakonishok (1983, 420), for instance, find that the average market-to-book ratio of electric utilities in the U.S. fell from 1.398 in 1971 to 0.727 in 1980.

Commitment plays a twofold role: The regulated firm has to make a strong commitment because of the high degree of irreversibility of the investment in regulated industries that potentially exposes it to high risk.[85] At the same time, the regulator cannot credibly commit in advance to allow-

81 Of course, the risk of a change of the risk-less interest rate during the economic asset life would still exist, making the investment more or less advantageous *ex post*.

82 Cf. Myers (1972, 73ff.); Gordon (1977, 1502f.); Brennan/Schwartz (1982a); Carleton/Chambers/Lakonishok (1983, 420); Houston (1996, 3).

83 Cf. Gordon (1977, 1503): "A utility share … is like a one period note if regulation is periodic and perfect." See also Robichek (1978, 701f.).

84 For the consequences of releasing of these assumptions, see section 5.2.

85 Without this irreversibility, even a natural monopoly with strong economies of scale could be disciplined by potential competition.

ing the firm an appropriate rate of return on this investment. Firstly, the regulatory contract necessarily remains incomplete due to incomplete information, and secondly, the regulator lacks credible mechanisms for commitment. Even if the regulatory commission could be bound by the legislator, the legislator for his part could not credibly commit himself to an announced course of action, i.e. the behavior of the regulatory commission and the legislator is subject to a potential *time-consistency* problem. The government that has the ultimate responsibility for rate regulation is sovereign and cannot bind itself by a 'commitment of last resort'. It will always have discretionary power to deviate from an announced course of action and to change the regulatory system.

If investors anticipate that regulatory announcements are time-inconsistent, they will adjust their investment and financing decisions.[86] This two-fold commitment problem is aggravated by the fact that the typical asset life time in regulated industries is much longer than the regulatory review period. The commitment problem gains importance with increasing regulatory lag, longer review periods and longer asset life, as costs have to be estimated for a longer period and rate setting is less strictly orientated towards actual costs of the regulated utility. Without perfect information, a complete commitment is not even desirable, as this would take away any flexibility from the regulator to correct his errors. This holds true all the more, if it is the aim of regulation to simulate competitive results or to stimulate competition.

In a realistic setting, therefore, it has to be assumed that both circularities are relevant. The above line of argument also shows, however, that the regulatory commission has the *discretionary power* to break up these circularities at any time by setting a fixed point, i.e. by setting a certain price for the regulated product or service.[87] After such an intervention, in any case, the capital market will revaluate the regulated firm such that capital owners will earn an appropriate rate of return (that might be higher than before due to a loss of trust in the regulatory commission) on the new market value. Of course, this involves windfall losses (or profits) for the capital owners at the time of the intervention, and, usually, cannot be done without lasting effects on incentives for future investment and financing decisions. Accordingly, Brennan and Schwartz (1982a, 509) "... define a *consistent regulatory policy* as a procedure for determining the holding of a rate hearing and setting the allowed rate of return at the hearing such that, when properly anticipated by investors, the procedure causes the

---

[86] See, for example, Biglaiser/Ma (1999).

[87] See the discussion of the use of market versus book values for the regulatory rate base in chapter 5.

market value of the regulated firm to be equal to the value of the rate base at the time the hearing is held."[88] In other words, the regulatory commission does not use its discretionary power such that windfall losses (or profits) would be induced.

A prominent example of an unanticipated regulatory intervention was the surprising reopening of the regulatory review process in the UK electricity industry by Steven Littlechild in March 1995, only a few months after the review had been closed and only weeks before it was supposed to come into force.[89] Even if there is no intervention between regulatory reviews according to schedule, utilities usually have to invest irreversibly for the entire economic asset life time that, for the most part of their infrastructure investments, is a multiple of the regulatory review period, exposing them to considerable risk.

Several approaches can be taken to mitigate the commitment problem at least partially. One possibility is to delegate rate regulation to a governmental agency such as a regulatory commission as is done in most countries in order to reduce the risk of unpredictable political interventions in the regulatory process.[90] Another approach consists in closing contracts between the government and the firm that are subject to civil law instead of using statutory instruments.[91] In addition, a regulatory commission "... can make expropriation of the utility's sunk capital stock less attractive by refusing to protect itself from the adverse consequences of supply shortages, ...",[92] e.g. by not purchasing backup power or by reducing investment in interconnection. Furthermore, the government can align its objective function with the one of private investors by holding shares of the regulated utility.[93] In the special case of the privatization of electricity distribution in developing countries, it has been proposed to backstop a pre-defined regulatory framework and process by a partial risk guarantee of the World Bank. Such a guarantee would cover the risk for private investors of the government deviating from the agreed-upon regulation and would present the government with the possibility of building up a credible regulatory track record.[94] Reasonable prospects for cost recovery depend on both an

---

88 Also cf. Appleyard/McLaren (1996) and Grayburn/Hern/Lay (2002, 7).
89 Cf. Grayburn/Hern/Lay (2002, 6).
90 Cf. Shuttleworth/MacKerron (2002, 34).
91 Cf. Shuttleworth/MacKerron (2002, 32).
92 Gilbert/Newberry (1994, 551).
93 On the other hand, governmental shareholdings in regulated utilities might entice the government to make regulatory laws more advantageous for incumbent utilities than would be efficient.
94 Cf. Gupta et al. (2002, 3ff.).

adequate revenue standard and an adequate procedural standard.[95] The regulated firm, for its part, can reduce its commitment by choosing a less specific and less capital intensive technology.[96]

It should be noted, that the existence of regulatory risk does not necessarily require the regulation itself be uncertain.[97] Certain regulation can absorb existing business risks by buffering the regulated firm against external shocks or increase existing business risks by taking away from the firm the flexibility to react to external shocks. Which effect is dominant, depends on the design of the regulatory system and process as well as on the characteristics of the underlying business risk.

3.3 Systematization and Analysis of the Effects of Rate Regulation on the Risk of a Regulated Firm

Regulatory risk is reflected in the overall cash flow risk of a firm.[98] By setting rates and accompanying directives concerning, for example, quality issues, technical standards or the provision of universal service, the regulator influences the cash flows of the regulated firm. The risk-adjusted cost of capital of the regulated firm depends, generally speaking, on the probability distribution of the expected cash flows. The impact of regulation on risk and cost of capital can be analyzed systematically by referring to the benchmark case without regulation, i.e. by comparing the expected distribution of cash flows with and without rate regulation (or an individual regulatory measure). A systematic analysis of regulatory risk should comprise its causes and effects as well as the transmission between causes and effects. The following analysis turns the cause-and-effect-chain upside down, i.e. it starts with the effects of rate regulation on risk, then gets to the transmission paths, and ends with the causes of regulatory risk, the individual design variables of the regulatory control panel.

When discussing the *effects* of regulation on risk, several questions need to be addressed: (1) Firstly, are rate-regulated companies exposed to any risk at all? If this is not the case, the cash flow distribution is reduced to one cash flow number that is realized with certainty. All risk that results

---

95 Cf. Shuttleworth/MacKerron (2002, 9f.)

96 For the impact of rate regulation on investment, see section 3.2.

97 This point is stressed also by Ergas et al. (2001, 8). For example, regulation in the model of Brennan and Schwartz (1982a) that investigates the influence of the regulatory process on the beta factor is certain; see section 4.1.4. For an extension to uncertain regulation cf. Ahn and Thompson (1989).

98 See section 2.7.

from uncertain parameters such as input prices and demand would be borne by the rate payers. It is clear from all evidence that under any existing regulatory regime, regulated firms are exposed to some risk. Nevertheless, it is worthwhile to analyze the conditions under which, in theory, a regulatory regime would abolish any risk as well as the reasons why a practically implemented regulatory regime necessarily deviates from this hypothetical reference point.

Provided that rate-regulated firms have to bear some risk, the second question arises: (2) Does rate regulation increase or decrease the risk of a regulated firm compared to a non-regulated firm? This question can be subdivided into two aspects:

(a) Does rate regulation decrease or increase the covariance of the cash flow distribution with a market portfolio? This systematic risk increases the risk-adjusted cost of capital and would be captured by beta in the Capital Asset Pricing Model (CAPM).[99] On the one hand, regulation may reduce the systematic risk by absorbing shocks that would otherwise enhance the covariance of cash flows. This is called the buffering effect of regulation.[100] At the same time, it reduces the scope of reaction for the regulated firm that, at the bottom line, might even increase the covariance of cash flows due to shocks. To determine the effect of regulation on risk, it is necessary to use the (hypothetical) situation without regulation as a point of reference. Due to interdependences with other risk influencing factors, it can be fairly problematic to isolate the effect of regulation. Time series analysis and analysis across regulatory systems can provide some empirical insights.

(b) Does regulation introduce asymmetry in the distribution of cash flows? Regulatory commissions can use their discretionary power to introduce a downward bias in the distribution of cash flows by cutting off the upside potential, i.e. the upper tail of the distribution, without limiting the downside risk.[101] If and to the extent that asymmetric regulatory risk exists, it has to be compensated to attain an appropriate rate of return on investment at the bottom line.

Each one of these questions is thoroughly analyzed in the following three sections.

---

99 Cf. Morin (1994, 38f.); Grayburn/Hern/Lay (2002, 2).

100 The buffering hypothesis goes back to the seminal paper of Peltzman (1976).

101 Kolbe/Tye/Myers (1993, 33) confine their definition of regulatory risk to this asymmetric type of risk.

3.3.1 Elimination of Risk by Rate Regulation?

If it is argued that rate regulation eliminates any risk for the regulated firm,[102] this view obviously refers to the hypothetical model of a perfect rate-of-return regulation that would guarantee the regulated firm the adequate (risk free) rate of return at any moment in time. This would require that the regulator is able to assess the cost of the regulated firm without any discretion, and that he could either continuously adjust the rates to any change in the costs or compensate exactly the regulated firm *ex post* for deviations of actual costs from the costs assessed ex ante by the regulator for setting rates. Practically implemented regulatory regimes deviate from this hypothetical benchmark in many respects. Firstly, the rate regulation process itself consumes resources. Alone for this reason, rates are not adjusted continuously but only in certain intervals that can be fixed review periods or flexible periods triggered by an automatic mechanism[103] or by request of one of the involved parties. As the rate setting process is time consuming, adjustments only can be made with a certain lag. Still, the regulator could try to compensate *ex post* deviations of actual costs from the cost estimated at the last review.

However, secondly, the regulator suffers from information asymmetries about costs (and demand) of the regulated firm, so that he cannot guarantee an exact compensation of costs even *ex post*. From the information asymmetry follows thirdly, that investment decisions should be taken by the firm, and not by the regulator and that, accordingly, the firm should bear investment risk to induce efficient investment decisions. As analyzed in section 3.2, the general problem underlying all of the aforementioned issues is one of commitment and time-consistency.[104] Resuming, it can be stated that a complete abolition of risk for the rate-regulated firm is neither possible nor desirable.

On the one hand, rate regulation must be cost-orientated in setting rates so that the regulated firm can expect *ex ante* an appropriate rate of return on its investment. On the other hand, it should not eliminate any risk by *ex post* reimbursement of all costs incurred. If the regulator does not protect the regulated firm from all cost and demand fluctuations and/or does not

[102] For example, in a recent decision against TEAG, the German Federal Cartel Office argues along this line; see Bundeskartellamt (2003, 23); see also Zimmermann (2003, 49), who supports the view of the Cartel Office.

[103] Such a mechanism is modelled by Brennan/Schwartz (1982a); the basic functioning and results of the model are outlined in section 4.1.4.

[104] Cf. also Spulber (1989, 610): "Perhaps the most important aspect of the regulatory bargain is the ability of regulators, customers, and the regulated firm to make commitments both to pricing policies and to irreversible investments."

accept in the rate base all investments made by the regulated firm, the regulated firm is exposed to risk that has to be compensated by an appropriate allowed rate of return. The same holds true, if the regulator uses yardsticks that are not strictly orientated towards the actual costs of the regulated firm with the aim in mind of improving the incentives for efficient investment and operation. Such yardsticks can be costs of comparable firms or costs derived from analytical cost models. They are beyond the control of the regulated firm.

For all these reasons, it is not surprising that empirical investigations unanimously confirm that rate-regulated firms are not risk-free, but are exposed to some risk. Part of this risk is systematic and, accordingly, relevant for the cost of capital, as, without exception, beta factors larger than zero are found.[105] From the analytical considerations as well as from the empirical investigations it is clear that rate regulation does not eliminate completely the (systematic) risk of the regulated firm.

3.3.2 Increase or Decrease of (Systematic) Risk by Rate Regulation?

The subsequent question is whether rate regulation increases or decreases the risk of the regulated firm (or leaves it unchanged), i.e. whether rate regulation exerts an overall buffering effect on the risk of the regulated firm. Provided there is an effect, it must be examined if it is reflected in the systematic part of risk that is relevant for the cost of capital of the regulated utility. It is not clear *a priori*, if rate regulation increases or decreases the (cash flow) risk of the regulated firm and if the effect of regulation is systematic or unsystematic. The CAPM shows that only systematic risk, i.e. the correlation of the firm's risk with the risk of the market portfolio of assets as measured by the beta factor, is rewarded by a higher return on the capital market. Unsystematic, i.e. firm specific, risk can be diversified for free on the capital market, and consequently is not rewarded. As only systematic risk results in a higher cost of capital, exclusively the effect of

[105] Cf., for example, Alexander/Mayer/Weeds (1996); Archer (1981); Binder/Norton (1999); Buckland/Fraser (2001); Davidson/Rangan/Rosenstein (1997); Dubin/Navarro (1982); Francis/Grout/Zalewska (2001); Morana/Sawkins (2000); Navarro (1982); Nwaeze (2000b); Riddick (1992); Robinson/Taylor (1998a) and (1998b); the predominant research object of these investigations is the question whether rate regulation increases or decreases risk, which is analyzed in the following section.

regulation on the systematic part of risk is of relevance for the impact of regulation on risk-adjusted cost of capital.[106]

On the one hand, a form of regulation, setting rates in such a way that a certain targeted rate of return should be attained, can be expected to have a buffering effect[107] on the volatility of cash flows compared to a setting without any regulation of rates. Rate reviews work towards adjusting revenues to costs and smoothing the return path. This effect is stronger the more cost-orientated the rate setting is. As described above, in the hypothetical benchmark case of a perfect rate-of-return regulation, the actual rate of return would be completely fixed by regulation. Cash flow risks existing because of uncertainties in the buying and selling markets as well as in the production process would be perfectly compensated as to guarantee the regulated firm a "fixed income".[108]

On the other hand, rate regulation takes away flexibility from the firm. If prices are fixed by the regulatory commission for a certain period, the regulated firm cannot adjust to (unexpected) changes on its selling market. If demand falls for whatever reason, the regulated firm cannot countersteer by lowering its prices, and *vice versa*. Alike, the firm cannot adjust its output prices flexibly to fluctuations in input prices. Either it has to wait until the next scheduled rate review or it can request an intermediate rate relief that will also be executed only with a lag, if at all. This problem can be mitigated by pass-through clauses for certain (exogenous) cost elements or by indexation of rates. But indexation with the overall retail price index – as done with price caps in UK – does not necessarily protect against specific price increases of the inputs used by the regulated firm.[109] Furthermore, the regulator makes his pricing decisions normally with less information than the regulated firm, which constitutes an additional source of risk. Finally, as described above, the regulated firm is always exposed to the risk of discretionary regulatory behavior, which makes the outcome of the regulatory process less predictable. Continuity in the regulatory track record, therefore, is of vital importance for the risk perception of private investors. All these factors are suited to reinforce the cash flow volatility of a regulated firm in comparison to a firm that is not subject to rate regulation. Which one of these two effects – buffering or reinforcing risk –

---

[106] Ergas et al. (2001, 6f.) confine their definition of regulatory risk to this systematic part that is reflected in the cost of capital.

[107] Cf. Peltzman (1976); Grayburn/Hern/Lay (2002, 2).

[108] The undesirable investment incentive effects of transforming equity in a kind of bond already have been discussed above.

[109] Cf. Grayburn/Hern/Lay (2002, 3).

prevails, depends on the design of the regulatory system and process; ultimately, this can only be answered empirically.

Assuming that there are effects of regulation on the (cash flow) risk of the regulated firm, it is to be investigated if they are correlated with the overall market risk, i.e. if they are systematic and affect the risk-adjusted cost of capital. One position is that this kind of regulatory risk is firm specific, can be completely diversified on the capital market and, consequently, has no effect on the beta factor and risk-adjusted cost of capital.[110]

The counter-position argues that regulatory risk actually can be correlated with the overall market risk, and puts forward different points to support this opinion. The first argument is that both the overall economic situation affecting all firms and the specific policy towards regulated firms are influenced in the same direction, depending on which political parties are ruling at the time. A second line of argument takes the overall economic situation and its impact on the regulatory commission as the starting-point. In periods of high inflation[111] and/or interest rates, for example, that in almost all instances are associated with a less favorable economic situation, the regulatory commission might be less inclined to raise rates of regulated firms in order to avoid additional burdens for consumers.[112] This would mean that regulated firms are negatively affected just as the overall market. Moreover, the pressure of associations of utilities' industrial and private consumers might be particularly high in such times reducing even more the willingness of the regulatory commission to increase rates. Finally, the voting behavior in political elections might be influenced by the overall economic situation. This could have an impact on regulation with a certain time lag. Gandolfi, Jenkinson and Mayer (1996) develop a model and run simulations, showing that regulatory risk can be systematic and depends on factors such as the type of the overall regulatory system and the length of the regulatory review period.

Most empirical investigations directly examine the impact of rate regulation on beta and cost of capital and neglect the unsystematic part of cash flow volatility.[113] The vast majority of empirical investigations find significant effects of regulation on the cost of capital of regulated utilities. An

[110] Cf. Appleyard/McLaren (1996, 21).

[111] Cf. Thompson (1991, 192), who supports the view that regulatory commissions are reluctant to increase rates in times of high inflation.

[112] This implies that actual costs are not completely passed-through to regulated rates without any delay.

[113] An exception are LaGattuta/Stein/Tennican/Usher (2000), who investigate the effect of rate regulation on cash flow volatility that about doubled in the late 1990s compared to the early 1990s.

early group of studies investigates the effect of *regulatory climate* on the cost of capital: Trout (1979), Archer (1981) as well as Dubin and Navarro (1982) each compare between 63 and 92 utilities across U.S. states, based upon rankings of the regulatory climate of each individual state by financial analysts. The regulatory climate is measured by factors such as length of the regulatory lag between rate reviews, the use of automatic adjustment clauses for certain (exogenous) cost components (usually pass-through clauses for fuel costs) and others.[114] A favorable regulatory climate is associated, among other things, with a shorter regulatory lag and with more costs that are passed through to rates. All the studies find a significant influence of regulatory climate on the cost of capital.[115] They confirm the conjectured correlation between a more favorable regulatory climate and a lower cost of capital. Obviously, a more continuous and cost-orientated regulation is associated with a lower risk, which can be understood as an indication that the buffering hypothesis proves true. However, the studies do not allow ultimate conclusions about risk buffering or reinforcing compared to companies that are not at all rate-regulated.[116]

Consistent with the buffering hypothesis, a regression analysis, run for regulated electric utilities across 33 U.S. states by Davidson, Rangan and Rostenstein (1997), confirms that systematic risk decreases significantly with regulatory intensity.[117] They run additional causality tests that show that rate regulation influences systematic risk and not the other way round. Nwaeze (2000a) finds that the share price reaction to earnings surprises is more favorable for utilities that are subject to a regulatory climate that is classified as more lenient.

Some studies directly *compare regulated utilities to unregulated firms.* Riddick (1992) compares a portfolio of regulated electric and gas distribution utilities with a portfolio of non-regulated firms as similar as possible except for the absence of regulation, and finds that regulation systematically lowers risk of the regulated firms compared to that of the unregulated

---

[114] These regulatory variables are discussed in more detail in chapter 4.

[115] The explanatory power of these investigations is constricted insofar as they use market to book ratio as a measure for cost of equity and bond rating as a measure for cost of debt.

[116] Navarro (1982) takes the studies on the impact of regulatory climate on cost of capital as a starting-point and goes one step further investigating the factors that influence regulatory climate itself. He found that in particular the method of selection of commissioners, their salary level, the length of the regulatory term, the method of funding of the regulatory commission and the expenditure size have a significant influence on the regulatory climate.

[117] See also Norton (1985).

firms, but does not completely eliminate risk.[118] Teets (1992) investigates the reaction of regulated and unregulated firms to earnings surprises that are found to be smaller for the regulated utilities.

A more recent group of investigations uses *event study* methodology to analyze the impact of announced changes of regulation on the cost of capital in most cases measured by the beta factor.[119] Part of this group are the studies by Sawkins (1996), Antoniou and Pescetto (1997), Robinson and Taylor (1998a and 1998b), Binder and Norton (1999), Nwaeze (2000b), Morana and Sawkins (2000), Buckland and Fraser (2001), Johanning and Ruhle (2004) as well as Rudolph and Johanning (2004). These studies find significant effects of announcements of regulatory changes on beta and the cost of capital. The findings cannot all be discussed here in detail, but summing up it can be said that the strongest influence is exerted by announcements concerning regulated prices and / or changing the perceived uncertainty about the behavior of the regulatory commission. The studies provide evidence that a more light-handed regulation increases systematic risk[120] and consequently risk-adjusted cost of capital. *Vice versa*, it can be concluded that stronger regulation has a buffering effect on risk-adjusted cost of capital[121] but does not reduce it to zero, which is in line with the observed beta factors of most utilities.

Cost of debt is less debated in regulatory hearings, as the cost of debt actually paid by the regulated firm can be observed by tracking credit contracts and bond emissions. Analogically to the line of argument and empirical findings of a buffering effect of regulation on the cost of equity, most regulated utilities have to pay a rather small risk premium compared

---

118 Clearly, the comparability of the portfolios is a somewhat heroic assumption, as there are no unregulated firms in the same business as electric and gas distribution firms.

119 An early event study by Rose (1985) finds that firm's values declined as a reaction to announcements of deregulation in the trucking industry from 1978 to 1980. This result is consistent with the buffering hypothesis.

120 An early event study by Davidson/Chandy/Walker (1985) does not support the buffering hypothesis. They examine reactions to the signing into law of the Motor Carrier Reform Act of 1980 that facilitated entry into new markets, thereby opening up new business opportunities and allowing for more regional diversification, and find positive abnormal returns after the event. Because of the special content of the act that is not just the removal or weakening of rate regulation, the result has to be interpreted with caution.

121 The buffering hypothesis is explicitly supported by Binder/Norton (1999), Nwaeze (2000b) and Johanning/Ruhle (2004).

to firms that are not subject to rate regulation.[122] Obviously, the risk of illiquidity is assessed small but non-zero by the capital market.[123] The empirical studies about regulatory climate cited above show a significant effect of regulatory climate not only on cost of equity, but also on cost of debt. While the return on debt is fixed by market forces to a great extent, actual return on equity depends largely on the actions of the firm, and additionally on the directives of the regulatory commission, in the special case of regulated firms. This is notwithstanding that the cost of debt *and* the cost of equity both are determined by capital market expectations *ex ante*. The actual rate of return *ex post* might differ from this cost of capital for a variety of reasons, some of which are discussed below.

3.3.3 Asymmetric Regulatory Risk

So far, the discussion has focused on systematic regulatory risk as measured by the beta factor in a capital asset pricing framework. The standard CAPM captures only the first and the second moment of a distribution, i.e. it models only symmetric distributions. In reality, however, it cannot strictly be assumed that regulation has a symmetric effect on the distribution of the firm's cash flows.

On the contrary, potential asymmetry is one of the most striking characteristics of regulatory risk.[124] Firstly, this asymmetry can be embedded already *ex ante*, i.e. before the regulated firm invests, in the existing rules of a regulatory system. If, for example, disallowances of the regulatory rate base, i.e. individual investments that are not included in the rate base, are principally admitted by existing regulatory rules, e.g. according to a used and useful standard or to a prudent investment review,[125] the regulated firm faces strictly downside risk about the future rate base and it anticipates that

---

[122] But of course this cannot be generalized. The bonds emitted in three different tranches by DTAG in May 2002 at the date of emission had a premium over corresponding interbank rates of 265 base points for a five year euro bond, 285 base points for a ten year euro bond, and 365 base points for a 30 year dollar bond. The day before, the rating of DTAG had been downgraded by Moody's; cf. Financial Times Deutschland, May 25, 2002.

[123] This also holds true for firms that consist of only one rate-regulated division.

[124] For an extended discussion of asymmetric regulatory risk cf. Kolbe/Tye/Myers (1993), who confine their definition of regulatory risk exactly to this asymmetric part of risk.

[125] For a detailed discussion of disallowances, see section 4.2.3.

it will earn the allowed rate of return only on part of its investments.[126] This can drive the expected rate of return on the entire investment way below the allowed rate of return on the regulatory rate base.

Secondly, as the regulatory commission cannot commit itself to a certain course of action, it cannot be excluded that, *ex post* after the regulated firm has made irreversible investments, the commission retroactively will change the regulatory rules to skim off rates of return actually turning out to be supernormal without, however, compensating for less than normal rates of return. Risks are shifted from the ratepayers to the capital owners. In both cases, rate regulation with a downside bias introduces skewness in the distribution of cash flows.[127] As payments to the debt holders are fixed, the financial consequences of these asymmetric regulatory risks have to be borne by the equity owners primarily, at least as long as the probability of financial distress is not changed substantially. If this asymmetric risk applies to access rates for competitors, it could be diversifiable for the investors of the regulated utility, at least partly, by investing in those competitors. If, however, this asymmetric risk applies to retail rates, it is at least not clear, how it could be diversified, as no other firm but consumers benefit from this redistribution, and investors cannot invest directly in claims on consumer income.[128]

The natural place to consider such a regulatory bias are the cash flows themselves. To avoid investment distortions, a compensating cash flow item is needed in the calculation of regulated rates. This cash flow item has the character of an insurance premium paid to the investor. If, however, the allowed rate of return instead is adjusted by an additional risk premium as to offset regulatory bias, rather strong adjustments might be necessary in some cases. This can be illustrated by the following numerical examples: The amount invested in regulated assets is € 100, the expected rate of return for alternative investments with corresponding risk is 10% and the

---

[126] Ergas et al. (2001, 10) show that a symmetric error in the setting of regulated prices results in an asymmetric, downward biased distribution of rate of return if the revenue function is concave and the cost function is convex. Of course, this is not relevant if the error of the regulator is mean preserving in return. Which kind of error actually is committed by the regulator would have to be investigated empirically.

[127] Extended forms of the CAPM capture this skewness, i.e. the third moment of the distribution; cf. Conine/Tamarkin (1985). This is one of the reasons why it is rather misleading to categorize asymmetric regulatory risk as "[n]on-diversifiable, non-systematic risk" (Ergas et al. (2001, 16)).

[128] Cf. Ergas et al. (2001, 17). Some diversification might be attainable by investing in companies that produce or sell consumer goods and might benefit from this redistribution towards consumers.

probability of a € 10 disallowance of the rate base is 50%. This means that investments of € 10 that were actually made by the regulated utility are not accepted in the rate base by the regulator, and, accordingly neither depreciation nor interest is earned on them. Assuming for simplicity a risk neutral investor,[129] the expected return on the regulated investment must equal the expected return of alternative investments (x denotes the allowed rate of return on the regulatory rate base):

$$0.5 * 100 * (1+x) + 0.5 * (100-10) * (1+x) = 100\,(1+0.1) \quad (3.1)$$

This yields an allowed rate of return of 15.79%. If, everything else unchanged, the possible disallowance is raised to € 25, the allowed rate of return is 25.71%. The considerably higher allowed rates of return are necessary to compensate the return of *and* on the disallowance.[130] The allowed rate of return is higher than the cost of capital resulting from symmetric systematic risk as measured in the standard CAPM. Table 3.1 shows compensating allowed rate of returns for further examples of different probabilities and percentages of disallowances.

If regulatory bias is not compensated by increasing the allowed rate of return and if this is anticipated by rational investors, investment distortions will result, which may lead to a serious underinvestment problem.[131] Even if the allowed rate of return is higher than the cost of capital, as measured by a standard CAPM, the expected rate of return taking into account asymmetries of regulation still might be lower than this cost of capital.[132] If it is not politically feasible to raise the allowed rate of return to the necessary level (and if there is no compensating cash flow item, which might be easier to implement), regulation itself must be made more symmetric to avoid potential investment distortions.[133]

---

[129] If the investor is risk averse, an additional risk premium has to be paid to compensate the effects of asymmetric regulation in this simplifying example. In reality, also the term on the right hand side of the equation is uncertain and the additional effect of risk aversion is less clear.

[130] A less strict form of regulatory standard would only disallow the return on but not the return of the amount invested; cf. Kolbe/Tye/Myers (1993, 20).

[131] For some current data regarding the investment in the energy sector cf. section 1. Kolbe/Tye/Myers (1993, 60) call this potential underinvestment problem a reverse Averch-Johnson effect. Cf. Averch/Johnson (1962).

[132] It should be noted, that ceteris paribus, the systematic symmetric risk, as measured by the beta factor, even is reduced by asymmetric regulation cutting off upside potential, as there is less correlation with (upside) movements of the overall market. Cf. Thompson (1991, 81). Cf. also the simulations in Ergas et al. (2001, 18).

[133] Cf. Kolbe/Tye/Myers (1993, 53).

Table 3.1. Impact of disallowances on the allowed rate of return

Table 3.1 shows numerical examples of how the probability and percentage of disallowances influence the allowed rate of return that exactly compensates the impact of disallowances on the expected rate of return

Probability of disallowance [%]	Percentage of disallowance [%]			
	5	10	25	50
5	10.28	10.55	11.39	12.82
10	10.55	11.11	12.82	15.79
25	11.39	12.82	17.33	25.71
50	12.82	15.79	25.71	46.67

Along an analogue line of argument, regulation could safeguard the regulated firm asymmetrically on the downside, i.e. cut off the lower tail of the cash flow distribution, in order to avoid financial distress of a utility and ensure security of supply. This acts as an insurance against bankruptcy,[134] and the regulated firm should be requested to ‘pay’ an appropriate insurance premium in the form of correspondingly lower rates.

The questions of the existence and the strength of the two outlined asymmetric effects of rate regulation ultimately only can be answered empirically. It is conjecturable that both effects actually do exist, as on the one hand regulators in very most instances do not accept all existing investments in the rate base[135] and as on the other hand regulators usually prevent regulated firms from going bankrupt. Conine and Tamarkin (1985) empirically investigate asymmetric regulatory risk by testing a three-moment CAPM that produced higher cost of equity estimates than the standard CAPM, on average 17.16% for the three-moment CAPM compared to 15.18% for the standard CAPM for their sample of 60 U.S. electric utilities for the two time periods 1971-1975 and 1976-1980. Obviously, cutting off upside potential dominated cushioning on the downside in the investigated sample.

134 The risk of bankruptcy may be small, but it will never be completely excluded.
135 See section 4.2.3.

3.4 Systematization and Analysis of the Transmission Paths of the Effects of Rate Regulation on the Risk of a Regulated Firm

While so far potential effects of rate regulation on the cash flow distribution of the regulated firm have been examined, the analysis now turns to the transmission paths between regulatory activity and the cash flow distribution, setting the stage for a thorough analysis of single regulatory design variables in chapter 4. Basically, effects of regulation on the cash flow distribution and risk-adjusted cost of capital can be either direct or indirect via changes of investment and financing of the regulated firm (see Figure 3.3).

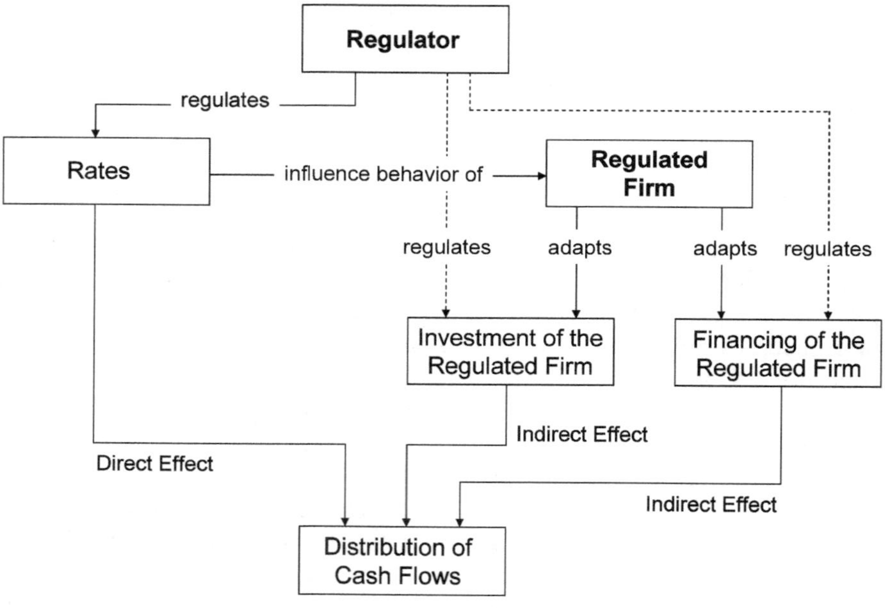

Figure 3.3. Transmission paths of the effects of rate regulation on the risk of a regulated firm

The outlined effects of rate regulation on the risk and risk-adjusted cost of capital of the regulated firm can be *transmitted* in different ways. They can be transmitted either directly or indirectly by altering investment and financing decisions. By setting rates and accompanying directives, the regulator influences directly the expected revenues level of the regulated firm as well as the reaction of revenues on changes of environmental factors, e.g. market parameters such as input prices.[136] Adjustments of investment and financing can be either decided deliberately by the regulated firm as a reaction to rate regulation or enacted by the regulator.

3.4.1 Direct Impact of Rate Regulation on Risk

By setting rates, the regulator directly influences the revenues of the regulated firm. Clearly, this effect is not independent from reactions of consumers and suppliers and, where applicable, of other involved third parties such as competitors. The influence on revenues is reflected in the probability distribution of cash flows and, possibly, in the risk-adjusted cost of capital.

3.4.2 Indirect Effects of Rate Regulation via Adjustments of Investment and Financing

Beyond its direct effect, rate regulation is suited to provoke reactions of the regulated firm in its investment and financing behavior. This requires that the firm actually has degrees of freedom in investment and financing decisions. Alternatively, adjustments of investment or financing also can be enacted by regulatory directives that accompany rate regulation.[137]

Adjustment of Investment

Volume of Investment. The discussion about the impact of rate regulation on optimal investment behavior goes back to the seminal paper by Averch and Johnson (1962). From a production model of rate-of-return regulation, they derive the conclusion that the firm has an incentive to overinvest, if the allowed rate of return is above the cost of capital.[138] Empirical investigations of the Averch-Johnson effect show mixed evidence.[139] This does not necessarily mean that the existence of the effect is questionable but could also be due to the possibility that, in some instances, the allowed rate of return might have been below the cost of capital.

---

[136] Cf. Prager (1989, 34).

[137] For regulatory interventions in investment and financing decisions, see section 4.3.1.

[138] Cf. Averch/Johnson (1962, 1059); see also Elton/Gruber/Lieber (1975), who construct a financial model.

[139] While Courville (1974), Spann (1974) and Petersen (1975) find evidence consistent with the conjectured effect, Boyes (1976) and Baron/Taggart (1977) find no evidence for it.

Elton and Gruber (1977) extend the analysis by constructing a financial model of the firm subject to a regulatory lag and comparing the results with the case of continuous rate-of-return regulation. Regulatory lag means that new investment earns its marginal rate of return until it is included in the rate base after a lag and the allowed rate of return thereafter. Clearly, the hurdle rate corresponds to that of an unregulated firm if the allowed rate of return equals the cost of capital, and is lower (higher) if the allowed rate of return earned on the investment after the lag is higher (lower) than cost of capital.[140] The interesting point with regard to investment incentives is that, with a lag, the regulated firm is induced to efficient investment behavior, independently of the length of the lag. Consistently varying the length of the lag in combination with the rate of return allowed after the lag, the regulator possesses a degree of freedom that he can use for alternative distributions of the gains from efficient investment between the investors of the regulated firm and its rate payers.

Brennan and Schwartz (1982b) model a rate-regulated firm that possesses discretion over its investment decisions. The actual rate of return follows a continuous stochastic process and is readjusted immediately to the allowed rate of return when a rate hearing takes place. Consistent with intuition, numerical solutions show that the optimal growth rate is an increasing function of the actual rate of return. Furthermore, it is derived that – for the same actual rate of return – the optimal growth rate increases with the probability of a rate hearing being held. This confirms the impact of the design of the regulatory process on the investment behavior of the regulated firm.

In all of these models, it is assumed that the regulator can commit to a predefined regulatory behavior, i.e. not to expropriate the regulated firm after it has irreversibly invested. As discussed in section 3.2, this assumption is of very limited validity. The regulator always retains some discretionary power that he can use to deviate from the announced regulatory behavior after the firm has sunk its investments. This is anticipated by the firm when making its investments decisions. The risk of regulatory opportunism reduces ceteris paribus investment incentives and brings about an underinvestment problem.[141]

Different approaches can be taken to mitigate the problem of regulatory opportunism.[142] A regulatory lag protects the regulated firm from expropriation. This is only a temporary effect, as the regulator can make a corre-

[140] Cf. Elton/Gruber (1977, 1490ff.).
[141] Cf. Spulber (1989, 610ff.).
[142] Cf. Gilbert/Newberry (1994, 551); Spiegel (1996, 193); Spiegel/Wilkie (1996, 254).

spondingly stronger adjustment of rates after the lag and, in addition, a regulatory lag is not a predetermined period, but can be largely influenced by the regulator. Furthermore, the regulated firm can use its informational advantages to confine the risk of opportunistic regulatory behavior.[143] Repetition of the regulatory game, in principle, is suited to cure at least partly the commitment problem. The government can also reduce the problem by delegating regulation to a regulatory commission and building up a regulatory bureaucracy. The firm can mitigate the risk of regulatory opportunism by adapting its financing and investment decisions. A larger proportion of debt increases the probability of financial distress and keeps the regulator from lowering rates. This is discussed in more detail in the next section. By reducing the investment volume, the regulated firm can limit its exposure to regulatory opportunism.

If the success of investments is uncertain, and if the regulator accepts only successful investment projects and does not reimburse the regulated firm for failed investment projects, asymmetry is introduced in the investment decision. If the successful investment projects earn only the cost of capital, the regulated company on average earns less than the cost of capital, as the failed investment projects earn nothing.[144] This clearly reduces investment incentives and becomes particularly relevant in the case of investments in new technologies with high uncertainty.[145]

Choice of Technology. Furthermore, regulation is not only suited to influence the optimal volume of investment but also the chosen technology.[146] For instance, the regulated firm can reduce its own commitment by choosing a production technology that requires less and less specific capital as a reaction to higher perceived regulatory risk. In Germany, for example, there is a tendency to construct power plants that necessitate less specific investment such as e.g. gas fired plants.[147] The risk of regulatory opportunism distorts the incentives to choose between technologies that differ in respect of cost structure. With the risk of expropriation being higher for fixed than for variable cost, regulated rates increase with marginal costs and the firm has an incentive to adopt technologies with higher variable

---

[143] Cf. Besanko/Spulber (1992).

[144] Cf. Cornell (1992, 9).

[145] This is analogue to the situation of non-regulated firms. These are only willing to invest if they expect to earn on average their cost of capital; that means the risk of investment failures must be compensated by the chance of a correspondingly higher return on successful investments.

[146] Cf., for example, Spiegel (1996); Baron/De Bondt (1982).

[147] Cf. Karl (2003), 43. For the U.S., see the evidence described in Gilbert/Newberry (1994, 551).

and lower fixed costs,[148] e.g. a power plant technology that requires less investment but has higher fuel costs. Decisions for a technology with lower fixed and higher variable costs decrease operating leverage and business risk.

Regulatory buffering reduces the volatility of cash flows, but brings about a similar effect. If rate regulation buffers the utility against cost fluctuations, the incentives of the utility to invest in mitigation measures against the risk of external cost shocks, e.g. in cost saving technologies or in hedging of input price fluctuations, are distorted downwards.[149]

Timing of Investment. The existence of real options influences the hurdle rate of new investment and raises the question of optimal investment timing. If, for example, an investment project is (partially) irreversible and can be delayed, if there is uncertainty in the sense that investing now could turn out to be disadvantageous later, and if the firm expects to receive new information about the advantageousness of the investment project in the future, the firm possesses a valuable option to postpone investment.[150] Foregone profits and possible competitive advantages have to be weighed up against the value of waiting to invest.[151] For a regulated firm, it must be assumed that it possesses degrees of freedom in its investment timing. If regulatory investment obligations completely eliminate delayability, it is obvious that waiting is not an option, at least from the perspective of the regulated firm.[152] If regulation eliminates the option of postponing investment by an investment obligation, the regulated utility *ceteris paribus* is put at a disadvantage compared to a non-regulated firm.[153]

In the hypothetical benchmark case of a perfect and continuous rate-of-return regulation, the regulated firm would always earn the cost of capital on its investment. From the above enumerated pre-requisites of a valuable option to wait, it is clear that, if there are no contingencies under that investment might turn out disadvantageous, an option to wait exists but has

[148] Cf. Spiegel (1996).

[149] Cf. Gandolfi/Jenkinson/Mayer (1996, 8).

[150] Cf. Dixit/Pindyck (1994, 135ff.). For the pre-requisites of a valuable option to postpone investment, see Pedell (2000, 176ff.).

[151] For the determinants of optimal investment timing, see Trigeorgis (1996, 275f.); Pedell (2000, 245f.).

[152] Analogically, the regulator can make his approval a pre-condition for any investment and delay investment by not giving timely approval of investment programs as soon as requested by the regulated firm.

[153] See section 4.3.1.

no value,[154] and investment would never be delayed.[155] The more the implemented regulatory system *de facto* deviates from perfect rate-of-return regulation, the higher tends to be the uncertainty regarding the advantageousness of an investment and, accordingly, the value of the option to wait, increasing *ceteris paribus* the incentive to postpone investment.[156] The uncertainty can result from incomplete buffering of external shocks or more directly from regulatory action, for example, if the possibility exists, that the regulator excludes some investments from the rate base. The option to postpone investment is not the only real option relevant for optimal investment timing.[157] Making an investment usually opens up new investment opportunities or growth options, the value of which must also be accounted for. Clearly, a growth option can only have some value if the possibility exists that the firm will earn more than the cost of capital on the investment. Therefore, under a regime of perfect and continuous rate-of-return regulation a growth option – such as an option to postpone investment – is valueless. Growth options become more important in the transition to more light-handed forms of regulation and to more liberalized markets with competition.

If competition is admitted in the regulated business, and if, at the same time, monopolistic bottlenecks of the incumbent remain, the question of (pricing) access to the essential facility for the new competitors arises.[158] In this context, it has to be looked not only at possible real options of the incumbent but also of the new competitors. As irreversibility characterizes investment in bottlenecks, the incumbent by investing gives up a valuable option to postpone investment, if the above-mentioned prerequisites are fulfilled. If new competitors had to invest themselves in the bottleneck fa-

---

[154] See also Teisberg (1994, 543), who shows that the value of an option to wait decreases if regulation has a buffering effect and concludes from this: "To the extent that the firm can mitigate bad outcomes by delay or abandonment of an investment project, regulatory loss protection is redundant and therefore adds less value than the firm loses as a result of a priori symmetrical profit restrictions."

[155] Interpreted the other way around, a regulator could induce immediate investment by guaranteeing the regulated firm to earn its cost of capital over the entire lifetime of the investment. But, as discussed above, this is neither possible nor desirable.

[156] The application of a perfect contestability standard that assumes reversibility of investment to irreversible investment boils down to ignoring this option; see Hausman/Myers (2002, 292ff.).

[157] For an overview of the different types of real options, see Trigeorgis (1993, 204).

[158] See section 4.3.2.

cility to enter the business, they would have to give up the same option value. If, on the other hand, they gain access to the bottleneck of the incumbent, they can compete without having to commit resources to the essential facility themselves. In other words, they are granted for free the option to use the bottleneck. This is an external effect of the incumbent's investment and has to be accounted for when setting efficient access prices. As the incumbent produces a positive externality, access prices have to be increased *ceteris paribus* to induce efficient investment.

Adjustment of Financing

Capital structure determines how cash flows and risks are shared between debt and equity holders, or, more generally speaking, how cash flows are shared between different groups of capital providers and across different states of nature. Under rate regulation, capital structure also becomes important for the distribution of wealth and risk between the regulated firm and consumers of the regulated service.

Rate regulation unfolds its influence on the capital structure of the regulated firm in two basic ways. First, as discussed, regulation is suited to change the business risk of the regulated firm and thereby the *incentives for financing decisions*. If the firm changes its capital structure, it is clear that the weights of the WACC are changed. A higher debt ratio results in a higher tax shield, which, ceteris paribus, decreases the overall cost of financing.[159] However, financing decisions for their part change risk and risk-adjusted cost of debt and equity. A higher debt ratio means that variations in cash flows are translated into higher variations of return on equity, driving up the cost of equity.[160] This makes clear that the cost of equity of different regulated utilities, even if doing business in the same industry, can only be meaningfully compared after having been adjusted for differences in gearing.[161] Furthermore, from a certain point on, a higher gearing might be associated with a higher risk of financial distress increasing the

---

[159] It is assumed that a free cash flow-approach is used and that, consequently, the cost of debt in the WACC is reduced by corporate taxes.

[160] This mechanical increase in cost of equity can be shown best by a simple arithmetical exercise keeping constant the business risk and the overall cost of capital; cf. Myers (1992, 13).

[161] This is only the most obvious argument showing that the fixing of a certain cost of equity for an entire industry, as done in the German gas industry with the Association Agreement II for Network Access in the Natural Gas Sector (Verbändevereinbarung II), BDI / VIK / BGW / VKU (2002), is conceptually wrong.

cost of debt. Additionally, financing effects on the corporate governance have to be taken into account.

Besides the effect via regulatory risk, financing incentives are also changed by regulation if the regulated firm anticipates that the level of rates is influenced by its capital structure decision.[162] If a higher leverage increases the probability of financial distress, and if the regulator wants to avoid this effect, he is more likely to allow higher rates to lower the probability of bankruptcy. This increases the incentive for the regulated firm to use debt, at least to a certain point, as there is a trade-off with higher bankruptcy costs. As a consequence, the distributions of wealth and risk between the regulated firm and consumers are shifted in favor of the regulated firm.

Along the same line of argument, the regulated firm can use this interactive effect of debt on regulated rates to mitigate the risk of regulatory opportunism.[163] Just as the choice of technology, debt becomes a means for the firm of substituting lacking regulatory commitment. Therefore, it is not surprising that the choice of capital structure and the distortion of investment are interdependent. The more debt is used by the regulated firm, i.e. the more financing decisions are distorted, the more regulatory opportunism is mitigated and the less investment decisions – choice of technology and investment volume – are distorted.[164]

With asymmetric information between the regulated firm, that has informational advantages about its cost and demand situation, and the regulator as well as investors, the capital structure, too, becomes a means of signalling information to the less informed parties.[165] While the regulated firm wants to signal with its leverage low cost, i.e. high value, to the capital market, at the same time it prefers to signal high costs to the regulator to get approval of higher rates. The direction of the net effect of these

---

162 Cf. Taggart (1981, 384ff.), who calls this the price-influence effect.

163 Cf. Spiegel/Spulber (1994), who show, that the underinvestment problem resulting from the risk of regulatory opportunism is not completely eliminated. Spiegel (1994) analyzes the effect of changes in regulatory climate on the capital structure.

164 Spiegel (1996) models this interdependence.

165 Cf. Spiegel/Spulber (1997). See also Spiegel/Wilkie (1996) who restrain their analysis to the signalling of information to outside investors and the effect of the risk of regulatory opportunism and the exposure of the regulated firm to this risk on this signalling. The signalling only works if the regulatory climate is not to unfavourable and the firm is not too strongly committed by sunk investments.

countervailing signalling incentives on the use of debt is not unambiguous and critically depends on parameters such as firm size.[166]

A significant correlation between rate regulation and capital structure of the regulated firm has been confirmed in a number of empirical studies. Hagerman and Ratchford (1978, 53) show that for 79 electric utilities from 33 U.S. states in 1975 the allowed rate of return on equity is a positive function of the debt-equity ratio supporting the view that regulators account for the risk increasing effect of leverage on equity when setting rates. Taggart (1985) examines 92 U.S. electric utilities in the years 1912, 1917 and 1922, and finds that the establishment of rate regulation was associated with an increase in leverage. This is consistent with the conjecture that rate regulation reduces risk, which allows for higher debt financing, but can also be explained by the intent of the regulated firm to influence the rate setting of the regulator.[167] Besley and Bolton (1990) show that these empirical findings correspond to the belief of the larger part of decision makers in regulatory commissions and regulated firms who ranked leverage as one of the most important determinants of the return on equity of regulated utilities in a questionnaire survey. Dasgupta and Nanda (1993) find that for U.S. electric utilities in the period 1972-1983 in less favorable regulatory climates regulated firms increase the debt-equity ratio, also consistent with the hypothesis that the regulated firm uses debt as a means to mitigate regulatory opportunism. Rao and Moyer (1994) use time-series and cross-sectional analysis to investigate U.S. electric utilities in the period 1978-1982, and confirm this correlation between regulatory climate and leverage. An alternative interpretation on their part is that, in a lenient regulatory climate, the rate of return on equity exceeds the cost of equity and, therefore, the incentive to use equity is increased.

Besides the impact of rate regulation on financing incentives, the regulator can more directly intervene in financing decisions and *dictate a certain capital structure* or calculate rates with a certain capital structure, leaving it up to the firm to actually adjust to this capital structure or not.[168] The mo-

---

[166] Spiegel/Spulber (1997, 4) take is as a possible explanation, why Miller and Modigliani (1966) in their seminal study on the cost of capital of electric utilities do not find a significant leverage effect.

[167] Taggart (1985, 271) interprets his findings as being consistent with the debt capacity model of capital structure and the political economy theory of regulation arguing that in times of depression the regulator protects producers whereas in times of expansion he acts more in favor of consumers.

[168] This is a form of micromanagement that either assumes that the regulatory commission has better information for taking financing decisions than the regulated firm itself (which is very unlikely) or bases its legitimacy on concerns of regulatory governance; see section 4.3.1.

tive for these regulatory directives is to lower the weighted average cost of capital by substituting debt for equity, assuming the existence of an optimal capital structure and insufficient use of debt by the regulated firm, i.e. that the regulated firm deviates intentionally from this capital structure to get higher rates or that the regulator is better able than the regulated firm to assess this optimal capital structure. The latter - better information of the regulator about the optimal capital structure - is very debatable, to say the least.[169] If the regulator dictates a certain capital structure or calculates rates with a certain capital structure different from the actual one, cost of equity and cost of debt have to be adjusted consistently to the new capital structure. Dictating a higher debt ratio without admitting a higher cost of equity, for example, would put the regulated firm at an unjustified disadvantage.

If the assessment of the capital structure considered optimal by the regulator does not depend on the actual capital structure, the firm has no incentive to adjust its financing decisions. The actual capital structure is a result of the regulated firm's optimization that, in this case, would be unaffected by the regulator's choice of another capital structure.[170] This gives rise to a gap between actual costs and calculated costs used for rate setting that might increase or decrease the risk of the regulated firm and correspondingly alters its investment decisions. If the regulator uses a lower weighted average cost of capital than the actual one, the firm expects to earn less than the appropriate rate of return and will reduce its investment. This underlines the informational dilemma faced by the regulator when he wants to induce both efficient investment and efficient financing.

[169] For a detailed discussion, see section 6.3.2.
[170] Cf. Taggart (1981, 391).

4 Development of a Regulatory Control Panel – Analysis of Individual Variables of Rate Regulation as Determinants of Regulatory Risk

In this chapter, the impact of single regulatory variables on risk (adjusted cost of capital) is analyzed. Variables of the regulatory commission are categorized in variables determining the scope of regulated markets, firms and decisions, variables defining the type of the overall regulatory system, as well as regulatory accounting directives establishing procedures to calculate regulated rates.

Regulatory risk can be traced back to the design variables of rate regulation as ultimate *causes*. Differences in the design of regulation are reflected in different effects on the risk of the regulated firm. In Figure 4.1, a *regulatory control panel* is developed. The design variables or regulatory directives of the panel can be grouped into several categories. *System* variables establish the basic functioning of the regulatory system. Regulatory systems can be classified with respect to the elements of cash flows covered by regulation.[171] The extent to which cash flow elements are covered by regulation determines the degree to which the firm is the master of its own destiny in the regulated business. While rate-of-return regulation covers all profit elements, price caps cover only prices. These forms are the poles of a spectrum of possible intermediate forms of regulatory systems. Furthermore, regulatory systems can be differentiated according the criterion whether and to which degree *ex post* adjustments are made by the regulator, should predictions underlying the earlier setting of rates prove to be wrong. In this regard, regulatory systems range between pure *ex ante* regulation and pure *ex post* regulation.

The rate setting process is characterized by numerous regulatory variables. The review period between scheduled rate adjustments can be either fixed or flexible. In the latter case, the opening of the rate adjustment procedure may be triggered by the actual rate of return hitting a lower or upper boundary of a bandwidth around the allowed rate of return. Intermediate rate adjustments between scheduled reviews may or may not be per-

[171] Cf. Alexander/Mayer/Weeds (1996) and section 4.1.1.

mitted. The question of who is entitled to request a revision of rates must be answered. Regulatory lag between the moment of a rate request and the actual adjustment of the rate determines how long the firm might be exposed to unforeseen cost shocks.

Variables Determining the Scope of Regulation		
Scope of Regulated Decisions - Investment Decisions - Financing Decisions - Risk Mitigation Measures	Scope of Regulated Firms - Scope of Competition and Entry Allowed - Access of New Entrants to Incumbents' Facilities - Symmetry of Regulation	Scope of Regulated Markets - Horizontal Scope of the Firm's Activities - Vertical Scope of Regulated Markets

Regulatory System Variables			
Profit Elements Covered by Regulation	Regulatory Lag / Regulatory Review Period	Degree of Regulatory Discretion	Bandwidth for the Actual Rate of Return

Regulatory Accounting Directives			
Regulatory Cost Concept			
Operating Expenditures - Automatic Cost Pass-Through - Tax Flow-Through or Normalization	Capital Expenditures		Cost Distribution Base
	Regulatory Asset Base - Historical Structure vs. Greenfield Approach - Disallowances - Stranded Assets - Market or Book Values - CWIP/AFUDC - Depreciation Scheme	Allowed Rate of Return - Interest Rate Risk - Debt and Equity Premium - Capital Structure	

Figure 4.1. Regulatory control panel - design variables of rate regulation as determinants of regulatory risk

Accounting directives stipulate how the cost of the regulated firm is calculated as a basis for setting rates. With regard to operating expenditure, this comprises, for example, the question of whether cost pass-through clauses are used, and whether tax effects due to accelerated depreciation are treated as a flow-through or are normalized. The calculation of capital expenditure requires the determination of the regulatory rate base and the assessment of the allowed rate of return. Finally, it has to be determined if costs are allocated on the total capacity or the actually marketed capacity, leaving the capacity utilization risk to the firm or to the consumers. If the firm offers several services, the allocation of costs across services arises as an additional accounting issue.

Variables determining the scope of regulation are not part of the rate setting itself.[172] However, the impact of rate regulation on the risk of the regulated firm is characterized by strong interaction with these variables. As far as the regulated business itself is concerned, the most prominent examples are investment obligations, e.g. in the form of a universal service obligation, and the admittance of competition. If competitors are in the same business, they may or may not be submitted to symmetric regulation. The accessibility of the regulated infrastructure for competitors depends on the regulation of technical standards. On top of that, the overall risk of the regulated firm depends on risk interdependences with other, vertically integrated or horizontally diversified businesses and the admittance of risk mitigation measures by the regulator.

4.1 Impact of the Overall Regulatory System Variables on Risk

4.1.1 Profit Elements Covered by Rate Regulation

Regulatory systems can be differentiated according to which profit elements are covered by regulation and which elements are completely left to the influence of the regulated firm. The following formula[173], in connection with Table 4.1, gives a schematic overview of idealized types of regulatory systems:

$$\Pi = PQ - C_x(Q) - C_n(Q) \qquad (4.1)$$

Π = total profits

P = unit price

Q = quantity sold

C_x = exogenous costs

C_n = endogenous costs

where endogenous costs can be influenced by the regulated utility, as in the case of administrative costs, and exogenous costs are beyond the influence of the regulated utility, as in the case of fuel costs.

---

172 Quality issues cannot be separated from rate setting. They belong to the definition and surveillance of the regulated service.

173 Cf. Alexander/Mayer/Weeds (1996, 7).

Table 4.1. Profit elements covered by alternative regulatory regimes

Regulatory system	Covered by regulation	Ignored by regulation
Price cap	P	Q, $C_{x,}$ C_n
Price cap with cost pass-through	P, C_x	Q, C_n
Revenue cap	PQ	$C_{x,}$ C_n
Rate-of-return regulation	PQ, $C_{x,}$ C_n	—

Source: Alexander/Mayer/Weeds (1996, 8)

Rate-of-return regulation and price caps can be interpreted as the poles of a spectrum of possible regulatory systems. Rate-of-return regulation covers all profit elements and guarantees the regulated firm in the (hypothetical) case of its perfect implementation a certain allowed rate of return on all its investment. Theoretically, this could be achieved by continuously adjusting rates to cost and demand changes. As this is unrealistic, the regulator rather compensates the regulated firm *ex post* by raising future rates, if in the past the firm earned less than the allowed rate of return, respectively claws back past returns above the allowed rate of return by decreasing future rates. A system of perfect *ex post* rate-of-return regulation would remove all risk from the regulated firm. As is well known, this would raise serious problems of regulatory governance,[174] e.g. regarding incentives for efficient investment and operation, as well as the reporting of true costs.

Therefore, more incentive-oriented regulatory systems such as price caps have been established. A pure type of price cap only covers the price or baskets of prices. A price cap is set *ex ante* for the whole regulatory review period, according to the expected development of consumer price index and productivity. If the firm realizes higher efficiency gains and earns supernormal profits, these remain with the firm in order to set incentives to invest efficiently and to improve operating cost efficiency. Except for the

[174] For an extensive treatment of problems of regulatory governance, see Laffont/Tirole (1993); for a recent overview of approaches of incentive based regulation and a discussion of its merits, see Vogelsang (2002).

price setting, the regulated firm is the master of its own destiny and accordingly bears considerable risk.

Two special types of an intermediate regulatory system are a price cap with a cost pass-through clause and a revenue cap. The basic idea of a price cap with a cost pass-through[175] is to shift risks associated with cost elements not controllable by the regulated firm to buyers of the regulated product. Leaving these risks with the regulated firm does not increase incentives for cost efficiency, as the cost elements cannot be influenced by the regulated firm anyway. A typical example for costs that are passed through to regulated rates are fuel costs in the energy sector.

A revenue cap is used, above all, if the proportion of fixed costs (that is not covered by fixed revenues) becomes very large. In this case, variations in demand cause high variations in profit. The revenue cap aims at reducing this risk without diminishing the incentives for cost savings.[176] However, if a revenue cap is applied in the case of a high proportion of variable costs, risk is on the contrary increased, as a higher demand increases cost and, consequently, reduces profits, unless the revenue cap is automatically adjusted upward.[177]

In a large empirical study, Alexander, Mayer and Weeds (1996) compared asset betas[178] of different types of regulatory systems by conducting time series and cross-country analyses. Table 4.2 shows their aggregate results for different regulated sectors and for different groups of regulatory systems with high-powered (i.e. close to the idealized type of a price cap), low-powered (i.e. close to the idealized type of a rate-of-return regulation) and intermediate incentives. It can be clearly seen that regulatory systems with high incentives, on average, have a higher asset beta. This holds true across all investigated industries, and confirms the conjecture that the risk to which a regulated utility is exposed depends on the profit elements covered by rate regulation. The more profit is determined by the regulatory system, the stronger the buffering effect seems to be and the lower the residual risk to be borne by a regulated firm is.[179]

---

175 For cost pass-through, see section 4.2.2.

176 Furthermore, revenue caps avoid incentives for high energy consumption that can be induced by price caps.

177 Cf. Vogelsang (2002) for a more detailed differentiation of regulatory systems.

178 For the calculation and use of asset betas, see section 6.2.4 and section 6.2.5.

179 These results are confirmed by Alexander/Estache/Oliveri (2000).

Table 4.2. Average asset beta values by regulatory regime and sector

Incentives	Electricity	Gas	Energy	Water	Telecoms	Average
High-powered	0.57	0.84	—	0.67	0.77	0.71
Intermediate	0.41	0.57	0.64	0.46	0.70	0.60
Low-powered	0.35	0.20	0.25	0.29	0.41	0.32

Source: Alexander/Mayer/Weeds (1996, 29).

From this empirical evidence can be concluded that, if a higher profitability is observed for firms subject to a price cap compared to firms that are rate-of-return regulated, this is justified, in principle, by higher risk. This does not exclude, however, that a lenient handling of price caps allows the firm an expected rate of return above its cost of capital. Such a regulatory upside bias would make investment in firms regulated by price caps less risky. The same argument applies to a very restrictive handling of a rate-of-return system with an asymmetric downside bias. Besides which, these effects would not be captured by beta in a two-moment CAPM.

4.1.2 Regulatory Review Period and Regulatory Lag

The frequency of regulatory reviews affects the risk sharing between the regulated firm and the rate payers. In the hypothetical case of a continuous and instantaneous adjustment of rates to exogenous cost (and demand) changes, the risks associated with these changes are completely borne by rate payers. On the one hand, if rates are never adjusted, all the risks remain with the regulated firm.[180] In principle, the longer the regulatory lag after a cost change or the longer the scheduled regulatory review period, the higher is the portion of risk that has to be borne by the regulated firm.[181] The more this risk is correlated with the overall market risk the more it raises the cost of capital. On the other hand, regulatory lag tends to

[180] Instead of a fixed review period boundaries within that the actual rate of return can vary without regulatory adjustments can be used. A review is triggered if the actual rate of return hits the lower or upper boundary. This results in a flexible review period. See section 4.1.4.

[181] Cf. also Thompson (1991, 204).

increase the incentives for the regulated utility to invest in cost-reducing technology.[182]

Gandolfi, Jenkinson and Mayer (1996, 2) analyze the impact of the length of the regulatory review period on systematic risk and, to this end, build a model consisting of two industries: one monopolistic rate-regulated utility and an unregulated industry with a number of firms engaged in Cournot competition in the market of a homogeneous good. The number of firms depends on the extent of sunk costs, the size of the market and the production cost. The intuition that a shorter review period reduces total risk, systematic risk and consequently the cost of capital of the regulated utility is confirmed by numerical simulations.[183] In other words, the buffering of market fluctuations by rate regulation is more complete with more frequent rate reviews. In an extension of the model, the cost structure is taken as endogenous, i.e. driven by cost-saving investment of the regulated firm. As cost-saving investment reduces the risk of the regulated firm compared to the exogenous cost case and as the incentive for such investment is reduced by frequent regulatory reviews, short review periods can work in the opposite direction and increase systematic risk and the cost of capital.

The model does not address the issue of asymmetric regulatory risk. If rate regulation is downward biased, as described in section 3.3.3, asymmetric regulatory risk is likely to increase with the number of rate reviews during the economic lifetime of a regulated asset. If the rate of return varies over the economic lifetime of an asset, and if supernormal rates of return are capped by regulation without compensating for rates of return below the normal level, the total effect on the rate of return over the economic lifetime of the asset is likely to be higher with more frequent rate reviews. Within longer review periods, supernormal profits and profits below the normal level are more likely to compensate each other without regulatory intervention. An asymmetric effect working in the opposite direction might be due to continuous cost increases. If the regulatory commission determines the rates for a certain time period based on the cost

---

182 See, for example, John/Saunders (1983).

183 Cf. Gandolfi,/Jenkinson/Mayer (1996, 11). Only in the case of a small degree of cost pass-through for the regulated utility and a relatively long adjustment process in the unregulated market to an exogenous cost shock, systematic risk slightly increases with the length of the review period. In this case, an exogenous cost shock affects the regulated firm stronger than the unregulated sector, reducing the correlation of market values of the regulated utility and the unregulated sector. Shortening the review period, on the other hand, attenuates this effect.

situation at a certain point in time and does not include future cost increases during the review period, the regulated firm faces a downward bias in its rates. Such a bias would be attenuated by more frequent rate reviews.

A hypothetical regulatory scheme of perfect rate-of-return regulation is characterized by a complete pass-through of all costs to rates without any lag (see Figure 4.2); *both* criteria have to be fulfilled to guarantee continuously a certain allowed rate of return to the regulated firm. A hypothetical scheme of pure incentive regulation would set rates once and for all at the very beginning of regulation and not pass through any costs to rates and/or would adjust rates with an infinite lag. *Either* zero cost pass-through *or* infinite lag is sufficient to establish pure incentive regulation. Intermediate schemes operate with a finite lag and partial cost pass-through. For a given cost pass-through, systematic risk of the regulated firm *ceteris paribus* increases with the length of the regulatory lag. Accordingly, for a given regulatory lag, systematic risk of the regulated firm *ceteris paribus* decreases with the share of costs passed through to rates. It has to be considered, however, that buffering by regulation, e.g. against external cost shocks, reduces the incentives for the regulated firm to adopt risk-mitigating measures, e.g. by investing in cost-saving technologies.[184] This indirect effect via the investment of the regulated firm works in the opposite direction of the direct buffering effect.[185]

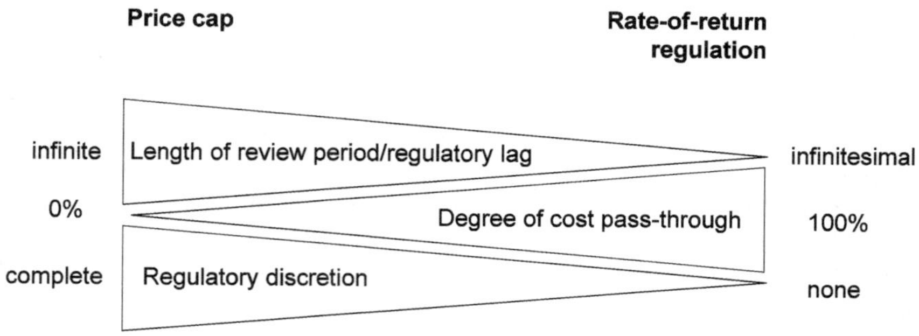

Figure 4.2. Characteristics of price caps and rate-of-return regulation

[184] For a theoretical and simulative investigation of these effects, see Gandolfi/Jenkinson/Mayer (1996, 2ff.) who to this end model an economy consisting of one regulated and one unregulated sector.

[185] Gandolfi/Jenkinson/Mayer (1996, 11ff.), in their simulations, show that this indirect effect can even outweigh the direct buffering effect.

Practical implementations of both regulatory systems are much more closely related than the hypothetical extreme forms. Regulatory commissions use cost and demand information to determine initial price caps and to review them. In a system of rate-of-return regulation, prices are only adjusted with a time lag to changes in cost and demand. To give the regulated firm an incentive for efficient investment, not all investment is necessarily accepted in the rate base.[186] Depending on the time intervals in which regulatory reviews take place and/or on the length of the regulatory lag, the effect of price cap and rate-of-return regulation on risk becomes more similar. The approach currently pursued in UK regulation can be described as accounting-based with the principle of granting an appropriate rate of return to the firm, but without *ex post* adjustments during the review period with the aim of keeping alive incentives for efficient investment and operation.[187]

4.1.3 Degree of Regulatory Discretion

Regulatory discretion arises for two reasons: On the one hand, the regulatory contract necessarily remains incomplete, as not all contingencies can be anticipated by the involved parties. On the other hand, the regulator ultimately cannot even commit to the well-specified parts of the regulatory contract, as the government standing behind the regulator will always be able to change the contract unilaterally.[188] Nevertheless, striving for establishing well-specified regulatory rules is not pointless, since the regulatory game is a repeated one and the regulator can build up reputation capital. The rate setting process should be as stable, predictable and transparent as possible in order to limit the perceived regulatory risk.[189] A dispute resolution process is needed for contingencies not unambiguously covered by the regulatory contract.

Modifications of the regulatory contract should be made with care and with sufficient lead time until they become effective. A special risk in this context is the tendency of policymakers "…to view any desirable change in policy as a "one-off improvement" that leads to a new and better environment. However, a series of "one-off" changes creates uncertainty over

---

[186] Cf. section 4.2.3.

[187] Cf. Burns/Estache (1999, 2).

[188] Grayburn/Hern/Lay (2002, 5ff.) refer to this risk as "regulatory intervention risk" delimiting it from "regulatory system risk". See section 3.2 for a discussion of regulatory commitment.

[189] See Shuttleworth/MacKerron (2002, 10).

what further changes will take place, especially if these improvements are being driven by multiple, and potentially conflicting, objectives."[190]

The possible problems resulting from the incompleteness of the regulatory contract are especially highlighted when a hitherto public monopolist is up for privatization. The better pre-specified the planned rate regulation is, the easier it is for private investors to build expectations consistent with the future rate regulation and to price the firm accordingly. Any *ad hoc* changes after privatization bring about windfall gains or losses for the current shareholders.[191] Therefore, governments should aim at defining the planned system of rate regulation to the greatest possible extent before privatization.

Empirical evidence confirms that unforeseen regulatory interventions are in principle apt to increase risk perceived by investors. Robinson and Taylor (1998b) show that the unexpected reopening of the already closed regulatory review in the UK electricity sector in March 1995 led to a significant and lasting increase of the volatility of share prices of most of the concerned electric utilities. In a further study with several events, they find the volatility increasing effect of unexpected regulatory interventions confirmed for most of the events investigated. However, Morana and Sawkins (2000) find a significant reduction in the share price volatility in the English and Welsh water industry following the announcement of a revision of the industry's price caps in 1994. They explain their findings with investors' "… confidence in the credibility and political sustainability of the settlement."[192] Obviously, the effect of an unforeseen regulatory intervention on the volatility of share prices crucially depends on whether the perceived risk of *future* interventions is increased or decreased. Furthermore, this effect cannot be separated from the content of the intervention, i.e. if the modification of the regulatory system *per se* has a buffering or reinforcing effect on the risk of the regulated firm.[193]

As to regulatory discretion, the assignment of a certain degree of discretion to a regulatory system is less clear than the assignment of regulatory lag and cost pass-through. In principle, the regulator can deviate from an announced course of action and change the regulatory regime in an *ad hoc* manner under any regulatory system.[194] The commitment quality of a regu-

---

[190] Shuttleworth/MacKerron (2002, 19).

[191] For a more detailed discussion of this issue in the context of market values versus book values for the regulatory rate base, see section 5.3.3.

[192] Morana/Sawkins (2000, 98).

[193] See the event studies referred to in section 3.3.2.

[194] This refers also to switches of the methods of rate base determination and cost of capital assessment that are analyzed in chapter 5 and chapter 6.

latory system ultimately depends less on the type of rate regulation, but more on its institutional establishment. It can be stated, however, that even a system of perfect rate-of-return regulation with complete cost pass-through and without any lag only guarantees an appropriate (risk-free) rate of return if it is supported by complete commitment not to change this system within the period over which the regulated firm commits capital to its investments. If there is the slightest possibility that the regulator will change the system, investors will demand a risk premium even under otherwise perfect rate-of-return regulation. In a dynamic perspective, complete regulatory commitment is the third condition that has to be fulfilled to eliminate any risk for the regulated firm (see Figure 4.2).

Practical implementations of rate regulation necessarily leave discretionary power to the regulator.[195] Rate-of-return regulation tends to be supported by stronger institutional commitment than price caps, e.g. by the establishment of a larger regulatory bureaucracy and more detailed laws and decrees.[196] Under price cap regulation, political pressure to claw back observed excess profits is likely to be considerable. However, there is no strict correlation between the type of rate regulation and its commitment quality. The importance of regulatory risk and the commitment quality of a regulatory scheme is underlined by Gilbert and Newberry (1994). They show that price cap regulation that is *a priori* supposed to have better incentive qualities than rate-of-return regulation might be inferior in its overall efficiency if a dynamic perspective is taken and rate-of-return regulation has better commitment quality. The lesson is that, ultimately, the advantageousness of price cap *versus* rate-of-return regulation cannot be judged without looking at their institutional establishment.

4.1.4 Bandwidth Within Which the Actual Rate of Return Can Vary

A regulatory system variable that is closely related to the issue of regulatory lag is the (explicit or implicit) fixing of boundaries around a certain rate of return assessed as appropriate by the regulatory commission within which the actual rate of return can vary without regulatory adjustment. In such a scheme, rates are only adjusted when the actual rate of return hits the lower or upper boundary. Rates can be adjusted such that the actual re-

---

[195] See the discussion of regulatory commitment in section 3.3.1, especially the argument regarding the lack of commitment of last resort for the government and its agencies.

[196] Cf. Houston (1996, 1), who attributes the rise of enormous regulatory discretion to the „... under-specified procedures in RPI-X regulation ..." in the UK.

turn is immediately reset to the allowed rate of return or that the actual rate of return is just prevented from overshooting the boundary or that the rate of return is admitted beyond the boundary, but from that point profits (or losses) are shared between the regulated firm and the consumers. The profit sharing scheme is also known as sliding-scale regulation. The wider apart the boundaries are set, the longer is the expected time between the starting point and the next regulatory review. Along the same line of argument as in the previous section, narrower boundaries reinforce the buffering effect of (symmetric) regulation and decrease the cost of capital. On the other hand, if the regulatory adjustments, taking place when the actual rate of return hits the upper or lower boundary, are downward biased, the risk associated with these interventions can be increased by narrower boundaries, i.e. by a shorter expected time between regulatory adjustments.

The setting of the bandwidth not only determines the sharing of profits between regulated firm and consumers but also the sharing of risk. The wider the bandwidth is set, the more risk remains with the regulated firm. By setting the bandwidth around the allowed rate of return within which the actual rate of return can vary without regulatory interventions, intermediate forms of regulation between non-regulation and perfect rate-of-return regulation can be realized. An unlimited bandwidth can be interpreted as non-regulation whereas an infinitesimal bandwidth boils down to a perfect and continuous rate-of-return regulation.

A dynamic model of rate regulation by Brennan and Schwartz (1982a) shows the effect of such boundaries on value and systematic risk of the regulated firm. In their model, a completely self-financed regulated firm is assumed with rate base B and actual rate of return r on this rate base. The actual rate of return r follows an exogenous stochastic process:

$$dr = \mu dt + \sigma dz \tag{4.2}$$

where μ denominates the expected change of the return, t is time, and dz is a Wiener process with expected value zero and variance dt. σ^2 is the variance of the change in r and represents the business risk. With a dividend yield $p(r)$ on B, the amount $(r - p(r))\,B$ remains for self-financing after distributed profits, and B follows the stochastic process

$$dB = (r - p(r))Bdt \tag{4.3}$$

At the starting point, rates are set such that the actual return equals a certain allowed rate of return r^* for which the market-to-book ratio m equals one.[197] This is what is called a "...consistent regulatory policy..."

[197] In the model, this means, that the return just equals the cost of capital.

by Brennan and Schwartz (1982a, 509). The regulatory commission fixes boundaries around this *a priori* allowed rate of return r^* within which the actual rate of return can vary without regulatory intervention. As soon as the actual rate of return hits the lower boundary r^l or the upper boundary r^u, the regulator adjusts the rates of the firm such that the actual rate of return equals again the allowed rate of return r^* (see Figure 4.3).

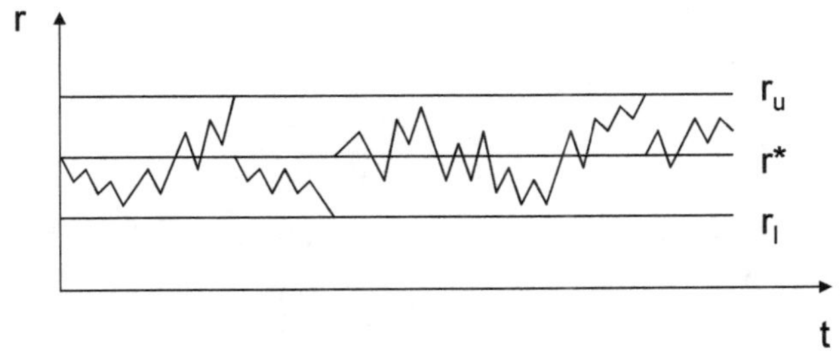

Figure 4.3. Development of the actual rate or return under a rate correction mechanism

In equilibrium, the return of the regulated firm equals the risk-less interest rate plus a risk premium (*P* denotes the share price of the firm)[198]

$$\frac{E(dP(r,B)) + pB + \pi(r)[P(r^*(r),B) - P(r,B)]}{P(r,B)} = r_f + \lambda\sigma\frac{P_r(r,B)}{P(r,B)} \quad (4.4)$$

$$\pi(r) = 0,\ \mathrm{r_l} < r < r_u$$

$$\pi(r_l) = \pi(r_u) = 1$$

$$m(r^*) = 1$$

On the left hand side of the differential equation is the expected share price change plus dividend plus change in value due to rate regulation all in relation to the share price; on the right hand side is the risk-less interest rate plus market price of risk times the firm specific risk. $\lambda\sigma$ denotes the covariance between changes in *r* and market return, where

$$\lambda = [E(r_M) - r]\cdot\left[\frac{Cov(dz, r_M)}{\sigma_M^2}\right] \quad (4.5)$$

A higher λ means a higher systematic risk of the regulated firm. π is a regulatory parameter that depends on the actual rate of return and indicates

198 Cf. also Thompson (1991, 72ff.).

the probability for a review of rates. In the simplest case of deterministic regulation, it is zero as long as r is within the bandwidth and it is set to one as soon as r touches the upper or lower bound.

From equation (5), under certain premises[199] the following differential equation can be derived giving a functional relationship between the market-to-book ratio m and the return r on the capital base B that is determined by regulation.

$$\frac{1}{2}\sigma^2 m_{rr} + (\mu - \lambda\sigma)m_r + (g - r_f)m + r - g + \pi(r)[m(r^*(r)) - m(r)] = 0 \quad (4.6)$$

$$m(r) = \frac{P(r)}{B}$$

In this setting, the value of the firm is a function of the actual rate of return, as shown by Figure 4.4. If the actual rate of return r is above the allowed rate of return r^*, it is expected that the regulated firm will earn supernormal profits for a certain time. This expected time is longest, if the actual rate of return lies in the middle between the allowed rate of return and the upper boundary r_u. Closer to r^*, profits closer to normal profits are expected to be earned on average; closer to r_u, a rate adjustment, bringing the actual rate of return back to r^* instantaneously, becomes more likely. This trade-off yields a maximum of market-to-book ratio m somewhere between r^* and r_u. The effect of an actual rate of return below the allowed rate of return on value can be explained by reversed reasoning. Narrower boundaries limit the deviations of m from unity. If the bandwidth is reduced symmetrically, the expected frequency of rate adjustments increases. The actual rate of return will deviate for shorter periods from r^*, and the value function converges to a horizontal line with the value of one that is attained in the extreme case that the bandwidth is set to zero.

[199] Cf. Brennan/Schwartz (1982a, 511); among other things, it is assumed that the capacity of the regulated firm develops proportionally to B, and that the regulated firm can be obligated by the regulator to adjusts its capacity to the exogenous demand growth g. Furthermore, it is assumed that the rate adjustments made by the regulator in order to keep r within the bandwidth have no effect on g.

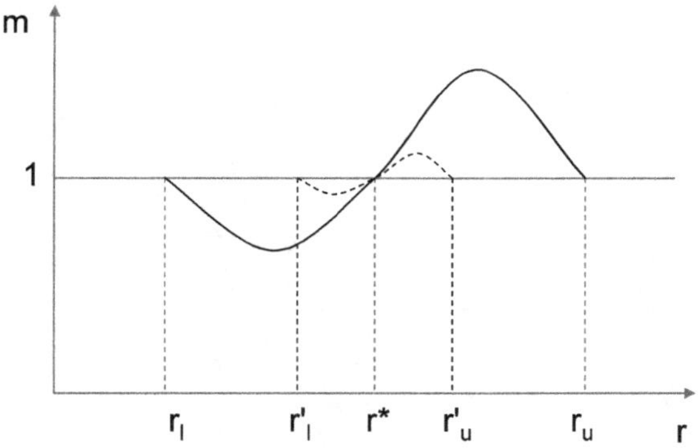

Figure 4.4. Value as a function of the actual rate of return with deterministic regulatory rate adjustments (Source: Thompson (1991, 74))

If the lower boundary is unilaterally brought down, the value function exhibits stronger amplitude between r^* and r^l, and r^* is shifted to the right (see Figure 4.5). As a consequence of lowering r^l, longer periods of below normal actual returns are expected, and, with constant r^u, r^* has to be increased as compensation in order to attain the same expected rate of return at the bottom line. The reverse argument applies, when the upper limit r^u is raised unilaterally.

Furthermore, not only value, but also beta and cost of capital are functions of the actual rate of return in this model, where beta is defined as

$$\beta = \frac{m_r}{m}\left[\frac{\lambda\sigma}{\sigma_M^2}\right] \tag{4.7}$$

σ_M denotes the variance of the overall market. The expression in brackets corresponds to the beta of the standard CAPM, the term before the brackets is the additional effect due to rate regulation.[200]

[200] Cf. also Riddick (1992, 143).

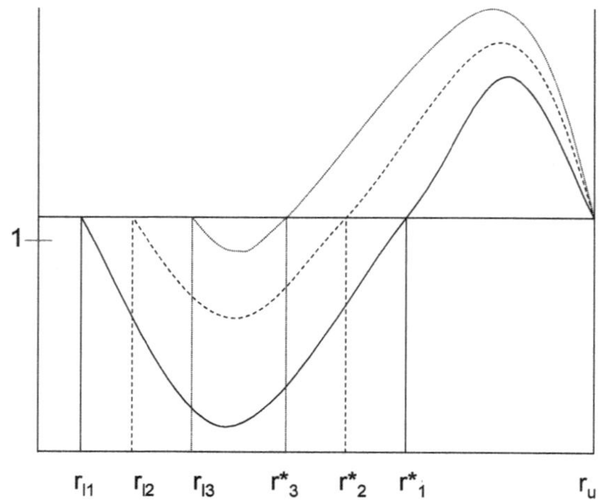

Figure 4.5. Influence of the lower boundary on market value and allowed rate of return (Source: Thompson (1991, 79))

The form of the beta function is exhibited in Figure 4.6. If the actual rate of return is close to the allowed rate of return, it is very likely to follow the exogenous stochastic process (that, by assumption, corresponds to the development of the return on the market portfolio of assets) over a relative long time before hitting one of the boundaries. Therefore, beta is close to one. The closer the actual rate of return to one of the boundaries, the more likely becomes a regulatory adjustment that drives the rate of return of the regulated firm in the opposite direction of the overall market return. This negative correlation is reflected by a negative beta.

The form of the function depends on the rate-resetting mechanism. Beta values are lowest at the boundaries, if the actual rate of return is completely reset to the allowed rate of return (reverting mechanism). Beta is higher, but still negative, at the upper boundary for a regulatory regime that just keeps the actual rate of return within the boundaries (reflecting mechanism), and still higher in the case that the regulatory commission allows the regulated firm to keep a portion of its profits above the upper boundary.[201] A scheme that shares profits with rate payers, for example by way of discounts, is also known as sliding-scale regulation. In this case, beta decreases above r*, but does not take negative values, as the actual return of the regulated firm is driven in the same direction as the overall market return even at and above the upper boundary.

201 Cf. Lewellen/Mauer (1993, 268ff.).

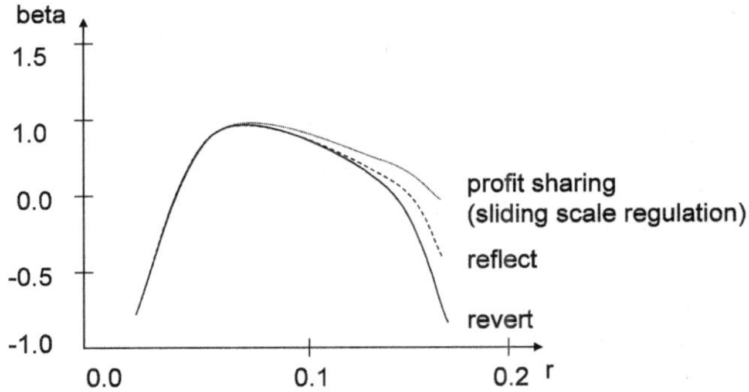

Figure 4.6. Beta as a function of the actual rate of return with deterministic regulatory rate adjustments (Source: Lewellen/Mauer (1993, 279))

Notwithstanding its fairly restrictive assumptions, this model contains several lessons. The beta factor of a rate-regulated firm is not necessarily a strictly (or even linearly) increasing function of the actual rate of return as implied by the CAPM. It might be subject to strong fluctuations, even if the actual rate of return can only vary within a relatively small bandwidth. Therefore, a beta factor estimated by capital market data should be interpreted very carefully for the purpose of assessing the cost of capital and the appropriate rate of return of a regulated firm. The estimation period for the beta factor should not be chosen too short, i.e. should not comprehend only a short time interval immediately before an adjustment of rates. The model suggests that in this case the beta factor and the cost of capital would be underestimated.[202] However, this result seems to depend crucially on the assumption of a consistent regulatory policy, and empirical evidence exists that contradicts this aspect of the model. It has been found that the volatility of the share price of regulated utilities is particularly high when the rate review process is reopened and especially low immediately after a review.[203] This underlines the importance of the risk from regulatory discretion for the beta factor and the cost of capital of a regulated utility.

[202] This result is confirmed by Gandolfi, Jenkinson and Mayer (1996, 12). Simulations of their model show that beta factors fall when the rate review approaches resulting in a saw-tooth cycle of cost of capital.

[203] Cf. Morana/Sawkins (2000); see also Robinson/Taylor (1998b).

4.2 Impact of Regulatory Accounting Directives on Risk

Regulatory accounting directives determine how rates are calculated. As discussed in section 2.2, every form of rate regulation should be cost-orientated to a certain degree. This section analyzes how individual calculation directives for cost elements feed back on risk (adjusted cost of capital) of a regulated firm.

4.2.1 Regulatory Cost Concept

A fundamental accounting variable is the cost concept employed by the regulator. Basically, either actual costs or some other form of cost concept can be applied. As already discussed in section 4.1.1, a hypothetical regulatory system that continuously and completely reimburses all costs actually incurred by the regulated utility, including an adequate allowed rate of return, would remove any risk from the regulated firm.[204] The regulatory cost concept employed in reality by the regulator considerably influences the deviations from this benchmark case, i.e. the risks to be borne by the regulated firm.

A prominent cost concept applied in rate regulation is LRIC. As discussed in section 2.4, these are the costs that could be saved, if an increment of demand were not served and all inputs were completely flexible.[205] In principle, LRIC is oriented towards the future. As a consequence, in many instances, not the technology actually in place is used for the determination of costs, but a more efficient or even the most efficient technology available. If technological progress occurs, the regulated firm gets compensated unilaterally less than its actual costs, i.e. it is exposed to an asymmetric downside risk by the use of LRIC.[206] For instance, the concept of 'cost of efficient service provision'[207] that is applied in the German telecommunications sector does not refer to actual costs, but to an efficiency criterion that needs to be qualified. The German Monopoly Commission, in a special report about the telecommunications and postal sector, recog-

---

[204] In reality, even if the regulator aims at reimbursing actual costs, frictions will arise alone taking into account adjustment lags and information asymmetries.

[205] Cf. Bromwich/Vass (2002, 1684).

[206] For a more detailed discussion of this issue in the context of the quantity structure of the regulatory rate base, see section 4.2.3.

[207] § 31 (1) of the German Telekommunikationsgesetz (TKG) [Telecommunications Act] states that regulated rates have to be orientated towards the 'Kosten der effizienten Leistungsbereitstellung'.

nizes that this exposes DTAG to certain risks as the development of costs of efficient service provision in the future is uncertain.[208]

The cost concept of total element long run incremental costs (TELRIC) uses the most efficient technology that would be employed in a competitive market. Consistently, The U.S. Federal Communications Commission (FCC) consistently acknowledges in its Triennial Review Order that the use of TELRIC requires compensation of the regulated utility by a higher cost of capital to "...reflect the risk of a competitive market."[209] Along the same line of argument, an asymmetric risk arises if the regulator uses the lowest (internationally) available cost benchmark. Apart from the fact that the regulatory system - to which the benchmark company is subject - has to be comparable, utilities, on average, will earn less than their cost of capital, if the most efficient firm is always used as a benchmark.[210] Hausman (1997, 28ff.) criticizes TELRIC on the grounds that it adopts a perfect contestability standard by giving competitors access to successful investments without a mark-up over cost that, under uncertainty, would be required to compensate the regulated utility for failed investments; he reasons by analogy to patent protection in competitive markets.[211] Furthermore, he criticizes that TELRIC assumes that every investment permanently operates at full capacity[212] and that, for all these reasons, the efficiency criterion underlying TELRIC is a static one, which distorts investment incentives.

Furthermore, LRIC critically depends on the definition of the increment. An increment can be a complete service offered by the regulated firm or a single unit of this service. Alternatively, LRIC can refer to a certain network element. If all services offered by a regulated firm are included in the increment, LRIC corresponds to average cost, while LRIC equals marginal cost, if the increment consists only of a marginal service unit.[213] In a natural monopoly with economies of scale, marginal cost is below average cost; therefore, revenues will not be sufficient to cover fixed costs, if such

208 Cf. Monopolkommission (2003, 72).

209 FCC (2003, 419, para. 680).

210 Cf. NECG (2003, 3).

211 See also Hausman/Myers (2002, 292f.), who criticize the application of the perfect contestability standard to irreversible investments, on the grounds that "...[i]n a contestable market, worse-than-expected outcomes will not attract competitive entry while better than expected outcomes are likely to attract competitive entry...", which introduces asymmetry in the distribution of expected cash flows from an investment.

212 See the discussion of capacity utilization risk in section 4.2.4.

213 Cf. utilityregulation.com (2003), section 'Incremental cost, and how this concept differs from marginal cost.'

an increment is used that LRIC is below average cost.[214] This, again, boils down to an asymmetric treatment of the regulated firm's investments and will bar the regulated firm from earning an appropriate return on all of its investments on average, unless compensated otherwise.

4.2.2 Accounting Directives Determining Operating Expenditures

Automatic Cost Pass-Through Clauses

The basic idea of an automatic pass-through of price changes of certain inputs to regulated rates without a formal rate review is to shift to the rate payers risks associated with costs that cannot be influenced by the regulated firm. Leaving the responsibility for these costs with the regulated firm does not improve incentives for cost efficiency, but, on the other hand, increases the risk faced by the regulated firm.[215] An automatic cost pass-through in principle is characterized by a shorter adjustment lag and better predictability than an ordinary rate review process. In times of high price increases of the inputs of the regulated firm, e.g. sharp fuel cost increases for electric utilities, a long regulatory lag endangers the financial viability of a regulated firm. An automatic cost pass-through protects the firm against this risk and can be expected to decrease its cost of capital.[216]

Of course, a pass-through of costs only reduces cost of capital to the extent that these costs are correlated with market development, which has to be debated in each individual case. A prominent example for costs passed-through are fuel costs in the energy sector.[217] As it is widely accepted that price spikes of fuel costs affect the overall economic development, a pass-through of fuel costs most likely reduces cost of capital. Clearly, if a pass-through is applied asymmetrically, the risk of the regulated firm can be increased instead.

Automatic (fuel) adjustment clauses not only have a direct buffering effect on the risk of the rate-regulated firm, but also distort incentives for in-

---

[214] Crespo/Giacchino (2003, 50ff.) show that the use of marginal cost bidding rules for electricity peaking units distorts the choice of technology towards plants with a low average-cost-to-marginal-cost ratio.

[215] Cf. Golec (1990, 166).

[216] As alternatives to automatic cost pass-through clauses, interim rate relief and the use of future test years are proposed; see Baron/DeBondt (1979, 245).

[217] Fuel costs are not necessarily completely exogenous in a dynamic perspective, as, in principle, the regulated firm has the possibility to smooth out fluctuations of fuel costs by long-term contracting and hedging, provided that the necessary markets exist.

put choices and investment decisions, if in this way the costs passed-through and, accordingly, rates can be influenced in a predictable way by the regulated firm.[218] This problem can arise, if pass-through clauses are extended to endogenous cost elements.[219] Generally speaking, there is less of an incentive for the regulated firm to save on these costs. More specifically, it can be argued, that if the firm has a choice between different sources of supply of the same fuel, it has less incentive to choose the cheapest source. Furthermore, there is less incentive to substitute capital for fuel costs and invest in fuel saving technologies, giving rise to an underinvestment problem.[220] Finally, a firm that is protected by an automatic fuel adjustment clause against volatile input prices has less of an incentive for vertical integration with upstream activities or for investment in technologies operating with less price-volatile inputs.

In the light of these incentive problems, it has been suggested to admit only a portion of the costs in question for pass-through to keep incentives for efficiency alive.[221] It can be replied that even with an automatic adjustment clause, there is always a certain lag that provides incentives for efficiency. This lag can be controlled to a certain extent by the regulator in order to adjust incentives. The longer the lag, the higher the incentives for efficient fuel choice and investment are.

Simulations of the model of Gandolfi/Jenkinson/Mayer (1996, 11ff.) show that, all else equal, the (systematic) risk of the regulated firm decreases monotonically as the degree of cost pass-through is increased. If, however, incentives for investments in cost saving technologies are accounted for, beta continues to be a decreasing function of the degree of cost pass-through when starting from low pass-through ratios, but an increasing function when starting from already very high pass-through ratios. There is a trade-off between the direct buffering effect of cost pass-through and the indirect effect via reduced incentives for investment in cost saving technologies.

For 50 electric companies in the U.S. for the period 1965-1974, Clarke (1980) finds evidence that the use of fuel adjustment clauses reduces systematic risk by approximately 10%. In the empirical investigation of Dubin/Navarro (1982), fuel adjustment clauses are one element defining a more favorable regulatory climate that, consistent with the above conjecture, reduces cost of capital. However, the effect on the cost of capital is

218 Likewise the behavior of consumers might be changed if more of the risk of input price volatility is shifted to them; cf. Marshall (1980, 385).

219 For examples in the U.S. electricity sector, see Baron/DeBondt (1979, 247).

220 Cf. Baron/DeBondt (1981).

221 Cf. Baron/DeBondt (1979, 247).

only investigated for the overall regulatory climate, but not for its individual elements.

Tax Flow-Through Versus Normalization of Taxes

It is undoubted, that corporate tax payments have to be covered by regulated rates, just as any other cost element. However, in case they vary widely over time, the question is raised whether they should flow through to rates in the period they have to be paid or if they rather should be normalized over several periods, e.g. over the assets' life. If the depreciation scheme that is employed for tax purposes results in a sum of tax-deductible depreciation and interest that is higher at the beginning than at the end of assets' life; *ceteris paribus* less taxes are paid at the beginning of assets' life and more taxes towards the end of assets' life. In this case, flow-through of taxes results in lower regulated rates at the beginning of assets' life and higher regulated rates towards the end of assets' life compared to tax normalization. The benefits of tax deferrals are passed on to the current generation of rate payers, and the tax burden is shifted to future generations. This approach necessitates quite frequent rate adjustments. If the necessary adjustments are delayed, the regulated firm earns less than the allowed rate of return. Normalization of taxes is usually associated with a more favorable regulatory climate,[222] as it allows the firm to keep the benefits of deferred taxes. With increasing tax payments over time, flow-through of taxes results in a backloading of revenues. This exposes the regulated firm to a higher risk, as the more distant the revenues are in the future the higher the uncertainty is as to whether the necessary rate increases actually will be made.[223] If the market already has been opened up for competition or if the admission of competition is planned, it should be scrutinized if these increasing rates will be achievable at all under competition.[224]

If tax flow-through is handled as a complete cost pass-through, including *ex post* compensation of deviations between actual and expected tax payments, the additional problem from the point of view of the regulator arises that taxes cease to have any incentive effect on the investment be-

[222] Cf. Dubin/Navarro (1982, 144).

[223] Cf. Houston et al. (1999, 16).

[224] Along the same line of argument, it is suggested to adjust the depreciation profile to the development of replacement costs if competition is admitted and input prices are declining with the aim in mind that regulated rates still will be achievable in the market towards the end of assets' life; cf. Crew/Kleindorfer (1992a); Carne/Currie/Siner (1999); Knieps/Küpper/Langen (2001).

havior of the regulated utility, as the latter expects that exactly hundred percent of its tax payments are covered at the bottom line.

In the case of normalization of taxes, the regulated utility makes an allowance for deferred tax payments at the beginning of the assets' life. The predominant approach in the U.S. is that regulated utilities have to keep separate accounts of deferred taxes and no return on deferred taxes is allowed in the calculation of rates.[225] By this means, the consumers of the regulated service ultimately reap the benefits of deferred taxes. At the present time, the normalization approach to taxes is widely accepted by all involved parties in the U.S.

In empirical investigations, it has been shown that tax normalization has a positive impact on utility share prices,[226] which is plausible, as it provides the regulated firm with an unambiguous cash flow advantage compared to tax flow-through. Furthermore, it has been shown that it improves the bond rating, presumably due to smaller capital requirements, and thereby decreases cost of debt.[227] Even if tax normalization smoothes out cash flow fluctuations, its effect on cost of equity is less clear. If investment of the utility is pro-cyclical, it benefits from tax deferral above all in phases of high overall economic activity, which might be taken as an indication of an increase in the correlation of firm specific risk with the overall market risk, which, counterintuitively, would mean an increase in the cost of equity. Admittedly, without empirical evidence, this remains speculative.[228]

4.2.3 Accounting Directives Determining Capital Expenditures

As interest and depreciation are the major cost drivers of most regulated utilities, regulatory accounting directives for the assessment of the allowed rate of return and the determination of the regulatory rate base bring about the highest risk potential for a regulated firm.[229]

---

[225] Cf. Houston et al. (1999, 15f.).
[226] Cf. Trout (1979, 30).
[227] Cf. Dubin/Navarro (1982, 157).
[228] As has been discussed in the context of depreciation, there are additional effects of normalization compared to flow-through, in the case that competition is admitted.
[229] Cf. also Houston (1996, 1).

Impact of Procedures for the Assessment of the Allowed Rate of Return

The methods applied to assess the risk-adjusted cost of capital and to determine the allowed rate of return affect the risk sharing between the regulated firm and consumers on the one hand as well as between debt and equity owners on the other hand. Accordingly, they feed back on the cost of capital of the regulated firm. This interrelation is analyzed on the basis of individual parameters of the weighted average cost of capital.

Sharing of Market Interest Rate Risk and Market Equity Premium Risk. With respect to interest rate risk, the primary question is whether, to what extent and with how much regulatory lag interest rate changes are passed through to the allowed rate of return. These regulatory variables predominantly determine the *sharing of interest rate risk between the regulated firm and ratepayers*. If the allowed rate of return is not adjusted at all to interest rate changes, the entire interest rate risk remains with the regulated firm, whereas complete and immediate pass-through of interest rate changes to the allowed rate of return shifts interest rate risk completely to rate payers.[230] In the latter case, the regulated firm bears no risk in the sense that it continuously earns the current market rate of interest on its regulatory rate base.[231] Therefore, its market value is protected against interest rate changes.

The length of the regulatory review period, respectively of the regulatory lag, also plays an important role in the sharing of interest rate risk between the regulated firm and rate payers. If rates are set for a review period of several years, the expected development of the market rate of interest within this period has to be accounted for when setting rates. If it is intended by the regulator to just cover costs during the review period, the imputed cost of capital has to be higher (lower) than the current cost of capital if the market rate of interest is expected to increase (decrease).[232] Put the other way round, if the regulator uses only the interest rate prevailing at the outset of the review period to determine regulated rates and an increase (decrease) of the interest rate during the review period is ex-

---

[230] Cf. Haugen/Stroyny/Wichern (1978, 719).

[231] Due to possible asymmetric regulatory risk this does not necessarily mean that the regulated firm earns the market rate of interest on its capital invested. For a discussion of asymmetric regulatory risk, see section 3.3.3.

[232] Clearly, this argument becomes irrelevant if all payments on debt are already contractually fixed at the beginning of the review period and no new debt will be issued during the review period.

pected, the regulated firm is set at an asymmetric disadvantage (advantage).

Methodologically, this means that the risk-less interest rate as an input parameter of the weighted average cost of capital has to be estimated for the entire review period.[233] This, in turn, has implications for the length of the appropriate estimation period. If no clear trend in the development of the market interest rate is discernable, it is plausible to use an estimation period as long as the regulatory review period. If the regulator wants to smooth the impact of interest rate fluctuations on regulated rates over the asset life time that usually comprises several review periods, he has to estimate the risk-less interest rate for the entire asset life time, which calls for a correspondingly longer estimation period. In this context it becomes important that the regulator can credibly signal not to deviate asymmetrically from the asset life time average interest rate in periods during which below average interest rates prevail.

These arguments can be applied analogically to the *market equity premium*. For the purposes of cost-orientated rate regulation, it has to be estimated for the entire review period, which should be reflected in the length of the estimation period. If there are no structural changes, it is plausible to use an estimation period as long as the regulatory review period. If it is intended by the regulator to flatten fluctuations of the market equity premium over the asset life time, a correspondingly longer estimation period should be used. If the regulator aims at flattening rates as much as possible, the longest possible estimation period should be used. As with the interest rate, a consistent and credible handling by the regulator is essential; otherwise capital owners are exposed to an asymmetric regulatory risk and will ask for a correspondingly higher risk premium. On the other hand, the flattening of parameter changes over time *per se* is likely to have a buffering effect on the firm's cash flow distribution.

The *sharing of the interest rate risk remaining with the regulated firm between debt and equity holders* depends on the financing decisions made by the regulated firm (or by the regulator if the firm has no complete autonomy on its financing decisions). The most important financing variables are the debt-equity ratio and the maturity structure, respectively the duration, of debt. If the duration of capital investment is considerably longer than the duration of debt, large parts of the financing risk are borne by shareholders. *Ceteris paribus*, i.e. with the same maturity structure of debt, the effect of interest rate changes on share prices is stronger, the higher the financial leverage. The regulated firm can shift financing risk to

233 See section 6.2.1.

debt holders by extending the duration of debt, e.g. by choosing a longer maturity.

So far in this section, it has been implicitly assumed that the regulator bases his cost calculation and rate setting on the embedded cost of debt determined by existing bonds and credit contracts. If the regulator does not set rates on the basis of embedded costs but applies other criteria such as current costs of a (potential) competitor, the argument is changed fundamentally. In this case, long term debt does not provide a protection against future interest rate changes for the shareholders. If regulated rates fluctuate with the prevailing market interest rate, but actual payments on debt are fixed by long-term contracts, equity holders are, on the contrary, exposed to a higher residual interest rate risk than with short-term revolving debt.

Haugen, Stroyny and Wichern (1978) compare 78 U.S. electric utility stocks and 163 stocks of non-regulated firms for the period from 1967 to1975, and find that utility stocks are more sensitive to interest rate changes than the stocks of non-regulated firms.[234] Furthermore, they show that the largest share of interest rate risk of the utilities is borne by shareholders, which can be explained by the conjecture that usually the duration of debt is shorter than the duration of capital investment.[235] Carleton, Chambers and Lakonishok (1983) investigate U.S. electric utilities for the period from 1971 to 1980 and find that the allowed rate of return on equity lagged considerably behind the then inflation driven increases of interest rates, but they do not find a significant correlation between equity risk premiums and the level of interest rates.

Assessment of the Firm Specific Debt and Equity Premium. Just as any other parameter, the firm specific debt premium and the firm specific beta factor have to be estimated for the entire future review period, if it is the intention of the regulator to just cover costs by regulated rates. The risk of changes of these parameters is borne by the regulated firm to a higher degree, if there is less and less frequent adaptation of rates to these changes. The risk of unforeseen structural changes is higher for these firm specific parameters than for market parameters such as the risk-less interest rate and the market equity premium. Discretionary modifications of rate regulation itself are a primary possible source for such structural changes of the firm specific debt premium and beta factor.

In a system of cost-of-service regulation, the regulator uses actual cost of debt. The embedded debt premium can be observed relatively easily by registering existing debt contracts. Very recently closed debt contracts

[234] Cf. Haugen/Stroyny/Wichern (1978, 708).

[235] Cf. Haugen/Stroyny/Wichern (1978, 718f.).

show the currently prevailing debt premium. If no contracts have been closed or renewed recently, the currently prevailing bond rating allows conclusions on the debt premium of the regulated firm. If there is no clear evidence how the debt premium will develop during the review period, the debt premium prevailing at the outset of the review period should be used to calculate the cost of debt for new (or renewed) debt financing during the review period. Cost-of-service regulation tends to free the regulated firm from risks of debt premium changes by passing them through to rates and thereby shifting them to rate payers. If the regulator does not use embedded costs but long run incremental costs in order to set efficient incentives for competition, he will base the setting of rates only on the debt premium currently prevailing or predicted for the review period. This debt premium can deviate considerably from the embedded debt premium in existing contracts, e.g. due to major changes in the regulatory regime. As the payment obligations to debt holders are contractually fixed, the risk of these deviations is borne by the equity holders of the regulated firm.

With respect to the beta factor, the possibility of structural changes induced by modifications of rate regulation implies, on the one hand, that its estimation period should not reach as far in the past that it would include data before relevant modifications of rate regulation. In times of frequent regulatory modifications this supports the use of relatively short estimation periods. Clearly, the exclusion of structural changes comes at the cost of more serious effects of statistical problems; e.g. estimated beta might decrease in spite of an increase in systematic risk if at the same time the reference index rises, which leads to a stronger distortion when the estimation period is shorter.[236] On the other hand, anticipated changes during the future review period should be accounted for as far as possible when setting rates for the entire review period.

If it is the regulator's policy to smooth out fluctuations of the debt and equity premium between regulatory review periods over the asset life time, a consistent and credible handling of this policy by the regulator is essential; otherwise capital owners are exposed to a (perceived) asymmetric regulatory risk and will ask for a correspondingly higher risk premium.

Capital Structure Employed by the Regulator. Regulatory calculation directives also determine the debt ratio and the equity ratio that enter in the WACC as weights of cost of debt and cost of equity. In the following, it is assumed that a free cash flow-approach is used and that, consequently, cost

[236] For a more extensive discussion of methodological issues regarding the appropriate estimation period for the beta factor of a rate-regulated firm, see section 6.2.4.

of debt is reduced by corporate taxes in the WACC.[237] There is a broad consensus that market values of debt and equity should be used to calculate the debt-equity ratio.[238] If changes of the capital structure are planned during the regulatory review period, sub period specific target debt-equity ratios are relevant; otherwise the actual debt-equity ratio prevailing at the outset of the review period should be used. The regulator is only likely to accept changes of the capital structure in the calculation of rates if they are verified by detailed finance and investment plans. If future changes of the capital structure are planned and accepted by the regulator, cost of debt and cost of equity have to be adjusted consistently to the new capital structure. A higher leverage means that the same cash flow volatility is transmitted into a higher volatility of return on equity which *ceteris paribus* increases cost of equity.[239] If a higher leverage raises the firm's likelihood of getting into financial distress, cost of debt also increases.[240] On the other hand, the use of more debt increases the tax shield, which *per se* reduces cost of capital.

If the regulatory commission does not accept the actual capital structure, but uses another capital structure deemed optimal in its calculations,[241] then the regulated firm bears the risks that arise from the deviation between the actual and the imputed capital structure. In most cases, the regulatory commission will use for its calculations a higher leverage than the actual one to reduce the incentive for the regulated firm to use more equity than without rate regulation, as conjectured by the Averch-Johnson effect.[242] If a higher than actual debt-equity ratio is used by the regulator, at least cost of

---

237 For an analysis of the free cash flow-approach, see Ballwieser (2004, 140ff.).

238 See, for example, Robichek (1978, 701); Oftel (1992, 5); Ballwieser (1998, 85); Ickenroth (1998, 4); Busse von Colbe (2002); Knieps (2003, 994); Küpper (2002, 27); Kempf (2002, 27). For a more extensive discussion of the issue, see section 6.3.

239 In the context of rate regulation and with numerical examples, see Myers (1992, 13ff.).

240 Cf. Myers (1992, 19).

241 Clearly, no comprehensive theory exists to determine the optimal capital structure. As a consequence the use of an "optimal" capital structure by a regulatory commission necessarily has the character of an *ad hoc* adjustment. The CAA (2001, 25, para. 4.49) shares the view that "... the firm itself working with its financiers is best placed in deciding on its appropriate financial structure." Therefore, the CAA does not ordinate a capital structure; however, it does not accept an increase of the cost of capital as a consequence of a changed capital structure, which seems a reasonable approach.

242 Empirical evidence on the effect of rate regulation on the incentive to use equity is not unambiguous; see section 3.4.2.

debt and cost of equity have to be adjusted consistently, as discussed above. If the regulatory commission calculates with a higher debt ratio than the actual one without adjusting the cost of equity (and if necessary cost of debt), the regulated firm is exposed to an asymmetric downside risk, as, on average, it will not earn its actual cost of capital. In any case, the regulated firm should be given enough time to adopt the imputed capital structure in order to avoid the risks associated with deviations of the actual from the imputed capital structure if it wishes to do so.

Impact of Procedures for the Determination of the Regulatory Rate Base

Quantity Structure and Valuation of the Regulatory Rate Base. The regulatory rate base can be broken down into a quantity component and a value component, as shown by Figure 4.7. Either one of these components can be assessed in different ways.

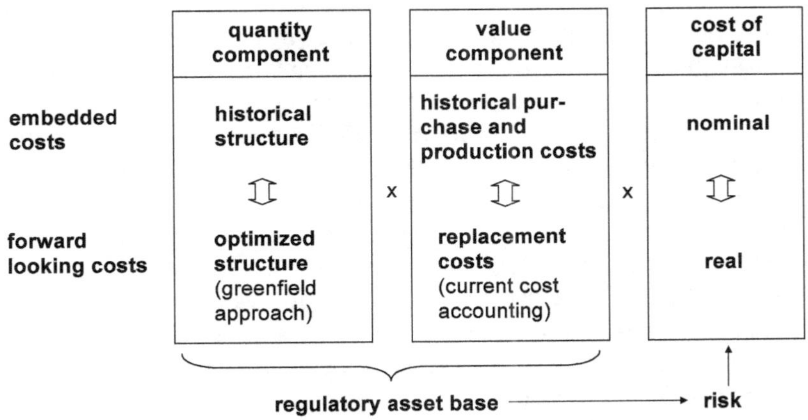

Figure 4.7. Components of the regulatory rate base and risk-adjusted cost of capital

The *quantity component* of the rate base can use the *de facto* existing, historical quantity structure that is subject to path dependences and not necessarily optimal from a today's point of view.[243] Due to unexpected demand changes, the existing capacity might be too small or too large for actual demand. Existing infrastructure might not be optimally located from today's perspective. Due to path dependences, e.g. several small gas pipe-

[243] For a discussion of methodical issues associated with the determination of the quantity structure of the rate base, see section 5.2.1.

lines might have been built successively in the past, while the same capacity could be provided at less cost by one large pipeline. If the historical quantity structure is used by the regulator, the risk of becoming sub-optimal due to technological progress and demand changes is borne by rate payers.

Alternatively, a structure deemed to be optimal under currently prevailing conditions can be applied. To this purpose analytical cost models have been developed. Hereby, a greenfield approach is pursued, assuming that the optimal structure can be planned without any inherited burdens from the past. Instead of existing assets procured in the past, so-called modern equivalent assets are used in the calculation of the rate base. If the regulator uses an optimized quantity structure for his cost calculations, the risk of the infrastructure becoming sub-optimal due to technological progress and demand changes is shifted to the regulated firm.[244] Of course, there is a spectrum of intermediate forms of quantity structure between these two poles.[245]

If the calculation of the regulatory rate base is based upon a quantity structure better than the historical structure (in case there is such a better structure), technological progress and demand changes will introduce a downward bias in the distribution of outcomes for the regulated firm. As soon as there is any technical progress, the firm will not receive a return on its assets in place but only on the modern, more efficient assets. Analogically, demand changes render sub-optimal existing capacity dimensions or locations of infrastructure investment. These are clearly examples of the asymmetric regulatory risk discussed in section 3.3.3. To compensate for this effect, the rate of return on the modern equivalent assets has to be increased *ceteris paribus* to be equivalent to an appropriate rate of return on the historical assets. Without such compensation, investment incentives would be seriously reduced.[246]

Furthermore, even if the allowed rate of return on the modern equivalent assets is raised sufficiently to yield on average the same expected revenues

---

[244] See already Gordon (1977, 1504), who states that, if the regulated "...product price provides a return ... not on the actual investment but on what the investment would be at the start of each period if the best available technology were incorporated in the plant ... [i]nvestors would ... require a higher return to reflect the higher risk."

[245] See section 5.2.1.

[246] This is somewhat analogical to a situation with exogenous technological progress and perfect competition in that a firm would never be willing to invest. The same non-investment result would be obtained with endogenous technological progress that is not protected by patents or other mechanisms that establish market entry barriers; see Pedell (2000, 220ff.).

as the appropriate rate of return on the historical assets, with uncertain technological progress and demand development, the use of the optimal quantity structure increases the volatility of cash flows. To the extent that this volatility increase is correlated with the overall market volatility, the cost of capital is raised.

Regarding the *valuation* of the regulatory rate base, several issues are relevant for the level of risk-adjusted cost of capital. Basically, market or book values can be used.[247] If the overall market value of the regulated firm or a regulated division is taken as regulatory rate base, there is no need for a separate analysis of the quantity structure of the regulated business. The use of market values reinforces external cost and demand shocks as well as estimation errors of the appropriate cost of capital. This leads to a higher volatility of returns, and it is not guaranteed that a stable equilibrium will be attained. For these and a number of other reasons, in practically implemented regulatory regimes, the calculation of the regulatory rate base is based on book values. Compared to market values, these act as an anchor against external cost and demand shocks as well as estimation errors of the appropriate cost of capital and thereby reduce the volatility of returns.

If the regulator opts for the use of book values, there is still a subordinate decision to be made as to *which* book values to employ. There is wide acceptance that, principally, either historical purchase and production cost and the nominal cost of capital or replacement cost and the specific real cost of capital[248] can be combined for calculating depreciation[249] and interest (see Figure 4.7). If applied consistently, both methods yield the same net present value of the sum of depreciation and interest, equal to the initial investment.[250]

However, the methods result in different profiles of cash flows over the economic lifetime of the assets. In the case of price increases for the assets of the regulated firm, the use of purchase and production cost results in earlier cash flows than the use of replacement cost. Depreciation is higher if replacement cost is employed but this effect is more than overcompensated by the interest effect. In the case of price decreases, the use of pur-

---

[247] For a discussion of the use of market versus book values for the purposes of rate regulation, see chapter 5.

[248] This specific real cost of capital is calculated by subtracting the specific price increase rate of the assets of the regulated firm – not the overall inflation rate – from the nominal cost of capital.

[249] The impact of regulatory depreciation schemes on risk-adjusted cost of capital is discussed in section 4.2.2. The choice of a regulatory depreciation scheme is analyzed in detail in section 5.1.1.

[250] Cf. Knieps/Küpper/Langen (2001, 763).

chase and production cost correspondingly results in later cash flows than the use of replacement costs. Due to the different profiles of cash flows over the lifetime of the assets, the method of purchase and production cost with the nominal cost of capital on the one hand and the method of replacement cost with the specific real cost of capital on the other hand are not necessarily equivalent, neither from the perspective of rate payers nor from the perspective of the regulated firm. If regulated rates follow the periodic costs, different shares of the same return of and on the investment are earned in the single periods and possibly are paid by different generation of rate payers.[251] The distribution of cash flows over time also feeds back on risk-adjusted cost of capital. The uncertainty about future regulation tends to increase the further a regulatory review lies in the future. Put differently, the risk of discretionary regulatory behavior tends to rise. Therefore, the expected variance of the overall return on an investment tends to be higher if cash flows are expected further in the future. This effect is neglected if the same discount factor is used irrespective of the time profile of cash flows.

Disallowances by Used and Useful Tests or Prudence Reviews. The issue of disallowances is closely related to (or even can be interpreted as a sub-case of) the above discussion of the quantity structure of the rate base. A disallowance is made when an individual investment is not admitted in the rate base by the regulator, as it is deemed inefficient according to a certain standard. The need for disallowances is justified by the argument that under pure cost-of-service regulation there would be no incentives for efficient capital investment without the possibility of disallowances.[252] The two most common standards for the assessment of efficiency of investment employed by regulatory commissions are used and useful tests and prudence reviews.[253] Each standard takes a different perspective in time:

1. In a so-called used and useful test the regulator audits if the investments (made in the past) are, as the name implies, used and useful from today's point of view. If, in the extreme case, he resorts to the hypothetical quantity structure deemed optimal from today's point of view as the

[251] For a large utility with many overlapping investments, this issue is of minor importance.

[252] See the seminal paper by Averch/Johnson (1962).

[253] Cf. Kolbe/Tye/Myers (1993, 20ff.); in addition intermediate forms can be distinguished: The modified prudent investment standard allows for the return *of* investments deemed imprudent but not for the return *on* them. The fair value standard, just as the used and useful test, excludes any unused and useless investment from the rate base but allows for a rate of return above cost of capital on successful investments as compensation.

benchmark for the assessment of usefulness, this method boils down to the above discussed approach of using an optimized quantity structure for the rate base.

2. In a so-called prudence review, the regulator audits investments according to the criterion, whether they were made with sufficient prudence at the time of investment with the information that was available then.[254] Only investments that have been incurred imprudently at the outset are excluded from the rate base.

The used and useful test is the more restrictive standard, disallowing more investments from the regulatory rate base than a prudence review. Both approaches lead to a kind of micromanagement of investment by the regulator and open up scope for judgment. If the regulatory commission has the (discretionary) power to disallow single investments from the rate base, the regulated firm is exposed to an asymmetric downside risk. In the best case, all investments remain in the rate base, in all other cases, some investments are disallowed from the rate base. Consequently, if the cost of capital is applied to this rate base, the regulated firm, on average, does not earn its cost of capital on all investments. A higher rate of return on the remaining assets is necessary to offset the effect of disallowances on the overall expected rate of return.[255]

In the case of Germany, the TKG requires rate setting for DTAG to be based on the costs of efficient service provision [Kosten der effizienten Leistungsbereitstellung].[256] Even if the notion of efficiency is not qualified and not operationalized, it can be concluded from this that the costs reported by DTAG will be adjusted for inefficiencies according to certain criteria. The issue of disallowances is not explicitly addressed, and, in particular, it is not specified, which perspective over time should be taken in order to assess efficiency, i.e. whether the perspective of a used and useful test or of a prudence review should be assumed. However, efficiency corrections, in all probability, will result *de facto* in disallowances and produce an additional asymmetric risk for the regulated utility, which calls for appropriate compensation.

---

[254] Kahn (1988, xxvi) argues in favor of this second approach: "But judgments of prudence can, in principle – and in fairness – be made only as of the time when the pertinent commitments and expenditures were made."

[255] See the numerical examples in section 3.3.3.

[256] § 31 (1) Telekommunikationsgesetz [Telecommunications Act] and § 3 (2) Telekommunikations-Entgeltregulierungsverordnung [Ordinance on rate regulation in the telecommunications sector].

Stranded Asset Risk. "Assets are considered stranded, when they were prudently acquired but have lost economic value as a direct result of an unforeseeable regulatory or legislative change specific to the industry in question."[257] This definition of stranded assets requires several preconditions to be fulfilled. Firstly, the investments must have been *incurred prudently* at the outset. This implies that e.g. disallowances according to a prudence review are not suited to produce stranded assets, whereas disallowances according to a used and useful test, principally, can give rise to stranded assets but only to the extent that the investments in question are considered prudent and if the used and useful test is employed surprisingly instead of a prudence review or a pure cost-of-service regulation without any disallowances. Clearly, there are many other modifications of a regulatory regime that can give rise to stranded assets, some of which are discussed below.[258]

Secondly, the loss of economic value must be *directly attributable to regulatory or legislative activities*. This has to be distinguished from other possible causes of losses. Principally, a loss in value of assets can be due to a variety of causes: bad management foresight and decisions regarding investment and financing,[259] world states proving to be unfavorable or unanticipated regulatory changes. Stranded assets must not be mixed up with assets that have lost value due to managerial misjudgment or unfavorable development of environmental factors; the latter are risks that also have to be borne by any non-regulated firm. The central problem lies in assessing *ex post* why assets actually have lost value. This difficulty is aggravated by information asymmetries between the regulator and the regulated firm. From the context of rate regulation, it is implicitly clear, that not only alterations of regulation have to be responsible for the loss in value of stranded assets, but also the design of the regulatory scheme must have been relevant for the decision to invest capital in those assets in the first place.[260] To assess the loss induced by unforeseeable regulatory change, the

---

[257] Crew/Kleindorfer (1999, 64). See also Shuttleworth/MacKerron (2002, 38).

[258] Therefore, the issue of stranded assets is considerably wider than the one of disallowances. On the other hand, imprudent investment, which might be the reason for disallowances, is excluded as a reason for stranded assets.

[259] Clearly, management can only be held responsible for investment and financing, if it has the power to decide on them without regulatory restrictions. Investment obligations and capital structure prescriptions by the regulator can restrain the freedom of decision and, accordingly, the responsibility; for a detailed analysis of investment obligations, see section 4.3.1.

[260] Brennan (1999, 82) makes this point explicit.

net effect of gains and losses of a measure taken by the regulator on all assets of the regulated firm has to be calculated.[261]

Some authors assign the entire difference between the book value of assets and their market value to stranded assets.[262] This is too broad a definition of stranded assets, as it attributes all losses to regulation irrespective of the underlying causes. If the firm receives compensation for its stranded assets, this broad definition would act as a comprehensive insurance without a deductible for the regulated firm. This would bring about distorting effects on investment and operational efficiency.

Thirdly, the regulatory modifications must not have been anticipated but must come as a *surprise* to the regulated firm. If the planned and announced course of action of the regulator at the time of investment already foresees alterations of the regulatory scheme for the future, these alterations are by definition not suited to generate stranded assets. The less that is known about future regulation from explicit announcements of the regulator at the time of the investment, the more difficult it becomes to assess whether or not a certain course of action of the regulator was foreseeable. As the expectations of investors are not observable, this becomes necessarily a very discretionary matter.[263]

It is important to note that the fact that assets have become stranded does not necessarily mean that they are no longer used.[264] Assets are only withdrawn from operation if the decision relevant costs at a certain moment in time are no longer covered. Assets in rate-regulated industries usually are characterized by a very high degree of irreversibility, i.e. the salvage value of used assets on secondary markets is very low. Assuming for a moment that investment is completely irreversible, operation would not be shut down unless operating costs exceed revenues. Since assets are locked-in, they can become stranded when the regulator uses his discretionary power for unexpected changes. If the regulated firm had anticipated these changes at the time of original investment decision, it would not have committed capital to the investment, as, over its economic lifetime, the investment is not profitable any more. As the phenomenon of becoming stranded is a financial one, not a physical one, it is more appropriate to use the term ‘stranded investments’ (or ‘stranded costs’). From this, Maloney, McCormick and Sauer (1997, 90) conclude “... that stranded

261 Cf. Crew/Kleindorfer (1999, 68).

262 Cf. Loxley (1999, 99); see also Maloney/McCormick/Sauer (1997; 63).

263 For the same reason it is important to give potential investors a clear picture of future regulation before a utility is privatized.

264 This point is illustrated with examples by Maloney/McCormick/Sauer (1997, 64).

cost recovery is primarily an issue of wealth redistribution, with little or no impact on the utilization or allocation of capital." This is a somewhat naïve view, as expectations about future behavior of the regulator are of paramount importance for investment incentives and these expectations are strongly influenced by the current regulatory behavior.

Stranded investments can be classified into three categories:[265] physical assets, deferred expenses and long-term contractual obligations. The issue of stranded investments becomes especially manifest in the transition from protected monopoly to the opening up for competition.[266] One of the most prominent examples of *physical assets* are power generation facilities, especially nuclear power plants, in the U.S. electricity industry in the mid 90s after the market had been opened up for competition for independent power producers.[267] The Public Utility Regulatory Policy Act of 1978 (PURPA) obligated established utilities to purchase electricity from renewable energy sources and from cogeneration. The Energy Policy Act of 1992 (EPAct) gave all power producers access to the electricity transmission network. At the same time, technological progress reduced the minimum efficient scale of power generation by gas fired plants. These developments left many utilities with relatively inefficient and therefore unutilized generation capacity, especially from nuclear power plants. However, it is discussed controversially if this is a case of stranded investments. To the extent that the admission of competition was foreseeable, utilities were able to account for it in their demand forecasts that, some authors argue, were erroneous in consideration of the information available at the time of the original investment decision.[268] This example underlines the difficulties that arise when sorting out the causes for a loss in value of assets.

Maloney, McCormick and Sauer (1997) go even further and flatly dispute the existence of an effective regulatory compact in the U.S. electricity industry. They argue that, if a regulatory compact existed, the regulated firm should pay only the risk-free interest rate on its debt on capital mar-

---

[265] See Loxley (1999, 96ff.); see also Blacconière/Johnson/Johnson (1997, 203).

[266] Maloney/McCormick/Sauer (1997, 60) even confine their definition to the loss in value of assets due to the admission of competition in former monopolistic markets. This view is too narrow to embrace the phenomenon of unanticipated discretionary regulatory behavior.

[267] See Brennan (1999, 82ff.); Studness (1995, 38) underlines the paramount importance of this issue: "Recovery of stranded investment today marks the central issue in the debate over electric utility competition."

[268] See Brennan (1999, 92); Maloney/McCormick/Sauer (1997, 83); Studness (1995, 40); the assessment of excess generation capacity as stranded investment is supported by Loxley (1999, 99ff.).

kets. As risk premiums on debt can be observed, they draw the reverse conclusion that there exists no effective regulatory compact. Their argument is misleading insofar as even an effective regulatory compact never acts nor should act as a perfect buffering mechanism against all external shocks and internal managerial misjudgment; therefore, the observation of risk premiums on debt does not allow the conclusion that no effective regulatory compact exists.

Also, in the U.S. telecommunications industry, the issue of stranded investments arose in the transition to more competition but the actual causes were somewhat different.[269] The Telecommunications Act of 1996 opened up access to unbundled network elements to promote entry into local telephone markets. The FCC used the TELRIC-approach to determine access rates.[270] This is a current cost accounting approach based on the best available technology.[271] As discussed above, such an approach does not cover embedded costs in the case of any technological progress and puts the regulated firm in a situation of asymmetric downside risk. However, it is not the fact that TELRIC is used *per se* that is suited to produce stranded assets, but the unanticipated switch to competition and TELRIC-based access prices that could not be foreseen by the incumbent utilities at the time of their original investment. On the other hand, it can be observed that many assets in telecommunications gained value after the admission of competition thanks to growing demand and technological progress that increased the capacity of existing network elements.[272]

So called *regulatory assets* are a specialty of rate-regulated businesses. From the viewpoint of accounting they "... represent *deferred expenses* that are capitalized in accordance with *Statement of Financial Accounting Standards Number 71* (SFAS No. 71)."[273] This accounting directive allows regulated firms to expand the capitalization of expenses compared to non-regulated firms when a regulatory commission orders an accounting method deviating from US-GAAP. This is done on the grounds that recovery of the deferred expenses by future regulated rates can be expected. Typical examples of regulatory assets are deferred income taxes and deferred fuel costs. If current tax or fuel payments are deemed to be extraordinarily high compared to the long-term average by the regulator, he might not accept them completely in current rates but defer part of them to future

[269] See Crew/Kleindorfer (1999, 66ff.); Brennan (1999, 84ff.).

[270] See the discussion of the impact of regulatory cost concepts on risk in section 4.2.1.

[271] For the concept of current cost accounting, see also section 5.1.1.

[272] Cf. Crew/Kleindorfer (1999, 67).

[273] Blacconière/Johnson/Johnson (1997, 204, no bold type in the original text).

periods in order to normalize costs and regulated rates. Other examples are exceptionally high or one-off expenses for pension plans, for DSM (demand-side management) programs and for abandoned plant construction projects as well as extraordinary property losses that are normalized by spreading them over several periods.

Regulatory assets can become stranded if the regulator decides to change his policy regarding their recovery and does not accept the deferred expenses anymore in his calculation of regulated rates. It has been proposed by representatives of electric utilities to securitize regulatory assets to avoid the risk of expropriation by discretionary regulatory behavior.[274] Loudder, Khurana and Boatsman (1996) find evidence that investors are well aware of the risk of expropriation by discretionary changes of the regulatory regime to which regulatory assets are exposed. For 109 U.S. electric and natural gas utilities for the period 1984-93, they show that the valuation of regulatory assets significantly depends on favorableness of the regulatory climate in a state.

Finally, stranded investments can be due to *long-term contractual obligations*, e.g. stemming from long-term power or fuel purchase contracts.[275] In many cases, the use of such contracts is even ordered by regulatory commissions with the purpose of ensuring security of supply and smoothing out price fluctuations. If power or fuel prices later turn out to be lower than prices fixed by the long-term contract, the regulator might be tempted to no longer allow the pass-through of contractually fixed fuel costs to regulated rates but to use current fuel costs instead. This devaluates the compensation for the contractually committed payment obligations.

Blacconière, Johnson and Johnson (1997) investigate 111 investor owned U.S. electric utilities for the period from 1991 to 1994, and find evidence consistent with this categorization of stranded investments. Based on an assessment of stranded investments by the rating agency Moody's, they find that the extent of stranded investment is positively and significantly correlated with power generation assets, especially nuclear power plants, regulatory assets and fixed expenses. Intraregional and interregional differences in cost structures became significant only after EPAct opened up electricity markets for more competition. The role of competition is confirmed by a significant and positive correlation with the share of industrial revenues, as only industrial rate payers were able to change their energy supplier.

---

[274] Cf. Loxley (1999, 102f.).

[275] Cf. Loxley (1999, 96ff.).

There are different approaches regulatory commissions can embark on to deal with the stranded investment issue.[276] The first approach does not give the regulated firm any compensation for the recovery of investments that are stranded, e.g. due to the admission of competition. Supporter of this approach argue that, in a competitive market, assets are not specific any more. This argumentation ignores the fact that investments always are irreversible to a certain degree and investors are only willing to commit capital, as the irreversibility at the same time exposes the investments to risks and erects market entry barriers protecting the investment. Therefore, the benchmark of perfect competitive markets is misleading. If investors anticipate that they will receive no compensation for stranded investments and thereby are exposed to an asymmetric downside risk, they will demand a correspondingly higher allowed rate of return on investment in the first place or refrain from investing.

Secondly, the regulator can pursue a *quid pro quo* approach, as has been suggested by Crew and Kleindorfer (1999, 71). Here, the regulated firm gets conceded additional pricing flexibility to recover stranded investments. If it is intended to admit competition during the economic lifetime of an investment, the possibilities for capital recovery are no longer determined exclusively by the regulator, but are determined substantially by the market. This will expose the regulated firm to the risk that the investment becomes stranded, as cost recovering rates are not sustainable any more under competition, e.g. due to technological progress. A possible solution consists in frontloading cost recovery to early periods during which high rates are still enforceable.[277] This can be done by way of price caps with a high initial rate level and a high X factor in later periods. Strictly speaking, this is not an approach to recover stranded investments but to prevent investments from becoming stranded at all, i.e. a mitigation approach. So far, it has not been implemented formally, but long transition periods during which the incumbent continues to be protected from competition in market segments for certain services can be interpreted as a kind of *quid pro quo* approach.[278]

A third approach consists in identifying, quantifying and compensating stranded investments. Identification of stranded investments faces the prin-

[276] See Crew/Kleindorfer (1999, 68ff.).

[277] Frontloading of cost recovery is discussed in more detail in the context of regulatory depreciation schemes in section 5.1.1; see also Brennan (1999, 92).

[278] Cf. Crew/Kleindorfer (1999, 72), who cite the example of Deutsche Post AG (DPAG) [German Post Office] that got conceded long transition periods for its letter monopoly while the market for parcels already had been opened up for competition.

cipal problem of distinguishing discretionary regulatory behavior from managerial misjudgment and unfavorable environmental development as causes of a loss in value, as has been discussed above. Quantification raises general valuation problems and is complicated additionally by the fact that the value of many investments of utilities cannot be assessed independently from the rest of the network. Identification and quantification of stranded investments are interdependent insofar as the value of future payments that can be generated from an investment has to be determined to be able to judge *if* an investment actually has become stranded.[279] Compensation for stranded investments can be financed by general tax revenues, by imposing a per unit of output charge on new competitors,[280] or by levying an additional charge on consumers by introducing stranded investments as an additional cost element in the calculation of regulated rates of the incumbent.[281]

If not compensated otherwise by the regulatory commission,[282] stranded asset risk requires a higher allowed rate of return on the regulatory rate base for two reasons: Firstly, it reduces the expected rate base and thereby the expected cash flows. This drives the expected rate of return below the allowed rate of return.[283] Secondly, it increases the variability of the expected cash flows and, to the degree that this variability is correlated with the overall market variability, the cost of capital. Without the appropriate increase of the allowed rate of return, incentives for future investment are severely distorted and underinvestment will occur. Kolbe and Borucki (1998) use event study methodology to investigate the impact of the California Public Utility Commission's Blue Book in 1994 that came as a surprise to investors and announced the introduction of more competition.

---

279 Auctioning off stranded assets, as proposed for example by Lesser and Ainspan (1996), is a way to assess the liquidation value. However, in most instances, this value will deviate from the capitalized earnings value.

280 See Crew/Kleindorfer (1999, 72ff.) who make an analysis of the effects on overall welfare.

281 See Shuttleworth/MacKerron (2002, 38). Maloney/McCormick/Sauer (1997, 88f.) propose levying the compensation of stranded investments with the fixed tariff element in a two-part tariff regime to minimize distortions and overall welfare loss.

282 This might raise unsolvable definition and valuation problems, as it cannot be determined without judgment which regulatory changes had been anticipated at the time of investment. One possibility to handle stranded assets are insurance-like schemes that are set up as public-private partnerships that take over stranded assets and to this end emit bonds, using the relative low financing cost of public authorities.

283 See Kolbe/Borucki (1998, 256).

They find significant negative share price reactions for two out of the three utilities they investigated, driving up dividend yield by 50 to 100 basis points. They use a model-based approach to convert this finding into the corresponding effect on the required rate of return under different assumptions and come up with an increase of the required rate of return in the range of 1.6 to 1.9 (respectively 3.2 to 3.7) percentage points for a 50 (respectively 100) basis points dividend yield increase.

Construction Work in Progress Versus Allowances for Funds Used During Construction. So far it has been discussed, *if* assets are allowed in the rate base by the regulatory commission at all. Another issue is, *at which time* they are included in the rate base, especially if there is a construction phase during which funds are committed but the corresponding assets are not yet operating. If assets only are allowed in the rate base from the commissioning date on, and if investors are not compensated for committing funds before this date, they will not receive the appropriate rate of return over the entire lifecycle of the investment beginning with the first cash outflow. This reduces investment incentives and *per se* gives rise to underinvestment.

In the U.S. regulatory practice, two approaches have emerged to handle this issue. The first approach is known under the name of *construction work in progress* (CWIP) and applies the principle of including any (part of an) investment in the regulatory rate base at the very moment when the payment is made, even if the facility is not yet operating. In contrast, the second approach capitalizes the return on capital employed that is forgone during the construction phase and builds up a so-called *allowance for funds used during construction* (AFUDC) that, together with the actual investment, is accepted in the rate base at the beginning of operation. If applied consistently, both approaches allow an adequate rate of return on the capital employed, i.e. they are neutral with respect to net present value.

However, the approaches differ with respect to the allocation of cost of capital over generations of ratepayers. While AFUDC stipulates that the generation of rate payers that actually benefits from a facility also finances this facility during its period of operation, CWIP puts the burden of financing the provision of capital before the beginning of operation of a facility on generations of rate payers before the actual consumer generation. This is of substantial importance, particularly when investment volume is subject to strong fluctuations over time.

From the perspective of the capital owners of a regulated utility, it is principally favorable if the return of and on an investment flows back to the regulated firm as soon as possible, as in most cases this will involve a lower variance of the expected return than with later cash flows, as uncertainty about regulation and environmental factors increases over time. For this reason, the use of AFUDC or CWIP feeds back on the risk-adjusted cost of capital. Especially under uncertainty about future regulation, it is advantageous for the regulated firm if investment is included in the rate base as soon as possible, as the cash flows generated from the investment are less subject to possible discretionary regulatory activities, which reduces the asymmetric to which risk capital owners are exposed. The application of AFUDC might cause a temporary liquidity problem, which, in turn, might lead to a downgrading of bond rating and, as a consequence, to an increase of cost of debt. For these reasons, the two methods do not yield the same net present value without the appropriate adjustment of the allowed rate of return.

It has been confirmed empirically that the CWIP method is associated by capital markets with a more favorable regulatory climate[284] and lower risk-adjusted cost of capital than the AFUDC approach.[285] Fitzpatrick and Stitzel (1978) investigate 95 U.S. investor-owned electric utilities for the period from 1969 to 1975, and find that the impact of AFUDC on stock prices was significantly negative for the sub-period from 1972 to 1975. Trout (1979) finds that, for 86 U.S. utilities in the year 1976, cost of capital increases with the AFUDC to income ratio. Chandrasekaran and Dukes (1981) survey 39 investment banking firms with a questionnaire, and show that regulated utilities with a large amount of AFUDC are classified as riskier. Prager (1989) focuses on the impact of regulation on cost of debt, and, to this end, investigates 100 U.S. investor-owned electric utilities in 1979. He shows that the use of the CWIP approach significantly decreases cost of debt and that CWIP is one of the most influencing factors of the cost of debt.

Choice of the Regulatory Depreciation Scheme. While the approach of including new investment in the rate base determines from which moment onwards the return of and on investment actually starts flowing back from rate payers to the regulated firm, the regulatory depreciation scheme de-

[284] The construct of regulatory climate is well established in empirical investigations in the U.S. since the beginning of the 80s. Besides the timing of the inclusion of investments in the rate base it comprises among other things the tenure and the appointment or election procedure of regulatory commissioners as well as the extent of the use of cost pass-through clauses; see Dubin/Navarro (1982), Navarro (1982).

[285] See Brigham/Tapley (1986), S. 16.14f.

termines the distribution over time of this return from that moment.[286] These three dimensions open up the universe of possible depreciation schemes. For the purposes of cost-orientated rate regulation, net present value neutrality of the regulatory depreciation scheme is usually required, i.e. the discounted value of depreciation and interest must equal the initial investment.[287]

Consistent with this requirement is a multitude of depreciation schemes with different *valuations of the rate base*, provided that they are combined with the appropriate allowed rate of return. The most commonly used methods are valuation of the rate base with historical purchase and production costs combined with the nominal cost of capital or valuation of the rate base with current replacement costs combined with the real cost of capital, where the specific rate of price increase of the regulated firm's assets is used for the conversion of the nominal into the real cost of capital. Both methods fulfill the requirement of net present value neutrality.[288]

However, if the uncertainty about the prospects for capital recovery increases with time (giving rise to higher variance of the return on investment), and especially if the perceived risk of discretionary regulatory behavior increases with time (causing higher asymmetric downside risk), the distribution of cash flows over time affects risk-adjusted cost of capital.[289] Under these circumstances, regulatory depreciation schemes that backload the recovery of capital towards the end of the investment period are perceived as riskier than schemes that allow for frontloading of capital recovery and capital owners will demand an appropriate compensation in the allowed rate of return. This interaction between the regulatory depreciation scheme and the risk-adjusted allowed rate of return has been so far widely ignored.

If the assets of a regulated firm exhibit price increases (respectively price decreases), and if straight-line depreciation is applied, the use of a historical purchase and production cost-based depreciation scheme entails frontloading (respectively backloading) of capital recovery in comparison

286 In this section regulatory depreciation schemes are only discussed with respect to their effect on risk-adjusted cost of capital. For a thorough analysis of the choice of regulatory depreciation schemes, see section 5.1.1.

287 For the criterion of net present value neutrality in the context of rate regulation, see Knieps/Küpper/Langen (2001, 760ff.). Yard (2004) discusses the criterion of value-consistency in the context of changes of regulatory calculation methods in Sweden.

288 Cf. Swoboda (1973); Gordon (1977).

289 This has already been discussed in the context of CWIP versus AFUDC in the preceding section.

with a current replacement cost-based depreciation scheme.[290] Due to the interaction with the risk-adjusted cost of capital, under uncertainty, the two methods cease to be equivalent without the appropriate adjustment of the allowed rate of return.

Furthermore, if *competition* is admitted in the market, above all, if regulation is asymmetric, i.e. competitors are not rate-regulated, the regulatory commission has to take into account the effect on (potential) competition when imposing a certain depreciation scheme on the firm. If, for example, depreciation and interest are calculated as an annuity and regulated rates are kept constant over time, and if, at the same time, technological progress reduces the input price of the assets, potential competitors will be able to enter the market from a certain moment on and undercut the regulated rates that are no longer sustainable. Put differently, if competition is admitted, only price paths that are replacement cost-orientated are sustainable. If the regulator does not adapt the price path to the development of replacement cost, the allowed rate of return cannot be achieved over the investment's economic lifetime. This, in turn, exposes the regulated firm to an asymmetric downside risk and gives rise to an underinvestment problem.

To avoid this problem, frontloading depreciation has been proposed, such that depreciation follows the path of replacement cost and at the same time the sum of depreciation allowances still equals the initial investment.[291] With rising input prices, a backloading of depreciation to later periods in the economic lifetime of an asset can be justified along the same line of argument, as otherwise competitors investing later would not be able to match the regulated rates. Here again, under uncertainty, the distribution of capital recovery over time not only has an effect on the sustainability of regulated rates, but also affects risk-adjusted cost of capital and the appropriate allowed rate of return.

4.2.4 Impact of the Cost Distribution Base on the Capacity Utilization Risk

Calculation directives not only concern cost elements, but also the output side of a regulated utility. Depending on whether costs are allocated on total capacity or marketed capacity, the capacity utilization risk remains with

[290] With increasing prices, depreciation amounts are higher in early periods if replacement costs are used, but this effect is more than offset by lower (real) interest. See also the numerical example for price decreases in Knieps/Küpper/Langen (2001, 763) as well as Table 5.5 in section 5.1.1.

[291] See Crew/Kleindorfer (1992a); Knieps/Küpper/Langen (2001).

the regulated firm or is borne by the rate-payers. This risk is likely to be strongly correlated with the overall market development and therefore increases the cost of capital of the regulated firm. The capacity utilization risk can be interpreted as a reflection of the cost concept employed by the regulator. If TELRIC is used, it is implicitly assumed that the regulated facility is permanently utilized at full capacity.[292]

If costs are allocated on total capacity, it has to be taken into account that a hundred per cent capacity utilization cannot be achieved realistically. This can be done either by applying a realistic capacity utilization rate to avoid the downside bias or by raising the allowed rate of return or implementing a capacity payment to compensate for the downside bias. In this context, it has to be considered that in many cases the targeted capacity utilization rate is only attained gradually so that the realistic average utilization rate is additionally reduced. In the U.S. electricity industry, in some instances, this is accounted for by shifting part of the depreciation and the interest toward the end of the useful life of power plants and network elements.[293] Moreover, in the calculation of rates, a lower-than-average utilization rate is appropriate, as a higher utilization in later periods does not compensate for a lower utilization in earlier periods due to discounting. Along the same line of argument, symmetric uncertainty about the economic lifetime of an investment introduces a bias in the calculation, as the gain of discounted cash flows of an additional period is worth less than the loss of discounted cash flows, when the economic lifetime is reduced by one period.

4.3 Impact of Variables Determining the Scope of Regulation

While so far it has been analyzed how the design of the rate regulation mechanism and of the regulatory accounting methods influence risk and the appropriate allowed rate of return for the regulated firm, a wider perspective is now taken and the impact of variables determining the scope of regulation is investigated. Scope of regulation can be measured in three hierarchically dependent dimensions: Which *markets* and market segments are comprehended by regulation? Which *firms* or firm divisions are admitted and regulated in these markets? And which firm *decisions* are regulated?

---

[292] Cf. Hausman (1997, 33).

[293] Cf. Swoboda (1996, 374).

4.3.1 Scope of Regulated Decisions

This investigation presupposes the regulation of pricing decisions in some way. However, the regulation of investment and financing decisions as well as the admission of risk mitigation measures possibly interacts with rate regulation with regard to its effect on risk-adjusted cost of capital.[294]

Regulatory Interventions in Investment Decisions - Universal Service Obligations

Regulatory intervention in investment decisions possibly occurs in one of the two following forms. On the one hand, regulatory commissions can make investments generally subject to *authorization*. This is done above all in regulatory systems that guarantee the regulated firm a certain rate of return on all or near to all of their investment, i.e. in cost-of-service-type systems of rate regulation, in order to prevent overinvestment as conjectured by the Averch-Johnson hypothesis.[295] This results in a kind of micromanagement by the regulator with all its well-known drawbacks, e.g. due to information asymmetries between the regulator and the regulated firm, and possibly causes distortions of the efficient investment volume. Moreover, the lag between request and permission of investment creates additional uncertainty about the advantageousness of investment that increases cost of capital.[296]

Things are further complicated if investments have to be approved by another regulatory commission than the one that sets rates, as is the case in California, where the California Energy Commission supervises investments, whereas rates are regulated by the California Public Utilities Commission. However, in a regulated monopoly, it is not likely that this has a considerable effect on the profitability of the investments actually made.

On the other hand, the regulatory commission can impose investment obligations on the regulated firm, which is made, for example, in the context of a universal service obligation.[297] A *universal service obligation* is

---

[294] See the analysis of indirect transmission paths in section 3.4.2.

[295] See Averch/Johnson (1962).

[296] Cf. Shuttleworth/MacKerron (2002, 23).

[297] Another prominent example is the Resource Adequacy Requirement included in the recent Standard Market Design Notice of Proposed Rulemaking of the U.S. FERC that foresees a generation capacity obligation mechanism and is the subject of intensive discussion; see Remedying Undue Discrimination through Open Access Transmission Service and Standard Electricity Market Design, Notice of Proposed Rulemaking, Docket No. RM01-12-000 (July 31, 2002).

defined by the following three characteristics:[298] Firstly, the regulated firm has to provide a certain service completely covering a certain geographic area and/or group of customers. Secondly, the service has to be provided at a non-differentiated, uniform price. Thirdly, the service has to be provided at a standard uniform quality. The reasoning for establishing such a universal service obligation can be distributional considerations aiming at geographical equity.[299] Another rationale are externalities within the network or expected impulses on the overall economic development. If competition is admitted,[300] a default service obligation usually includes coverage by the regulated firm when a competitive service has been temporarily interrupted or permanently cancelled.[301]

Cross-subsidization between low-cost and high-cost areas or customers is necessary to finance a universal service with a uniform price. In a protected *monopoly*, this is, in principle, a feasible way to implement a universal service obligation that in this case *per se* is not associated with a higher risk, provided that the regulatory commission guarantees that the regulated firm earns the allowed rate of return on average over all of its areas and/or customers. In the context of U.S. utility regulation, a universal service obligation is part of the so-called *regulatory compact*. The regulatory compact is a more or less implicit contract between the regulatory commission and the utilities. In principle, it submits utilities to a universal service obligation and in exchange guarantees them a fair rate of return on their investments. The regulatory commission controls the admission of competitors to the market and thereby protects the incumbent utility from an erosion of its customer base. The regulated utility promises in return to make the necessary investments to ensure security of supply and to maintain service quality as well as to strive for operational efficiency and prudent investment behavior. On the same lines, in Germany, electric and gas utilities were protected until 1998 by so-called demarcation contracts that

[298] Cf. Crew/Kleindorfer (1998).

[299] For possible reasons for establishing a universal service obligation cf. Valletti/Hoernig/Barros (2001, 170). For universal service obligation in the German telecommunications sector, see Picot/Burr (1996, 180ff.).

[300] See section 4.3.2.

[301] For instance, Best-Energy, a new entrant in power supply in Berlin, ceased operation and cancelled all contracts with its clients by the end of December 2003. The local incumbent is obligated to take over the customers if they so wish; see Frankfurter Allgemeine Zeitung, Nr. 261, 10.11.2003.

established protected regional monopolies and imposed universal service obligations on them.[302]

An investment obligation only becomes *binding* if the regulated firm is forced to invest more or earlier than it would do voluntarily. As discussed in section 3.4.2, under a perfect and continuous rate-of-return regulation, an option of waiting to invest has no value. Existing regulatory systems deviate more or less from this hypothetical benchmark, and the value of waiting to invest tends to increase with the risks that have to be borne by the regulated firm. If a binding investment obligation is imposed on the regulated firm, it looses flexibility with regard to the optimal timing of investment; in other words, the option to wait is eliminated. This calls for compensation by way of a higher allowed rate of return. It has been shown formally, that if a regulatory system deviates from the benchmark of perfect rate-of-return regulation in the sense that there are regulatory lags or boundaries within which the actual rate of return can vary around the allowed rate of return, an investment obligation, e.g. resulting from a universal service obligation, requires a higher allowed rate of return.[303]

The optimal timing of an investment depends on numerous factors: the exclusivity of the investment opportunity and the uncertainty about the advantageousness of the investment project, competitive disadvantages, foregone cash flows and additional information about the advantageousness of the investment project that are expected for the waiting period as well as the interest advantage of postponing investment. This multitude of determinants makes optimal investment timing a very complex issue. The major problem in the context of regulatory investment obligations is that the investment timing that the regulated firm would choose without an investment obligation neither can be observed nor can be assessed without considerable arbitrariness. Furthermore, the regulated firm has an incentive to report to the regulator that it would prefer to invest less and later with the aim of driving up compensation for its investment. Put differently, the regulator faces the extremely difficult problem of judging if and to which extent an investment obligation actually is binding.

---

[302] On April 24, 1998, a new version of the German Energiewirtschaftsgesetz [energy industry act] came into effect that abolished the protected regional monopolies and opened up energy markets for competition.

[303] For a formal model and a numerical example, see Brennan/Schwartz (1982b, 297).

Regulatory Interventions in Financing Decisions

Some regulatory commissions intervene in financing decisions with the objective of avoiding possible distortions of financing triggered by rate regulation itself.[304] Either the regulatory commission dictates a certain capital structure to the regulated firm that actually has to be adopted or it uses in its cost calculations for rate setting purposes a certain capital structure and leaves it open to the regulated firm to actually adopt this imputed capital structure or to retain a deviating capital structure. In both cases, potential effects on risk-adjusted cost of capital have to be considered.

Usually, the regulator makes capital structure prescriptions that are based on a higher than actual leverage, with the intention to reduce the overall weighted average cost of capital by replacing equity with cheaper debt. However, a change in the capital structure does not leave cost of debt and cost of equity unchanged. Particularly, it has to be accounted for that a higher leverage increases risk for the remaining equity, which calls for a consistent increase of cost of equity.[305] If the regulator forces the regulated firm to adopt a higher debt-to-equity ratio deemed optimal by the regulator, and if at the same time he does not account for increases of cost of debt and especially cost of equity, the imputed weighted average cost of capital will be below its actually appropriate value. This gives rise to a potential underinvestment problem.

The same holds true if the imputed and the actual capital structure diverge. For the calculation of the imputed weighted average cost of capital, it is necessary to adjust cost of debt and cost of equity consistently. Additionally, even if this is done correctly, it is still not guaranteed that the imputed cost of capital coincides with the actual cost of capital. This would only be the case if the capital structure happens to be irrelevant to the weighted average cost of capital in the considered range between the imputed and the actual debt-to-equity-ratio, as the effects of more debt via weighting and via increasing cost of debt and cost of equity exactly offset each other. This is at least not very likely. Otherwise, there is a systematic difference between imputed and actual cost of capital, which results in an allowed rate of return systematically too low as measured by actual cost of capital and thereby contributes to a potential underinvestment problem. If

---

[304] For a discussion of the objectives and drawbacks of such an approach, see section 3.4.2. For an overview of the regulatory practice in the UK, see CAA (2001, 16); for an international overview, see Houston et al. (1999, 20).

[305] Cf. Myers (1992, 13ff.), who shows with numerical examples that the cost of equity has to increase with the debt-equity ratio if the overall cost of capital is kept constant in accordance with the irrelevance theorem of Modigliani and Miller (1958); see also section 6.3.2.

such capital structure prescriptions are introduced unexpectedly by the regulator, i.e. if the allowed rate of return is reduced unexpectedly, this boils down to an expropriation of the capital owners, especially the equity owners in place.

The effect of setting an allowed rate of return on systematic risk too low due to capital structure prescriptions is far from clear. Without adjustments of investment and financing decisions, a lower allowed rate of return would induce a shift of the cash flow distribution to the left and at the same time would compress the distribution. If this effect is translated into reduced systematic risk, it would even decrease *per se* cost of capital. However, as it can be expected that investment and financing decisions will be adjusted by the regulated firm, this is an oversimplification. An analysis of all the potential effects via adjusted investment and financing is beyond the scope of this analysis.

Even if the regulated firm anticipates that in the future the regulator will intervene in financing decisions by capital structure prescriptions and considers this when making its financing decisions, it is still exposed to an asymmetric risk. At best, the regulator will find the prevailing capital structure optimal and use it in his cost of capital calculations; in many cases, however, he will find it suboptimal and use a capital structure that he deems better and that yields a lower weighted average cost of capital. This means that, at best, the regulated firm earns its actual cost of capital, but in many cases less than its actual cost of capital, which drives the expected average rate of return below the cost of capital. If this asymmetric risk associated with capital structure prescriptions is not compensated, e.g. by a higher allowed rate of return, investment incentives will be reduced.

Regulatory Interventions in Risk Mitigation Decisions

The extent to which the regulated firm is allowed to take risk-mitigating measures is a driver of the remaining risk that, ultimately, has to be borne by the regulated firm. Part of this is the question whether or not *long-term contracts*, e.g. for the procurement of fuel or electricity, and *hedging* are allowed. If the regulated firm enjoys a complete and immediate cost pass-through, it bears no procurement risk and has no incentive to mitigate this risk. However, if the regulated firm cannot pass through the corresponding costs to its customers completely and immediately, the use of long-term contracts and hedging reduces the risk remaining with the firm. One of the factors that contributed to the California energy crisis was the fact that electricity distribution companies were not allowed long-term energy procurement contracts leaving them fully exposed to short-term price spikes on wholesale markets.[306] Furthermore, the regulated firm can reduce procurement risks by using futures markets for the procurement of debt, labor and material,[307] if this is admitted by the regulatory commission. In principle, this is suited to lower cost of equity and cost of debt.[308]

Correspondingly, the regulated firm can protect its infrastructure investment that, for the most part, is characterized by extraordinarily long commitment periods, by closing long-term contracts on the demand side, i.e. with retail customers and with competitors buying access to its infrastructure. In this way, a part of the capacity utilization risk could be shifted to these parties. However, many regulatory commissions do not admit long-term contracts with the objective to preventing lock-in of the existing customer base, which could hinder the development of competition.[309] The question of whether these risk mitigation measures actually would be efficient from an investors' point of view or whether diversification on the level of the investor's portfolio would be more efficient, is not investigated here.

4.3.2 Scope of Regulated Firms

The scope of regulated firms depends on which firms actually are admitted to the market and which of these firms subsequently are submitted to rate regulation. Not necessarily all the firms that are admitted to a market are rate-regulated. In some instances, only the rates of the incumbent utility are regulated, introducing asymmetry into the situation between the incumbent and new entrants.

Scope of Competition and Entry Allowed

Compared to the benchmark case of a protected monopoly, the admission of competition tends to increase the *demand uncertainty* faced by the regulated firm. Competitors can build up new infrastructure to bypass existing infrastructure, e.g. by laying new (pipe)lines, introducing an additional

---

306 For a discussion of the factors that interacted in creating the California energy crisis, see section 4.4.

307 Kolb/Morin/Gay (1983) investigate the corresponding risk mitigation strategies.

308 On the other hand the existence of rate regulation that has a buffering effect on the firms profitability reduces the incentive to use risk mitigation measures; see Kolb/Morin/Gay (1983, 413ff.); Gandolfi/Jenkinson/Mayer (1996, 8) and section 3.2.1.

309 See Shuttleworth/MacKerron (2002, 33).

element of uncertainty in the capacity utilization for the regulated firm. In many countries, established energy suppliers are bound by law to accept at fixed rates energy from renewable resources or from cogeneration by third parties, so that only a residual demand remains for their own capacity utilization, i.e. the uncertainty about the quantity of energy from third parties feeds back in the uncertainty about their own capacity utilization. Furthermore, regulation can create completely new kinds of risk. If, for example, the regulator starts enforcing access for new competitors to monopolistic bottlenecks of the regulated firm, new risks arise associated with the competitors' ability to pay. These effects can be interpreted as partly a reversal of the buffering effect of rate regulation.

In a monopolistic setting, the capacity utilization risk can be borne either by the regulated firm or, when rates are calculated on the basis of marketed capacity, by the ratepayers. However, if the regulated firm is exposed to competition, the second solution is not sustainable. If the regulated firm lost demand, fixed costs would have to be distributed over a smaller quantity ('who stays pays') and rates automatically would go up, inducing a further loss of demand and inevitably leading to a downward spiral.

This is a specific application of the more general argument that competition *restrains the possibilities to shift costs* from the regulated firm to consumers. If competitors have access to more efficient technologies, e.g. due to general technological progress or due to a specific efficiency advantage, the regulated firm cannot shift completely the higher costs of its own technology to consumers; otherwise it will loose market share. More specific for capital investments, only a constrained set of depreciation schemes is feasible. The path of depreciation has to be derived from the path of replacement cost to yield rates sustainable under competition with technological progress.[310] The regulated firm cannot postpone the adoption of new technologies until existing investments have paid off; the economic lifetime of assets becomes more uncertain. If technological progress is uncertain and rates are regulated such that the regulated firm can earn at best its allowed rate of return and if, at the same time, competition can prevent the firm in some cases from earning this allowed rate of return, the firm is exposed to an *asymmetric downside risk,* for which it must be compensated in some way. If the admission of competition comes as a surprising change on the part of the regulatory regime, it exposes investments of the regulated firm already in place to the risk of becoming *stranded*. This has a

[310] For a more detailed discussion of regulatory depreciations schemes, see section 5.1.1.

two-fold effect on the appropriate allowed rate of return:[311] Firstly, it increases the volatility of expected cash flows. Secondly, it cuts off the upper tail of cash flow distribution asymmetrically.

The economic consequences of a *universal service obligation* change fundamentally, if competition is admitted.[312] Cross-subsidization is not sustainable any more, as competitors will pursue a cream-skimming strategy, i.e. pick the demand that can be served at a cost below the uniform price leaving only the high-cost customers to the firm with the universal service obligation. This triggers a downward spiral.[313] The firm with the universal service obligation has to raise its rates to the average cost of serving its remaining customers. Even if this is allowed by the regulatory commission without any time lag, the higher rates give competitors new incentives for further cream-skimming, and the firm with the universal service obligation loses even more customers.

The U.S. electricity market for example was opened up for competition by independent power producers and cogeneration by the Public Utility Regulatory Policy Act (PURPA) in 1978. Until then, the regulatory compact had given incumbent investor-owned utilities a monopoly franchise with the guarantee of a fair rate of return on prudently incurred investment in exchange for a universal service obligation.[314] The Energy Policy Act (EPAct) of 1992 further promoted competition by giving all power producers access to the incumbents' transmission network. Even after the market for electricity generation was opened up for competition and the new competitors were given access to the incumbents' transmission system, the universal obligation of the incumbent distribution companies continued to exist. This created the described adverse selection risk with respect to the incumbents' customer base.

The effects of competition, which expose the regulated firm to an asymmetric downside risk, are aggravated by a universal service obligation. One possible way of handling this problem is to install a *universal service fund* to which all firms competing in the market must contribute so that the established firm is not put unilaterally at a cost disadvantage. Another possibility consists in *auctioning* off the universal service obligation. A further alternative would be the admission of price discrimination for the regulated firm, but, of course, this setting is no longer a real universal ser-

---

[311] See Kolbe/Borucki (1998, 256).

[312] For a discussion of the consequences of a universal service obligation in a protected monopoly situation, see section 4.3.1.

[313] Cf. Crew/Kleindorfer (2001) for a microstructure model for what they call a 'graveyard spiral'.

[314] Cf. Wilson (2002, 1329).

vice obligation. In any case, if competition is admitted, it becomes even more important that the burdens imposed by a universal service obligation and their financing are made explicit.[315]

If the established firm has to stand in when a competitor fails to provide its contracted service,[316] it can either procure the missing quantity on the spot market or permanently keep in reserve a certain capacity. In the first case, the spot market price risk can be passed through to the consumer or be borne by the regulated firm, driving up its risk-adjusted cost of capital. In the second case, the regulated firm can close long term contracts at a fixed price.[317] On the other hand, this creates an additional capacity utilization risk.

The conjecture that the admission of competition increases beta risk of rate-regulated firms is confirmed empirically by Nwaeze (2000b). In an event study using data of U.S. electric utilities for the period 1976 to 1997, he finds that liberalization of energy markets, especially the EPAct, increased utilities' systematic risk or, in other words, reduced the buffering effect of rate regulation.[318]

Access of New Entrants to the Incumbents' (Essential) Facilities

If competition is admitted in a hitherto protected monopoly and if some parts of the incumbents' network continue to be monopolistic bottlenecks, the issue of access and especially access pricing for new entrants to these essential facilities arises. For instance, in the U.S. the Telecommunications Act of 1996 gave competitors access to unbundled network elements of incumbent telecommunication firms. As monopolistic bottlenecks are investigated, the underlying investment is characterized by definition by a high degree of irreversibility, exposing the regulated firm to risks over the commitment period of the investment. Therefore, by committing resources, the regulated firm has given up in the past a valuable option to postpone investment, or has been forced to give it up by an investment obligation.[319]

---

[315] Cf. Wilson (2002, 1334).

[316] This can be a legal duty or a *de facto* obligation due to (expected) political pressure.

[317] However, the use of long-term contracts is not always allowed by the regulatory, see section 4.3.1.

[318] The general hypothesis that competition increases cost of capital receives further empirical support by the studies of Thomadakis (1976); Sullivan (1977) and Subrahmanyam/Thomadakis (1980).

[319] For a discussion of optimal investment timing under rate regulation, see section 3.4.2.

Competitors that are given access to the incumbents' essential facilities by the regulator usually can buy capacity on a flexible scale and at short notice.[320] New entrants benefit from the incumbents' existing investments without committing resources themselves. Put differently, they get the option to use the capacity of an essential facility without bearing the risks of the underlying investment, most notably, its capacity utilization risk, and they get it for free if this is not accounted for somehow in setting rates.[321] This would introduce an asymmetry in the competitive position of incumbents and new entrants.[322] There are different solutions to this problem. Either part of the capacity utilization risk is shifted to new entrants by long-term contracts or the incumbent receives compensation for sinking funds by a correspondingly higher allowed rate of return. The appropriate markup factor on the allowed rate of return increases with the uncertainty about capacity utilization.[323]

There are also effects working in the opposite direction. If the admission of competition does not only shift demand from the incumbent to new competitors but generates additional demand, the essential facilities' capacity utilization risk will be reduced *ceteris paribus*, that is, as long as no additional capacity is installed simultaneously. However, this effect can become a disadvantage for a vertically integrated incumbent, in the case of capacity bottlenecks. If he is not allowed to give priority to his own demand, he loses some of his own downstream business as a consequence of having to share the scarce capacity of an essential facility with his competitors. If so-far-above-normal returns have been earned in the downstream business, the value of this business is likely to be reduced due to both less volume and less margin. However, if new competitors are considerably more efficient than the incumbent in the downstream market, the net effect of access on the profitability of the incumbent even can be posi-

---

[320] Cf. Hausman (1999, 193).

[321] Real option theory does not necessarily assume that the investing firm is a monopolist as stated by Economides (1999, 7). It is true that under perfect competition all investment opportunities are publicly available and do not have any option value, but under oligopolistic competition with partly irreversible investment, investment opportunities that are exclusive to a certain degree are valuable.

[322] Nonetheless, Ergas et al. (2001, 21f.) suggest charging access seekers only if additional costs have to be incurred by the incumbent; this boils down to applying SRMC, which might be efficient in the short run, but destroys investment incentives in the long run; SRMC are analyzed in section 2.4.

[323] Cf. Hausman (1997, 34).

tive.[324] Due to the countervailing effects, the question of how risk and value of the existing platform are affected by giving access to competitors ultimately can be only answered empirically.

In principle, the same arguments hold true for new investment. If the regulated firm anticipates that its competitors will gain access to its essential facilities, compensation is required to induce efficient investment. This becomes especially evident in the context of investments in new services, when it is uncertain whether or not these services will be successful.[325] If a service is accepted by retail customers, competitors will buy access to this service from the incumbent. If, however, a new service is a failure on retail markets, competitors will not participate in covering the losses. Therefore, the incumbent faces an asymmetric risk that has to be compensated; otherwise he will not choose the efficient investment level voluntarily. This can be done by imposing a share of the losses of unsuccessful new services to new entrants or, more appropriate, as it corresponds to the outcome prevailing in unregulated markets,[326] by raising access charges for successful new services. Again, the higher the uncertainty about the advantageousness of new investment, the higher the appropriate markup on access charges has to be.

In the context of telecommunication infrastructure, it has been objected that investments are either not irreversible or do not face significant demand uncertainty.[327] However, as there is always some irreversibility[328] and some uncertainty, this objection is not suited to categorically deny the existence of the discussed effect but only to discuss in each individual case the degree of its importance. As several effects have to be measured and traded off, and as the required input parameters are not readily observable

---

324 For a discussion of the advantageousness of non-price discrimination (also called sabotage) to exclude competitors from access to essential facilities, see Mandy (2000) and Weisman/Kang (2001). Aside from efficiency differences between the incumbent and competitors, the intensity of competition and the degree of product differentiation in the downstream market are two of a number of further determinants.

325 See Hausman (1997).

326 In unregulated oligopolistic markets the prospect for supernormal profits in case of successful investments is supported by the fact that irreversible investment not only exposes the firm to risks but also is suited to erect market entry barriers that make competitive advantages sustainable over a certain period; see Pedell (2000, 113ff.).

327 See Economides (1999, 211f.).

328 See Pedell (2000, 77ff.). Complete irreversibility is not required to raise the issue, as is implied by Economides (1999, 7) by making the point that network "… elements do not have zero resale value."

by the regulator, especially in the case of the involved options, accounting for access in assessing the appropriate allowed rate of return and setting regulated rates poses serious informational and regulatory governance problems.

Symmetric or Asymmetric Regulation with Respect to Entrants

Asymmetric regulation treats the various participants in a market in a different way;[329] usually the incumbent is subject to regulatory directives that its competitors do not have to follow, e.g. rate regulations or universal or default service obligations. It is straightforward that asymmetric regulation, in this sense, only can become an issue if competition is admitted. If the rate of the incumbent firm is fixed and averaged over geographic regions, it has no flexibility to react to undercutting pricing moves of its competitors and is extremely vulnerable to cream-skimming, which introduces a downward bias in the expected rate of return of the incumbent. This problem is mitigated if the rates of competitors are regulated symmetrically or if the incumbent firm is given pricing flexibility across geographic regions.

A unilateral universal service obligation is *per se* an asymmetric regulatory directive. Its effects have been discussed above already. A universal service fund can be interpreted as one possibility to make the effects of a universal service obligation of the incumbent more symmetric with respect to entrants.

4.3.3 Scope of Regulated Markets

Beyond the delimitation of the spectrum of regulated decisions and regulated firms in a certain regulated business, the regulator lays down on a superior level the horizontal and vertical scope of regulation over businesses,[330] as well as defines the businesses in which a regulated firm may be active.

Regulation of the Horizontal Scope of the Regulated Firm's Activities

Determining the horizontal scope over businesses and industries in which a regulated firm is allowed to be active can be interpreted as setting the de-

[329] Cf. Picot/Burr (1996, 191f.).

[330] In the horizontal perspective across industries this will usually involve several regulatory commissions.

gree to which *horizontal diversification* is admitted by the regulator. If the regulated firm is allowed to diversify in other, regulated and/or non-regulated, industries, it may be able to take advantage of portfolio effects to decrease its overall risk and cost of capital.[331] The argumentation is directly in line with the admission of risk mitigation measures, discussed above in section 4.3.1. Empirically, it has been found by Antoniou and Pescetto (1997, 11f.) that an enlarged scope of services offered by the regulated firm decreases beta risk.

If a firm is diversified across several regulated industries that are supervised by different regulatory commissions, it has to be considered that the behavior of these commissions will be correlated in many cases, i.e. in particular regulatory risk will be correlated across regulated industries. This interdependence can be referred to as "*regulatory overlap*".[332] It is confirmed empirically by Appleyard and McLaren (1996) who investigate in an event study the effect of a change in the regulatory regime in the electricity industry in the UK from five year review periods to annual reviews on electricity and water companies. They find evidence for the expected capital market reaction not only in the case of electricity companies but also in the case of the water companies, supporting the conjecture that regulatory risk is spread over the entire sector of regulated industries.

Vertical Scope of Regulated Markets and Unbundling

Closely related to the diversification issue, but taking a vertical perspective, are regulatory directives concerning the unbundling of upstream or downstream activities. A fully vertically integrated utility can be taken as a benchmark to analyze the effects of unbundling on risk allocation over the supply chain.[333] Generally speaking, risks are added at each side of the market when the supply chain is split up, e.g. between the generation, transmission and distribution of electricity or gas. This becomes particularly evident in the case of unbundled electricity distribution companies. As a result of the non-storability of electricity, real-time balancing of demand and supply over the entire supply chain from generation over transmission and distribution to the consumer is necessary.

In a liberalized electricity generation market with independent power producers, generation companies need price spikes in periods of peak de-

[331] The question of whether such diversification is efficient, respectively whether diversification is more efficient on the investors' portfolio level is not discussed here. See the discussion of diversification discounts in section 6.2.5.

[332] Geoffrey Rothwell brought this point to my attention.

[333] Cf. Wilson (2002, 1329).

mand to cover their investments in generation capacity. While in the case of a vertically integrated regulated utility the financing of generation capacity can be spread over the entire demand (on-peak and off-peak), thus smoothing out price spikes, an unbundled distribution company is exposed to price spikes on electricity wholesale markets. If, at the same time, retail prices are set or capped by regulation, the distribution company gets squeezed between volatile input prices and fixed output prices. In this case, the complete procurement risk remains with the distribution company. This risk is aggravated in many cases by a deteriorated load shape due to the loss of large base-load consumers to independent power producers or to new distribution competitors.[334]

Generation companies for their part bear a very high investment risk in an unbundled supply chain, as they are in what can be called a *boom-or-bust situation*. If competition is working in electricity generation markets, and if there is excess capacity, they will only earn avoidable costs and will not be able to cover sunk investments. Only in periods during which capacity constraints become effective will they be able to earn a return on their sunk investments. If there is excess capacity even in on-peak times, they will not be able to cover their generation investments over the assets' economic lifetime. In completely liberalized electricity generation markets, there is a clear incentive not to invest in a reserve margin, as power producers would prevent themselves from covering not only the marginal investment but also the investment in capacity already in place.

Therefore, in many instances, the financing of generation capacity is regulated. This can be done either by capacity payments that are included in regulated retail rates and are levied not only upon on-peak demand but are spread over more or even all hours, seasons and/or consumers. An alternative consists in imposing capacity or contracting obligations on electricity distribution companies that obligate them to invest in enough capacity or to contract enough capacity to meet their peak load demand plus eventually a reserve margin. If electricity distribution companies are not allowed to align the duration of the contracts with their consumers with the duration of these obligations, they are exposed to capacity utilization and/or price risk.

Furthermore, there is a trade-off between transmission and generation: Higher transmission capacity allows for more centralized electricity generation. As in this way supply and demand imbalances can be cleared to a certain extent over the different regions served by central generation, an accordingly smaller (peak) capacity of generation is adequate. Put the other way round, more local generation capacity reduces the demand for

[334] Cf. Chao (2002, 10).

transmission capacity. This trade-off is solved differently, if these activities are individually optimized by independent firms. Accordingly, it can be interpreted as an indicator of inefficient risk sharing when the cost of capital increases in the course of the unbundling of upstream or downstream activities.

4.4 Case Study: California Energy Crisis as the Result of an Incompatible Combination of Regulatory Variables

The summer of the year 2000 marks the beginning of the California energy crisis, a vivid and instructive example of how incompatible choice of regulatory variables can endanger the viability of regulated utilities.[335] A long drought period had significantly reduced the generation capacity of hydroelectric power plants in the Northwest and as a consequence cut down imports into California.[336] At the same time, demand was very high, as during the heat most air-conditioning systems run at their maximum. In order to fill the resulting gap, generation of gas-fired thermal plants in California was increased as far as possible. But still, this was not sufficient to completely close the gap. Due to the low level of investment in generation capacity in the decade before the crisis, the reserve margin had significantly dropped during that period. Restricted transmission capacity for the import of electricity and the main fuel for electricity generation, natural gas, from the Southwest additionally aggravated the problem. The difference in gas prices between Texas and California that is an indicator of gas transmission cost from Texas to California went up dramatically during the crisis. This could point to attempts by transmission companies to take advantage of the shortage of gas supply in California. As a consequence of these developments, extreme price spikes on the wholesale market for electricity could be observed. These price spikes continued throughout the winter when the Northwest had to import electricity from California and gas-fired plants had to be shut down alternately for inspection.

This situation posed serious problems first of all for the incumbent electricity distribution companies that had been unbundled from transmission and generation activities by the regulator. They were caught between volatile wholesale prices with extreme spikes on the one hand and retail prices

[335] This section benefited strongly from discussions with Paul Kleindorfer, Geoffrey Rothwell, James Sweeney and Robert Wilson.

[336] For a description of the process that lead to the crisis, see Wilson (2002, 1331ff.). For a comprehensive analysis of the California power sector, see Rothwell/Gomez (2003, 210ff.).

that could not be raised due to the prevailing price caps on the other hand.[337] Figure 4.8 depicts the causes that interacted in creating the California Energy Crisis. The load shape of the incumbent electricity distribution companies made them particularly vulnerable to price spikes. The liberalization of energy markets had set off an adverse selection process during which primarily large industrial base-load consumers had decided to switch from the incumbent distribution companies to new competitors or directly to independent power producers. This restricted the potential scope for cross-subsidization and left incumbent distribution companies with a more variable load shape. Furthermore, they had a default service obligation, according to which they could not refuse to provide electricity to customers from new competitors that were no longer able to meet their electricity supply duties. This deteriorated the actual load shape even more. One way to re-attract large base load consumers would be price discrimination with respect to load shape[338] and the ability to interrupt power supply.

Making demand price-responsive increases the risk-bearing capacity of consumers and therefore is a prerequisite for shifting some of the price risk to them. However, the electricity distribution companies had no possibility of making their customers' demand responsive to the price increases on the wholesale market by differentiating prices by the hour and passing through electricity procurement costs.[339] This would have been a way to prevent at least the most extreme price spikes. Sufficient price discrimination with respect to on-peak and off-peak hours was prevented by the prevailing price cap on retail prices. Besides, the technical preconditions for price discrimination by the hour were not fulfilled, as private households do not have the necessary real time metering equipment installed. Furthermore, it is unlikely that private consumers would be willing to supervise the development of energy prices by the hour. Therefore, an automatic mechanism to reduce or to cut off power supply in on-peak hours would be needed, where the consumer must be able to override this mechanism if he is willing to pay the relatively high electricity rates of these hours.[340]

---

337 The California price cap rarely had been binding until then but became binding most of the time from June 2000 to June 2001. I am indebted to Lee-Ken Choo and David Hunger of the U.S. Federal Energy Regulatory Commission (FERC) for bringing this point to my attention.

338 Cf. Chao (2002, 14).

339 Cf. Kahn (2002, 46).

340 I am indebted to Robert Wilson for bringing this argument to my attention.

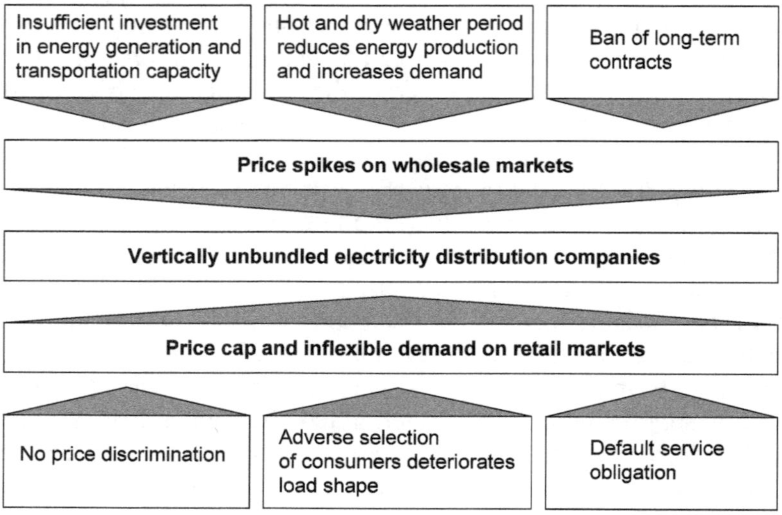

Figure 4.8. Causes of the California energy crisis

In addition, electricity distribution companies were precluded from taking mitigation measures against the risk of wholesale price spikes by the regulatory regime's refusal to admit long-term electricity procurement contracts. The ban of long-term contracts had been introduced in order to facilitate regulatory governance, as spot market prices can be observed more easily and open less space for judgment than long-term contracts, especially if the latter are closed with affiliated companies.

The case of the California energy crisis underlines the importance of scrutinizing the interaction of regulatory variables when making changes to a regulatory regime, especially when embarking on a process of market liberalization. The flaws of a piecemeal deregulation[341] can seriously endanger the financial viability of regulated utilities, especially when elements of competition and regulation are combined in an inconsistent way. The unbundling of supply chains adds new risks at each side of the market and makes the development of elaborate risk sharing mechanisms even more important. Therefore, the use of risk transfer mechanisms such as long-term contracts as well as futures and options should not be restricted if not inevitable for reasons of regulatory governance. Universal service obligations cannot be financed by cross-subsidization if competition is

341 The expression "piecemeal deregulation" is taken from Crew/Kleindorfer (2001c, 20).

admitted. The burdens associated with universal service obligations and their financing have to be made explicit.[342]

The example of Californian electricity distribution companies adds to the evidence that the different markets of a supply chain cannot be liberalized independently from each other. Caps on retail prices not allowing for pass-trough of wholesale prices and default service obligations of incumbent distribution companies were not sustainable under a regime of liberalized wholesale markets that became very volatile because of insufficient generation and transmission capacity. Setting incentives for efficient investment in generation and transmission capacity is of paramount importance not only for the functioning of wholesale markets but also for the regulation on the distribution level.[343] In the first place, predictable and consistent regulatory behavior is required to encourage investment and to attain resource adequacy in the long run.

[342] Cf. Wilson (2002, 1334).

[343] In the summer of 2002, the FERC proposed a Standard Market Design as a reaction to the California energy crisis and other events such as the Enron collapse. This proposal aims at re-regulating wholesale markets with price caps to avoid price spikes. As this tends to decrease incentives for new investment in generation and transmission capacity, it imposes at the same time an obligation on electricity distribution companies to contract enough capacity to meet their peak load demand plus a reserve margin, which is intensively discussed under the keyword of 'resource adequacy requirement'.

5 Determination of the Regulatory Rate Base

In the current discussion of the cost of capital for rate-regulated firms, the assessment of the appropriate rate of cost of capital is, in most instances, the predominant issue.[344] The determination of the regulatory rate base attracts less attention, although the regulatory rate base is inextricably interwoven with the rate of cost of capital as to the computation of interest and depreciation.[345]

The guiding theme underlying the analysis in this chapter is the question of whether market values or book values should be employed in the regulatory rate base. It is motivated by the following conflict. On the one hand, from a financial theory perspective, it is clear that investors expect to earn a return (equal to the cost of capital) on market value. From the point of view of capital owners, the current market value constitutes the capital that could be freed by selling shares and reinvested in alternative assets. Therefore, it seems that in a capital market-based approach, market values have to be used for the regulatory rate base for reasons of consistency.[346] On the other hand, throughout the international regulatory practice, some form of book values is used for the regulatory rate base, without which this would even be a major point of discussion between the regulator and regulated utilities in regulatory hearings.[347] It should be noted in this context that book values are not necessarily based on historical acquisition and production costs, but, in principle, can be based on replacement costs or some other form of current cost accounting. It should also be noted that regula-

---

[344] For the discussion in Germany, see, for example, Schneider (2001); Busse von Colbe (2002); Kempf (2002); Knieps (2002); Siegel (2002); Gerke (2003); Pedell (2004a). See in detail chapter 6. In the UK, the issue of the regulatory rate base is discussed more intensely; see section 5.3.3.

[345] Cf. Kahn (1988, 48/Iff.) and Bonbright/Danielsen/Kamerschen (1988, 202f.), who discuss this aspect with regard to the setting of regulated rates.

[346] In the context of rate regulation, this view is supported, for example, by Busse von Colbe (2002, 15f.); Küpper (2002, 53); Knieps (2003, 1002).

[347] For the U.S., see the overview in Bonbright/Danielsen/Kamerschen (1988, 229f.).

tory book values are not necessarily identical to the book values that are used for financial accounting or for tax accounting.[348]

There is a deficit in the academic debate with regard to (1) detecting and analyzing explanations for this conflict between the rationale for market values founded in financial theory and the predominant application of book values in the regulatory practice as well as with regard to (2) showing how this conflict can be reconciled in different situations. The following analysis aims at contributing towards closing these gaps. To this end, a hypothetical benchmark system of rate regulation that would establish equality between market values and book values is described in section 5.1. Section 5.2 identifies and analyzes reasons why market values and book values of rate-regulated firms differ, and brings to light the rationale for using book values in the regulatory rate base. In section 5.3 it is shown how, in different situations, the use of book values in the regulatory rate base can be reconciled with the return required by investors.

5.1 Characterization of a Hypothetical Benchmark System of Rate Regulation Establishing Equality of Book Values and Market Values

As starting point for the analysis of issues associated with the determination of the regulatory rate base, the hypothetical benchmark situation of a system of rate regulation, which establishes the regulated firm's equality of book value and market value, is investigated. It is assumed that (1) a new firm starts operating in t_0 and invests all its capital in one rate-regulated business; alternatively it could be assumed that the firms consists of several businesses (regulated or unregulated) whose value is additive, (2) rate regulation is perfect in the sense that it guarantees that the regulated firm will earn its cost of capital on all investments in the regulated business at any moment in time, i.e. actual costs are passed through to rates completely and without any lag, (3) the regulatory system is credible, i.e. investors do not expect the regulator to deviate from this regulatory policy, and (4) this situation extends for the entire life of the firm. In such a hypothetical benchmark situation, there are no synergies and no goodwill and the market values will not deviate from book values. Investors are not exposed to any risk, their equity *de facto* is converted to a risk-less bond,

[348] See also the discussion on tax flow-through versus normalization of taxes in section 4.2.2.

and, accordingly, they should earn the risk-less interest rate on their investment.[349]

The following sub-sections analyze how regulatory accounting procedures regarding the regulatory rate base must be designed so as to maintain equality of book values and market values. Firstly, the consistent treatment of the regulatory rate base, depreciation, and interest is investigated for the cases of non-wasting and wasting assets. Secondly, the inclusion of new investment in the regulatory rate base is analyzed and, thirdly, the treatment of investments accounted for as operating expenditures is discussed.

5.1.1 Consistent Treatment of the Regulatory Rate Base, Depreciation, and Interest

At the bottom line, different alternatives of rate base values yield the same return, if the rate of cost of capital is chosen consistently. It can be shown that an entire class of such consistent combinations of rate base valuations and rate of return exists.[350] The equivalence of nominal return on *historical acquisition and production costs* and the corresponding real return on *current replacement costs* is widely accepted in the relevant literature;[351] when using replacement costs, the specific price increase rate for the regulated facilities is needed for the conversion of the nominal return to the appropriate real return. Although, from the capital owners' perspective, the overall price increase is relevant to their consumption possibilities and, accordingly, to the appropriateness of the return on their capital, the equivalence between acquisition costs combined with nominal interest – containing the *overall* inflation rate – and replacement cost combined with real interest is established by using the *specific* price increase rate for the conversion. As the specific rate of price increase would have to be assessed for a multitude of regulated facilities, the determination of the specific real interest rate in most instances is more complex than using the readily available nominal interest rate; it creates more informational problems and increases the scope for discretion.[352]

---

349 Cf. section 3.2 and section 3.3, where it is shown that such a regulatory system is neither possible nor desirable.

350 See Greenwald (1980) and (1984).

351 Cf. Swoboda (1973, 363f.) and (1996). See the numerical examples and the formal proof in Knieps/Küpper/Langen (2001, 762ff.) as well as Table 5.5. See also Oftel (1992, 3) and the detailed discussion of original *versus* replacement costs in the rate base in Bonbright/Danielsen/Kamerschen (1988, 233ff.).

352 Cf. Swoboda (1996, 367). Moreover, the conversion of a post-tax to a pre-tax rate of cost of capital is additionally complicated; see section 6.4.3.

Regulatory Rate Base, Depreciation, and Interest in the Case of Non-Wasting Assets

The consistency of regulatory rate base, depreciation, and interest can be analyzed most clearly by considering in the first instance a simple numerical example of a non-wasting asset in order to isolate and better understand the effects of specific price changes of regulated assets.

Specific Price Change Equal to the Overall Inflation Rate. It is assumed that a regulated utility in t_0 invests in a non-wasting asset, e.g. undeveloped real estate to build a pipeline, and that the price of the real estate increases at a rate of 5% per year. The overall inflation rate relevant for the consumption possibilities of the capital owners is also 5%. The simplifying assumption that the specific price increase of the regulated utility's asset equals the overall inflation rate is released below. The annual cost of capital is 10% in nominal terms and, accordingly, 4.76% in real terms.[353] In this scenario, the capital owners of the regulated utility are exactly compensated for the overall inflation by the value increase of the real estate. If the nominal cost of capital of 10% is applied to the replacement costs at the beginning of each period to calculate the cost of capital in absolute terms, if regulated rates are based on this cost, and if at the same time gains realized by sale of the real estate are not considered by a reduction of rates, capital owners will obtain a double inflationary compensation.

The example in Table 5.1 assumes that the regulated firm buys the real estate in t_0 at the price of € 100 and resells it in t_6 at a price of € 134. If the nominal interest rate is applied to the replacement costs of the rate base (Panel A), a net present value of revenues from regulated rates and of the selling price of more than € 100 results, i.e. this procedure is not performance neutral with respect to net present value.[354] If the gains realized by reselling the asset in t_6 is accounted for by reducing revenues from regulated rates in t_6, the above normal return is reduced, but not completely eliminated (Panel B). If, in contrast, the real interest rate is applied to the replacement costs of the rate base, the net present value of revenues from

[353] Real interest rate = (nominal interest rate – inflation rate) / (1 + inflation rate). The same result is obtained if, instead of the interest rate, the rate base is divided by (1 + inflation rate). In this case, in order to be consistent, interest has to be calculated on used replacement value at the beginning of a period, whereas depreciation has to be calculated on the basis of replacement cost at the end of a period; see Küpper/Pedell (2005b, 6f.). Net present value neutrality for this case was shown by Sieben/Diedrich/Price Waterhouse (1996, 72); see also Diedrich (2004, 36ff.).

[354] For the criterion of net present value neutrality in the context of regulatory depreciation, see Knieps/Küpper/Langen (2001, 760); see also Yard (2004, 2).

regulated rates and of the selling price just equals € 100 (Panel C). The same cash flow series results if, in each individual period, the price increase is accounted for by an appreciation and revenues from regulated rates are reduced by the amount of this appreciation, i.e. for example € 100 * 10% - € 5 = € 5 in t_1 (Panel D).

If acquisition costs are used for the regulatory rate base, it is self-evident that they should be combined with the nominal interest rate. Table 5.2 resumes the numerical example of Table 5.1, but uses acquisition costs instead of replacement costs. It can be seen that the gains realized by reselling the real estate have to be offset by a reduction of regulated rates in t_6 (Panel B),[355] as otherwise capital owners again would obtain a double inflationary compensation (Panel A). If this aspect is accounted for, a net present value of revenues from regulated rates and of the selling price of € 100 will result. If the real interest rate is applied to acquisition costs, the net present value is reduced below the targeted amount of € 100 (Panel C).

The numerical examples show that rate regulation somehow has to take account of the price increase of the regulated asset, as otherwise investors are overcompensated for inflation, which *ceteris paribus* would drive net present value and market value above book value at the outset. Consistent combinations of regulatory rate base, depreciation and interest rate are either replacement cost in the rate base without separate depreciation and with real interest rate (Panel C in Table 5.1) or replacement cost in the rate base with rate diminishing appreciation and nominal interest rate (Panel D in Table 5.1) or acquisition cost in the rate base with rate diminishing sales gain of the non-wasting asset in t_6 and with nominal interest rate (Panel B in Table 5.2). These three methods yield a net present value of 100 in t_0, i.e. they produce quality of market value and book value in t_0. The equality of market value and book value also is maintained at later moments by these methods, as the net present value of the still outstanding cash flows at each moment equals the current book value, which increases in the case of replacement costs and is constant at € 100 in the case of acquisition costs. This result also holds true in the case of specific price changes different from the overall inflation rate and in the case of wasting assets, as will be shown below.

The profile of cash flows over time in Panel C and D of Table 5.1 differs from the one in Panel B of Table 5.2, even if in all cases the same net

---

355 In this simple numerical example with one asset, revenues from regulated rates in t_6 are smaller than the gains realized from reselling the asset, so that either the regulator would have to claim a net payment from the regulated firm in t_6, or the subtraction of the gains would have to be spread over several periods. In reality, this situation is unlikely.

present value of € 100 equal to the initial acquisition payment is obtained. The profile of cash flows over time might be relevant for two reasons. (1) If there is uncertainty about future regulation, which so far has been excluded by assumption, and if this uncertainty is higher the further ahead regulation lies, risk averse investors will require a higher risk premium when the cash flow profile is shifted towards the end of an investment, i.e. the adequate rate of cost of capital no longer will be equal for the two cash flow profiles.[356] (2) If competition is admitted, and if the regulator wants to avoid distortions of competition, he will mimic the decision situation of competitors when setting rates by orienting regulated rates toward the development of replacement costs, which would then have to be paid by a competitor wishing to enter the market after t_0. The effect of the cash flow profile over time on risk-adjusted cost of capital as well as its relevance when competition is admitted are discussed in more detail below.

Specific Price Change Different from the Overall Inflation Rate. The issue becomes more complex, if the specific price increase rate of the real estate diverges from the overall inflation rate relevant for the consumption possibilities of the capital owners and, accordingly, for their discount rate. If, for example, the value of the real estate increases at a higher rate than the overall price level, capital owners require less revenues from regulated rates to be willing to invest in the real estate. In this case, part of the real return requested by capital owners (referring to their consumption possibilities) is covered by the enhancement in value of the regulated asset. If, in contrast, the price of the regulated asset continuously decreases over the six periods and if at the same time the overall price level increases, an additional compensation for the fall in value of the real estate is required by regulated revenues; otherwise capital owners are not willing to invest in the real estate in t_0 in order to be able to provide the regulated service.

[356] Cf. Gordon (1977, 1508), who shows that, in the case of uncertain inflation, "... [w]ith historical cost regulation a utility share is riskier, but the return he [the investor] requires and gets under perfect regulation is correspondingly higher."

Table 5.1. Net present value of the cash flows from the investment in a non-wasting asset under rate regulation, using *replacement costs* for the regulatory rate base

(acquisition payment € 100, specific price increase rate 5%, overall inflation rate 5%, nominal interest rate 10%, specific real interest rate 4.76%)

	t0 (acquisition)	t1	t2	t3	t4	t5	t6 (sale)	NPV
Panel A: Rates on the basis of replacement costs with nominal interest								
Replacement cost	100.00	105.00	110.25	115.76	121.55	127.63	134.01	
Sales revenue							134.01	
Revenue from regulated rates		10.50	11.03	11.58	12.16	12.76	13.40	
Inpayment		10.50	11.03	11.58	12.16	12.76	147.41	
Discount factor		1.10	1.21	1.33	1.46	1.61	1.77	
Discounted inpayment		9.55	9.11	8.70	8.30	7.92	83.21	126.79
Panel B: Rates on the basis of replacement costs with nominal interest and rated diminishing sales gain								
Replacement cost	100.00	105.00	110.25	115.76	121.55	127.63	134.01	
Sales revenue							134.01	
thereof rate diminishing							-34.01	
Revenue from regulated rates		10.50	11.03	11.58	12.16	12.76	13.40	
Inpayment		10.50	11.03	11.58	12.16	12.76	113.40	
Discount factor		1.10	1.21	1.33	1.46	1.61	1.77	
Discounted inpayment		9.55	9.11	8.70	8.30	7.92	64.01	107.59
Panel C: Rates on the basis of replacement costs with specific real interest								
Replacement cost	100.00	105.00	110.25	115.76	121.55	127.63	134.01	
Sales revenue							134.01	
Revenue from regulated rates		5.00	5.25	5.51	5.79	6.08	6.38	
Inpayment		5.00	5.25	5.51	5.79	6.08	140.39	
Discount factor		1.10	1.21	1.33	1.46	1.61	1.77	
Discounted inpayment		4.55	4.34	4.14	3.95	3.77	79.25	100.00
Panel D: Rates on the basis of replacement costs with nominal interest and rate diminishing appreciation								
Replacement cost	100.00	105.00	110.25	115.76	121.55	127.63	134.01	
Appreciation (rate diminishing)		5.00	5.25	5.51	5.79	6.08	6.38	
Sales revenue							134.01	
Revenue from regulated rates		5.00	5.25	5.51	5.79	6.08	6.38	
Inpayment		5.00	5.25	5.51	5.79	6.08	140.39	
Discount factor		1.10	1.21	1.33	1.46	1.61	1.77	
Discounted inpayment		4.55	4.34	4.14	3.95	3.77	79.25	100.00

Table 5.2. Net present value of the cash flows from the investment in a non-wasting asset under rate regulation, using *acquisition costs* for the regulatory rate base

(acquisition payment € 100, specific price increase rate 5%, overall inflation rate 5%, nominal interest rate 10%, specific real interest rate 4.76%)

	t0 (acquisition)	t1	t2	t3	t4	t5	t6 (sale)	NPV
Panel A: Rates on the basis of acquisition costs with nominal interest								
Replacement cost	100.00	105.00	110.25	115.76	121.55	127.63	134.01	
Sales revenue							134.01	
Revenue from regulated rates		10.00	10.00	10.00	10.00	10.00	10.00	
Inpayment		10.00	10.00	10.00	10.00	10.00	144.01	
Discount factor		1.10	1.21	1.33	1.46	1.61	1.77	
Discounted inpayment		9.09	8.26	7.51	6.83	6.21	81.29	119.20
Panel B: Rates on the basis of acquisition costs with nominal interest and rate diminishing sales gain								
Replacement cost	100.00	105.00	110.25	115.76	121.55	127.63	134.01	
Sales revenue							134.01	
thereof rate diminishing							-34.01	
Revenue from regulated rates		10.00	10.00	10.00	10.00	10.00	10.00	
Inpayment		10.00	10.00	10.00	10.00	10.00	110.00	
Discount factor		1.10	1.21	1.33	1.46	1.61	1.77	
Discounted inpayment		9.09	8.26	7.51	6.83	6.21	62.09	100.00
Panel C: Rates on the basis of acquisition costs with specific real interest								
Replacement cost	100.00	105.00	110.25	115.76	121.55	127.63	134.01	
Sales revenue							134.01	
Revenue from regulated rates		4.76	4.76	4.76	4.76	4.76	4.76	
Inpayment		4.76	4.76	4.76	4.76	4.76	138.77	
Discount factor		1.10	1.21	1.33	1.46	1.61	1.77	
Discounted inpayment		4.33	3.94	3.58	3.25	2.96	78.33	96.38

Table 5.3 shows the situation of a specific annual price increase rate of the regulated asset of 7%, i.e. two percentage points above the overall inflation level. The numerical examples show that the approaches that yield a net present value of € 100 when the specific price increase rate equals the overall inflation rate, also are performance neutral in the case of a higher specific price increase rate. The same holds true, if the price of the regulated asset decreases at an annual rate of 5%, as can be seen in Table 5.4. In this case, the loss in value in each period is computed in Panel B as depreciation and compensated by regulated rates. As to the different cash

preciation and compensated by regulated rates. As to the different cash flow profiles over time, the same arguments apply that have been discussed in the preceding section. In particular, in Table 5.4 Panel C, it is debatable whether the sales loss realized in t_6 can and should be compensated by increasing regulated rates only in t_6. If the regulator wants to smooth rates, e.g. due to possible demand effects ignored by assumption in the numerical examples, he will spread the necessary compensation for the sales loss over the entire investment period. If competition is admitted, the price jump that is implied by the increase of total regulated revenues from € 10 in t_5 to € 36.49 in t_6 will not be achievable in the market, since a competitor, for example, could buy the asset in t_5 for € 77.38 and resell it in t_6 for € 73.51, and, accordingly, be willing to offer the same service for revenues of € 11.61 just covering the loss in value of the asset between t_5 and t_6 and a return of 10% on the capital invested in t_5.

Against this background, two cost concepts employed in the current regulatory practice for determining the regulatory rate base are briefly analyzed. In the German energy sector, the concept of the so-called *net substance maintenance* [Nettosubstanzerhaltung] has been applied for a fairly long time.[357] This concept uses acquisition cost combined with nominal interest for the debt financed part of the rate base and replacement cost combined with specific real interest for the equity financed part of the rate base. Net substance maintenance can be interpreted as a linear combination of the two above described methods and as the latter are equivalent if consistently applied, yields the same return at the bottom line. It made its way into the association agreements between energy producers and industrial consumers in the German electricity and natural gas sector.[358] Just as in the case of the use of pure replacement costs, this approach suffers from the problem that the specific price increase rates for all regulated facilities have to be assessed.

The concept of *current cost accounting*, which has been developed and applied mainly in the UK, might go beyond the mere use of replacement values in the regulatory rate base as, in some instances, not the actual quantity structure but modern equivalent assets valued at current procurement prices are employed. In other words, the concept applies the costs of service provision that would have to be incurred under current conditions by a (potential) competitor, and aims at stimulating or simulating competi-

[357] For the concept of net substance maintenance, see Sieben/Schildbach (1973); Sieben (1974); Schildbach (1993); for a critical view, see Zimmermann (1998); for an overview, see Reiners (2000; 60ff.); in the context of rate regulation see Männel (2003, 21ff.), Sieben/Maltry (2002a, 36ff.) and (2002b, 409ff.).

[358] Cf. BDI et al. (2001) for electricity, and BDI et al. (2002) for natural gas.

tion.[359] If assets more efficient than the assets actually installed are employed by the regulator for calculating rates, the regulatory rate base will be decreased and the revenues from regulated rates will not be sufficient to give investors an adequate return on the existing investments. Consequently, the market value of the regulated firm will decrease, unless the regulated firm receives compensation otherwise for the lower regulatory rate base, e.g. by a higher allowed rate of return.[360]

Regulatory Rate Base, Depreciation, and Interest in the Case of Wasting Assets

Regulatory Depreciation Schemes in the Monopolistic Case. The decrease in value of the assets contained in the regulatory rate base can be captured by different *regulatory depreciation schemes*. Elements of a depreciation scheme are the initial depreciation base, the profile over time and the total sum of depreciation amounts that can be larger, equal or smaller than the historical payments that were made for the acquisition or production of assets.[361] These dimensions open up the universe of possible depreciation schemes from which the regulator, in principle, can choose (see Figure 5.1).

For the purposes of cost-orientated rate regulation, a crucial criterion for the choice of a depreciation scheme is that cost of capital comprising interest and depreciation does not contain any above normal profit elements, i.e., from the perspective of investment theory, that the net present value of depreciation and interest just equals the acquisition payment of a facility (filter 1 in Figure 5.1),[362] assuming for simplicity's sake that there is no salvage value. This can be accomplished with different depreciation schemes: Acquisition costs and replacement costs are obviously possible candidates for the initial depreciation base. Both the combination of acquisition costs with nominal interest and the combination of replacement cost with specific real interest comply with the criterion of neutrality with respect to net present value, as has been shown for non-wasting assets in the preceding section.

---

[359] In principle, CCA can be based either on the concept of financial capital maintenance or on the concept of operating capability maintenance. From a financial theory perspective, the concept of financial capital maintenance should be applied. Cf. Oftel (1992, 3).

[360] For the use of a hypothetical quantity structure in the regulatory rate base, see section 5.2.1; for its feedback on risk-adjusted cost of capital, see section 4.2.3.

[361] Cf. Knieps/Küpper/Langen (2001, 762); Schweitzer/Küpper (2003, 102ff.).

[362] Criteria for the determination of regulatory depreciation are discussed in Knieps/Küpper/Langen (2001, 760ff.)

Table 5.3. Net present value of the cash flows from the investment in a non-wasting asset under rate regulation with a *specific price increase rate above the overall inflation rate*

(acquisition payment € 100 specific price increase rate 7%, overall inflation rate 5%, nominal interest rate 10%, specific real interest rate 2.80%)

	t0 (acquisition)	t1	t2	t3	t4	t5	t6 (sale)	NPV
Panel A: Rates on the basis of replacement costs with specific real interest								
Replacement costs	100.00	107.00	114.49	122.50	131.08	140.26	150.07	
Sales revenue							150.07	
Revenue from regulated rates		3.00	3.21	3.43	3.68	3.93	4.21	
Cash inflow		3.00	3.21	3.43	3.68	3.93	154.28	
Discount factor		1.10	1.21	1.33	1.46	1.61	1.77	
Discounted cash inflow		2.73	2.65	2.58	2.51	2.44	87.09	100.00
Panel B: Rates on the basis of replacement costs with nominal interest and rate diminishing appreciation								
Replacement costs	100.00	107.00	114.49	122.50	131.08	140.26	150.07	
Appreciation (rate diminishing)		7.00	7.49	8.01	8.58	9.18	9.82	
Sales revenue							150.07	
Revenue from regulated rates		3.00	3.21	3.43	3.68	3.93	4.21	
Cash inflow		3.00	3.21	3.43	3.68	3.93	154.28	
Discount factor		1.10	1.21	1.33	1.46	1.61	1.77	
Discounted cash inflow		2.73	2.65	2.58	2.51	2.44	87.09	100.00
Panel C: Rates on the basis of acquisition costs with nominal interest and rate diminishing sales gain								
Replacement cost	100.00	107.00	114.49	122.50	131.08	140.26	150.07	
Sales revenue							150.07	
thereof rate diminishing							-50.07	
Revenue from regulated rates		10.00	10.00	10.00	10.00	10.00	10.00	
Cash inflow		10.00	10.00	10.00	10.00	10.00	110.00	
Discount factor		1.10	1.21	1.33	1.46	1.61	1.77	
Discounted cash inflow		9.09	8.26	7.51	6.83	6.21	62.09	100.00

In Table 5.5, the initial example with a specific price increase rate of 5% equal to the overall inflation rate is resumed, but the case of a wasting asset with a life of six periods and which is used by the regulated firm over the entire six periods is investigated. As mentioned before, it is assumed for simplicity's sake that there is no salvage value. Again, the three approaches yield a net present value of € 100. In Panel B, depreciation is computed on replacement costs with the straight-line method.

Table 5.4. Net present value of the cash flows from the investment in a non-wasting asset under rate regulation with a *specific price decrease rate* (below the overall inflation rate)

(acquisition payment € 100, specific price decrease rate 5%, overall inflation rate 5%, nominal interest rate 10%, specific real interest rate 15.79%)

	t0 (acquisition)	t1	t2	t3	t4	t5	t6 (sale)	NPV
Panel A: Rates on the basis of replacement costs with specific real interest								
Replacement cost	100.00	95.00	90.25	85.74	81.45	77.38	73.51	
Sales revenue							73.51	
Revenue from regulated rates		15.00	14.25	13.54	12.86	12.22	11.61	
Cash inflow		15.00	14.25	13.54	12.86	12.22	85.12	
Discount factor		1.10	1.21	1.33	1.46	1.61	1.77	
Discounted cash inflow		13.64	11.78	10.17	8.78	7.59	48.05	100.00
Panel B: Rates on the basis of replacement costs with nominal interest and rate increasing depreciation								
Replacement cost	100.00	95.00	90.25	85.74	81.45	77.38	73.51	
Depreciation (rate increasing)		-5.00	-4.75	-4.51	-4.29	-4.07	-3.87	
Sales revenue							73.51	
Revenue from regulated rates		15.00	14.25	13.54	12.86	12.22	11.61	
Cash inflow		15.00	14.25	13.54	12.86	12.22	85.12	
Discount factor		1.10	1.21	1.33	1.46	1.61	1.77	
Discounted cash inflow		13.64	11.78	10.17	8.78	7.59	48.05	100.00
Panel C: Rates on the basis of acquisition costs with nominal interest and rate increasing sales loss								
Replacement cost	100.00	95.00	90.25	85.74	81.45	77.38	73.51	
Sales revenue							73.51	
thereof rate increasing							26.49	
Revenue from regulated rates		10.00	10.00	10.00	10.00	10.00	10.00	
Cash inflow		10.00	10.00	10.00	10.00	10.00	110.00	
Discount factor		1.10	1.21	1.33	1.46	1.61	1.77	
Discounted cash inflow		9.09	8.26	7.51	6.83	6.21	62.09	100.00

Even if the three methods in Table 5.5 yield the same net present value of capital service consisting of interest and depreciation, the allocation of capital service over time as well as its division into interest and depreciation are different. If acquisition costs are used (Panel C), the total sum of (undiscounted) depreciation amounts equals the historical acquisition payment; this corresponds to the theoretical separation of a return *of* capital by way of depreciation and a return *on* capital by way of interest.[363] If, in contrast, replacement costs are used and combined with the real interest rate and if specific prices of regulated assets are increasing (Panel B), the total sum of depreciation amounts is higher and interest is correspondingly lower than with the use of acquisition costs.

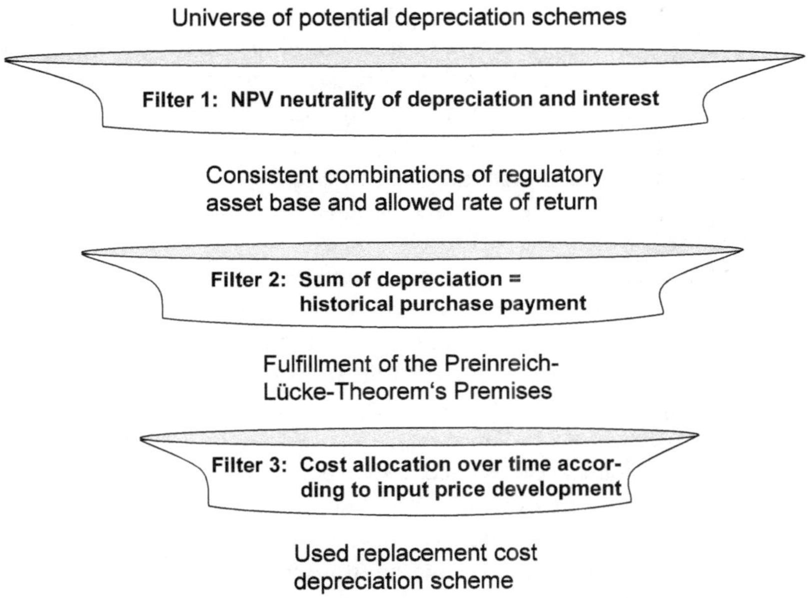

Figure 5.1. Regulatory depreciation schemes

Used replacement cost depreciation (Panel A) uses acquisition cost for the initial depreciation and computes depreciation in each period as the difference between used replacement costs at the beginning and at the end of the period. As the total sum of (undiscounted) depreciation equals the historical acquisition costs, used replacement cost depreciation has to be combined with nominal interest. It yields the same allocation of costs over time as replacement cost depreciation in Panel B, which is different from acquisition cost depreciation in Panel C.[364] The division of capital service into depreciation and interest is a different one for used replacement cost depreciation with nominal interest and for replacement cost depreciation with specific real interest; however, the denomination as depreciation or

[363] Cf. Kahn (1988, 32/I).

[364] See also Küpper/Pedell (2005a, 7ff.).

interest as well as the division of capital service into these categories has no substantial importance; at the bottom line, only the total level of capital service and its allocation over time are relevant.[365]

Table 5.6 shows that the results are robust if the asset is sold in t_4. It is assumed that the asset is sold for its used replacement value.[366] Selling off the asset before the end of its useful life truncates the investment cycle. In this case it is not sufficient that the overall investment cycle is neutral with respect to NPV; the truncated part also has to be neutral with respect to NPV. In other words, the allocation of capital service over time within the investment cycle becomes relevant. If used replacement cost depreciation (Panel A) or replacement cost depreciation (Panel B) is used and if the asset is sold for its used replacement value there are no payment frictions. The firm gets paid the used replacement value and the NPV of the truncated investment cycle is € 100.

In the case of *used* replacement cost depreciation, the asset's book value corresponds to its used replacement value and here too there is no friction in book values. In the case of plain replacement cost depreciation however, the asset's book value will deviate from its used replacement cost. If the price of the asset increases (decreases), replacement cost depreciation is higher (lower) than *used* replacement cost depreciation and the book value is lower (higher) than used replacement value. This book gain (loss) *must not* be accounted for in calculating regulated rates; as shown in Panel B of Table 5.6, the used replacement value has to flow back to investors to make the truncated investment cycle neutral with respect to NPV. *Used* replacement cost depreciation avoids this friction between book value and used replacement value. As the friction might not be intuitively clear, this is a reason for favoring used replacement cost depreciation over plain replacement cost depreciation.

---

[365] It is an obvious alternative to allocate depreciation over time in such way that an annuity of the sum of interest and depreciation in nominal or in real term results; cf. Ickenroth (1998); Yard (2004, 3f.).

[366] Clearly, the actual selling price can deviate from the used replacement value for numerous reasons; however, the used replacement value seems to be a reasonable assumption. This impact of rate regulation on the validity of this assumption is discussed below.

Table 5.5. Net present value of the cash flows from the investment in a *wasting* asset under rate regulation that is used until the end of its life

(acquisition payment € 100, specific price increase rate 5%, overall inflation rate 5%, nominal interest rate 10%, specific real interest rate 4.76%)

	t0 (acquisition)	t1	t2	t3	t4	t5	t6	NPV
Panel A: Rates on the basis of replacement costs with used replacement cost depreciation and nominal interest								
Replacement cost	100.00	105.00	110.25	115.76	121.55	127.63	134.01	
Used replacement cost	100.00	87.50	73.50	57.88	40.52	21.27	0.00	
Interest		10.00	8.75	7.35	5.79	4.05	2.13	
Depreciation		12.50	14.00	15.62	17.36	19.25	21.27	
Revenue from regulated rates		22.50	22.75	22.97	23.15	23.30	23.40	
Inpayment		22.50	22.75	22.97	23.15	23.30	23.40	
Discount factor		1.10	1.21	1.33	1.46	1.61	1.77	
Discounted inpayment		20.45	18.80	17.26	15.81	14.47	13.21	100.00
Panel B: Rates on the basis of replacement costs with replacement cost depreciation and specific real interest								
Replacement cost	100.00	105.00	110.25	115.76	121.55	127.63	134.01	
Used replacement cost	100.00	87.50	73.50	57.88	40.52	21.27	0.00	
Capital committed		105.00	91.88	77.18	60.78	42.54	22.33	
Interest		5.00	4.38	3.68	2.89	2.03	1.06	
Depreciation		17.50	18.38	19.29	20.26	21.27	22.33	
Revenue from regulated rates		22.50	22.75	22.97	23.15	23.30	23.40	
Inpayment		22.50	22.75	22.97	23.15	23.30	23.40	
Discount factor		1.10	1.21	1.33	1.46	1.61	1.77	
Discounted inpayment		20.45	18.80	17.26	15.81	14.47	13.21	100.00
Panel C: Rates on the basis of acquisition costs and nominal interest								
Book value	100.00	83.33	66.67	50.00	33.33	16.67	0.00	
Interest		10.00	8.33	6.67	5.00	3.33	1.67	
Depreciation		16.67	16.67	16.67	16.67	16.67	16.67	
Revenue from regulated rates		26.67	25.00	23.33	21.67	20.00	18.33	
Inpayment		26.67	25.00	23.33	21.67	20.00	18.33	
Discount factor		1.10	1.21	1.33	1.46	1.61	1.77	
Discounted inpayment		24.24	20.66	17.53	14.80	12.42	10.35	100.00

Table 5.6. Net present value of the cash flows from the investment in a wasting asset under rate regulation that is sold before the end of its life

(acquisition payment € 100, specific price increase rate 5%, overall inflation rate 5%, nominal interest rate 10%, specific real interest rate 4.76%)

	t0 (acquisition)	t1	t2	t3	t4 (sale)	NPV
Panel A: Rates on the basis of replacement costs with used replacement cost depreciation and nominal interest						
Replacement cost	100.00	105.00	110.25	115.76	121.55	
Used replacement cost	100.00	87.50	73.50	57.88	40.52	
Sales revenue					40.52	
Interest		10.00	8.75	7.35	5.79	
Depreciation		12.50	14.00	15.62	17.36	
Revenue from regulated rates		22.50	22.75	22.97	23.15	
Inpayment		22.50	22.75	22.97	63.67	
Discount factor		1.10	1.21	1.33	1.46	
Discounted inpayment		20.45	18.80	17.26	43.49	100.00
Panel B: Rates on the basis of replacement costs with replacement cost depreciation and specific real interest						
Replacement cost	100.00	105.00	110.25	115.76	121.55	
Used replacement cost	100.00	87.50	73.50	57.88	40.52	
Sales revenue					40.52	
Capital committed		105.00	91.88	77.18	60.78	
Interest		5.00	4.38	3.68	2.89	
Depreciation		17.50	18.38	19.29	20.26	
Revenue from regulated rates		22.50	22.75	22.97	23.15	
Inpayment		22.50	22.75	22.97	63.67	
Discount factor		1.10	1.21	1.33	1.46	
Discounted inpayment		20.45	18.80	17.26	43.49	100.00
Panel C: Rates on the basis of acquisition costs with nominal interest and rate diminishing sales gain						
Replacement cost	100.00	105.00	110.25	115.76	121.55	
Used replacement cost	100.00	87.50	73.50	57.88	40.52	
Sales revenue					40.52	
thereof rate diminishing					7.18	
Book value	100.00	83.33	66.67	50.00	33.33	
Interest		10.00	8.33	6.67	5.00	
Depreciation		16.67	16.67	16.67	16.67	
Revenue from regulated rates		26.67	25.00	23.33	21.67	
Inpayment		26.67	25.00	23.33	55.00	
Discount factor		1.10	1.21	1.33	1.46	
Discounted inpayment		24.24	20.66	17.53	37.57	100.00

In the case of the acquisition cost depreciation exhibited in Panel C, the gain of € 7.18 realized by reselling the regulated asset before the end of its life *has to* be accounted for by reducing revenues from regulated rates in t_4. Only then, is the NPV of the truncated investment cycle € 100. The underlying reason for this is the fact that the price increase is not accounted for at all by acquisition cost depreciation and that capital service accordingly is allocated differently over time. In the example of Table 5.6, capital service is shifted towards the beginning of the investment cycle; as can be seen in Table 5.5, cash inflows are higher in t_1, t_2 and t_3 and lower in t_4, t_5, and t_6 respectively. It is noteworthy that partial application of acquisition cost depreciation to the debt-financed part of assets as required by the concept of net substance maintenance, in principle produces the same problem.

So far, it has been assumed that the asset is sold for its used replacement value, which is a reasonable assumption when the asset is sold on a market unaffected by rate regulation. If, however, the asset just changes hands from one rate-regulated firm to another, the realized price will depend on expected future regulation. If the regulator accepts only the written down acquisition cost book value of the selling firm in the rate base of the buying firm, as laid down in the drafts for ordinances on rate regulation for the electricity and the gas sectors that are part of the new German Energy Act [Stromnetzentgeltverordnung and Gasnetzentgeltverordnung respectively], the price is unlikely to be higher than this book value. This approach suffers from a number of serious drawbacks. The prices on the secondary markets for the regulated assets are distorted, which is problematic, in particular when the assets can also be sold to firms that are not subject to rate regulation or when the assets can also be bought on primary markets. This kind of price distortion is avoided when the regulator accepts the price actually paid in the rate base of the buying firm. In this case, as argued above, the book gain (book loss) of the selling firm would have to be accounted for by reducing (increasing) the regulated rates of the selling firm accordingly. Book gains or losses are most likely to be avoided when used replacement cost depreciation is used. In addition, the regulator has to make sure that no excessive prices are paid, a risk that is immanent, in particular in the case of affiliated companies.

Where uncertainty exists, the allocation of cash flows over time becomes relevant for yet another reason. If uncertainty about the regulator's future behavior increases with the time-lag, it is favorable, from the perspective of capital owners, if capital flows back to them as soon as possible. The further ahead cash flows lie, the higher the expected fluctuation margin of the actual return over the life of an investment is. Risk averse investors require an additional risk premium, increasing cost of capital.[367] Depending on whether specific prices of regulated assets increase or decrease, the use of a replacement cost-based depreciation scheme either backloads or frontloads capital service over time compared to an acquisition cost-based depreciation scheme, assuming constant depreciation rates in each case;[368] accordingly, risk-adjusted cost of equity is increased or decreased, respectively. Taking this into account, the two methods no longer yield the same net present value of capital service over the life of an investment unless cost of capital is appropriately adjusted by the regulator when setting rates.

If the restricting convention is accepted, that the total sum of (undiscounted) depreciation amounts has to equal the acquisition payment of a facility (filter 2 in Figure 5.1),[369] this acquisition payment still can, in principle, be allocated arbitrarily over time, always assuming for simplicity that there is no salvage value. The Preinreich-Lücke theorem[370] applied to depreciation says that any depreciation scheme that allocates the acquisition payment over time and allows cost of capital to be earned on the respective residual book value in each period yields the same net present value of capital service that equals the acquisition payment.[371] It should be noted, that possible feedback effects of the allocation over time on the level of risk-adjusted cost of capital are not accounted for in this argument. In the context of rate regulation, the theorem can be interpreted as follows: The regulator can implement the principle of cost-orientated rate setting that allows capital owners an adequate return by any allocation of acquisition costs over time, and, therefore, possesses a degree of freedom that the regulator can use in order to pursue other objectives.

Governance of the regulated utility is among such objectives. Information asymmetries regarding the cost and demand functions of the regulated service exist between the regulator as principal and the regulated firm as

---

[367] Hitherto, this interdependence between depreciation scheme and cost of capital has been almost completely neglected in the relevant literature. See section 4.2.3.

[368] Though depreciation amounts are higher in the early periods of investment life if prices increase and replacement costs are used as depreciation basis, this effect is overcompensated by the lower (real) interest amounts.

[369] For example, this can be due to requirements of financial reporting, if the regulator explicitly demands that depreciation reported for purposes of rate regulation corresponds to depreciation documented in financial reporting.

[370] Cf. Preinreich (1937); Lücke (1955); in the context of rate regulation, see Schmalensee (1989).

[371] For a critical discussion of the theorem's assumptions in the context of its application to the calculation of regulated rates, see Awerbuch (1992, 64ff.).

agent.[372] In principle, the regulated firm can use these information asymmetries to its advantage; therefore the regulator adjusts his behavior and agency costs are caused. The allocation of depreciation over time can be used by the regulator in order to control the regulated firm's investment behavior[373] or in order to enhance incentives for cost savings or for truthful reporting on the cost and demand situation. Furthermore, he can control the distribution between generations of ratepayers.

Regulatory Depreciation Schemes with Admission of Competition. However, the regulator only possesses a degree of freedom with respect to the allocation of the acquisition payment over time in a protected monopoly market into which competitors cannot enter.[374] If *competition* is admitted in the market, as is the case for most infrastructure services due to the worldwide trend of market liberalization promoted, in particular, by the European Commission, the situation changes fundamentally.[375] A potential competitor's decision to enter the market as well as his pricing decision should he enter the market are both dependent on the prevailing procurement prices of the facilities needed to provide a certain service. If input prices fall after the incumbent regulated utility has invested, potential competitors have the option of buying lower-priced identical facilities at a later date. If potential or actual competition is working, the price reduction

---

372 For incentive-orientated regulation, see Laffont/Tirole (1993); Vogelsang (2002).

373 The structure of the problem is similar to the one of the governance of the investment behavior of divisional managers (with time preferences diverging from the time preference of capital owners) by a central office that has less information about investment-generated cash flows. Here, governance is also based on the use of a degree of freedom with respect to the allocation of depreciation on individual periods; see the seminal work by Rogerson (1997) and Reichelstein (1997). The implementation of the procedures makes high demands on the information available to central office, which has to know the profile of cash flows over time and consequently knows the complete cash flow series after the first period; for a critical discussion, see Küpper (2005, 254f.). For the problem of governing the investment behavior of a regulated firm, see the model of Friedl (2003), which allocates depreciation over time according to the profile of consumer utility; see also Burness/Patrick (1992). Rogerson (1992) investigates the interdependence between depreciation schedules and regulatory lag, and uses the depreciation profile over time to set incentives for an efficient choice of input-mix by the regulated firm, where the different inputs are affected differently by the regulatory lag.

374 In Germany, until liberalization the energy sector consisted of protected regional monopolies that were protected by so-called demarcation contracts.

375 Cf. Crew/Kleindorfer (1992a) and (1992b); Carne/Currie/Siner (1999).

of inputs is translated into an accordingly lower price of the regulated service.[376]

This means that the incumbent utility is forced to adjust its prices also to the development of input prices, otherwise it will loose market share and eventually will not be able to survive in the market. The regulator has to take this fact into account when setting rates from the very beginning of the incumbent's investment. On the one hand, the regulated utility needs flexibility to adjust its prices downwards as a reaction to competitors' prices or price threats. This can be accomplished relatively easily by using upper limits for prices, as e.g. in the case of price caps, instead of fixing certain prices. On the other hand, it has to be made sure that capital owners can expect an appropriate rate of return over the life of an investment. If a constant rate is fixed over the entire investment cycle,[377] it is not considered that this rate no longer will be achievable in the market from the moment of the admission of competition t^* on, as depicted in Figure 5.2. From t^* on, the expected rate of return lies below the allowed rate of return. Consequently, the average expected rate of return over the entire investment life lies below allowed rate of return, and investment incentives of the incumbent utility are distorted downwards. In this situation, the admission of competition only can be reconciled with the return requested by capital owners of the incumbent utility by using the scope for higher rates that exists until t^* so that at the bottom line capital owners earn an adequate return. If competition is already admitted in t_0, and if competitors have the same cost function as the incumbent utility, this can only be accomplished by completely adjusting rates to the development of input prices.

To this end, it has been proposed that a used replacement cost depreciation method be employed that uses acquisition costs for the initial depreciation base and that, at the same time, aligns the profile of depreciation over time with the development of input prices (filter 3 in Figure 5.1).[378] This means that the total sum of (undiscounted) depreciation equals the historical acquisition costs, while the depreciation profile over time reflects the development of replacement costs.[379] The alignment of cost allo-

---

376 Asymmetric regulation is assumed, i.e. the rates of the incumbent utility are subject to regulation, but not the prices of new competitors.

377 In the case of constant operating expenditures, this implies that capital expenditures are allocated as annuity over time.

378 Cf. Crew/Kleindorfer (1992a); Knieps/Küpper/Langen (2001).

379 For the used replacement cost depreciation scheme, see Knieps/Küpper/Langen (2001, 764ff.). For an overview of the recent discussion about the used replacement cost depreciation scheme in Germany, see Siegel (2002, 249ff.) who

cation over time with the development of input prices, in principle, is also achieved by using plain replacement cost depreciation; however, in this case the sum of (undiscounted) depreciation does not equal the historical acquisition payment (i.e. filter 2 in Figure 5.1 is not respected). Again, replacement cost depreciation would have to be applied not only to the equity financed part of assets as in the concept of net substance maintenance, but also to the debt financed part of assets.

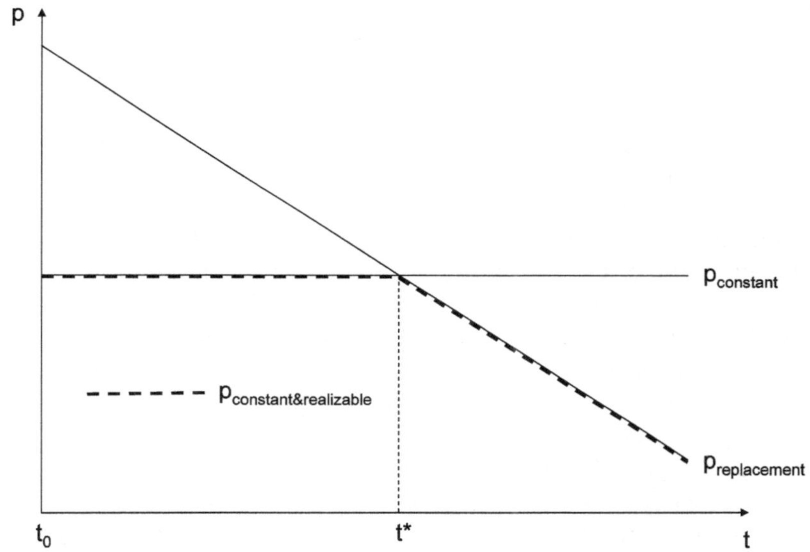

Figure 5.2. Price development in the case of declining input prices and admission of competition

Used replacement costs equal the share of the remaining service potential in the original total service potential at the beginning of operation of a facility[380] times the current replacement cost, i.e. input price, of a unit of

ultimately argues in favor of this scheme; for a critical position, see Busse von Colbe (2001, 54f.). The FCC (2003, 415, no. 671) accepts the necessity of accelerated depreciation if TELRIC methodology is applied, and suggests the use of an "economic depreciation" scheme that "reflects the true changes in economic value of an asset." Furthermore, in the U.S., used replacement costs are employed for the rate base in the regulation of oil pipelines. I am indebted to Bente Villadsen for bringing this point to my attention.

380 Possible determinants of the wear of service potential among others are time and/or utilization.

service potential in this period. This depreciation scheme is neutral with respect to net present value and at the same time ensures that regulated rates are aligned with the development of input prices[381] and that, therefore, these rates in principle are achievable in the market,[382] unless other reasons such as e.g. a lower cost efficiency compared to competitors prevents the incumbent utility from covering its actual costs. If the profile of depreciation over time is determined by the development of input prices due to the admission of competition, the degree of freedom for the choice of a depreciation scheme formally founded by the Preinreich-Lücke theorem is no longer available to the regulator. Put differently, the degree of freedom existing in the case of a protected monopoly is used up by the admission of competition.

An analog argument applies in the reversed case of increasing procurement prices for regulated facilities. Even if the regulated rate is kept constant over the entire investment cycle, in this case, the problem does not arise that this rate would not be achievable from a certain moment on due to the admission of competition. If, however, competitors do not invest in t_0, i.e. at the same time as the incumbent utility, they do not have the possibility to enter the market at a later date, as they could no longer compete due to the then increased input prices, assuming that their cost structure otherwise is identical with the one of the incumbent utility. In other words, if the regulated rate is kept constant over the entire investment cycle, the regulated rate in earlier periods can be interpreted to subsidize the regulated rate in later periods as compared to the development of input prices. If the regulator aims at promoting competition, it is not sufficient merely to admit competition, but he also has to align the regulated rates of the incumbent utility with the development of input prices, which is accomplished by the used replacement cost depreciation scheme.[383]

This line of argument is also applicable when a hitherto unregulated firm, whose assets are already written off below used replacement costs or even completely written off, becomes subject to rate regulation. In this case, used replacement cost depreciation based on true asset life seems an

---

[381] If used replacement costs are employed for the regulatory rate base, the gap between book values and market values is likely to be smaller than in the case of book values resulting from other depreciation schemes.

[382] Consequently, there is not necessarily a conflict between basing depreciation on acquisition costs and promoting competition, as argued by Ickenroth (1998, 3), provided that the profile of depreciation over time is chosen appropriately.

[383] Again, the alignment of cost allocation over time with the development of input prices is also achieved by using plain replacement cost depreciation; however, in this case the sum of (undiscounted) depreciation does not equal the historical acquisition payment.

appropriate approach for calculating regulated rates, so that efficient investment signals are given to (potential) competitors. If the value of already written off existing assets were not accounted for in regulated rates, the latter were not high enough to enable new investments of competitors.

So far, the discussion about depreciation schemes and admission of competition has not considered the fact that the allocation of depreciation over time feeds back on risk-adjusted cost of capital. If uncertainty about the future behavior of the regulator exists and if this uncertainty increases with the time lag, risk averse investors prefer invested capital to flow back to them as early as possible[384] and, accordingly, demand a higher risk premium if the invested capital flows back to them later. If depreciation is frontloaded in the case of declining input prices, the risk premium falls and cost of capital is correspondingly lower. If, in contrast, depreciation is backloaded in the case of rising input prices, risk-adjusted cost of capital increases.

5.1.2 Inclusion of New Investment in the Regulatory Rate Base

Particularly in the case of large investment projects for which payments are made in several steps during the construction phase, i.e. before the commissioning of the facility, the question arises of at which point in time the investment is accepted in the rate base. If this is not done until the commissioning date and if capital owners receive no compensation for the capital committed before this date, the investment does not earn an adequate return at the bottom line and investment incentives accordingly are biased downwards. Section 4.2.3 outlined and discussed the two basic approaches to deal with this issue, *AFUDC* and *CWIP*. Both approaches, if applied consistently, yield appropriate compensation for the fact that funds are committed before the commissioning date but involve different distributions of the financing burden over generations of rate payers. AFUDC puts the financing burden for a certain facility on the generation of consumers that actually benefits from its services.

Furthermore it is important to note that, under uncertainty about the future design of the regulatory scheme, it is advantageous from the perspective of risk averse capital owners if cost of capital is earned as early as possible, as, in this case, a narrower fluctuation margin of the actual rate of return is expected. Therefore, the decision as to whether to employ AFUDC or CWIP feeds back on risk-adjusted cost of capital, as the latter results in a frontloading of cash flows. It has been confirmed empirically

---

[384] It is noteworthy, that this effect is not due to investors' time preferences.

that the capital market associates CWIP with a more favorable regulatory climate and lower cost of capital than it does with AFUDC.[385] Moreover, the use of AFUDC is more likely to produce temporary liquidity squeezes, negatively affecting bond rating and increasing cost of debt.

If competition is admitted, a method assigning to an investment project all costs caused by the investment project should be employed, as this simulates the decision situation of a (potential) competitor. This argument speaks in favor of AFUDC, as a new competitor will not earn a return on his investments before the commissioning date of the facilities. Along the same line of argument as in the context of regulatory depreciation schemes, AFUDC leads to a profile over time of regulated rates that, in principle, are achievable under competition.

5.1.3 Investments Accounted for as Operating Expenditures

Part of the investments of a regulated utility in regulatory accounting – just as in financial reporting – is treated as operating expenditures (OPEX) and accordingly is not activated. R&D investments for example are assigned at least partially to OPEX and, consequently, not included in the book value of the firm. In a hypothetical benchmark system of rate regulation guaranteeing the regulated firm exact compensation for its actual costs, OPEX would be passed through to rates on a one-to-one basis and would not be accounted for afterwards, so that, in theory, market value should not be affected. However, in reality, such investments might increase (decrease) the market value of the firm at the time of investment, as far as it is expected that they will generate a positive (negative) net present value.[386] This can be due to deviations from the hypothetical benchmark system of rate regulation that has been outlined so far[387] and corresponds to the effect of such investments on the market value in the case of a non-regulated firm.

If the regulator accounts for one hundred per cent of these R&D investments as OPEX in the period in which they are incurred and calculates rates on this basis, these investments may not be included in the regulatory rate base even if they contribute to the market value of the regulated firm; otherwise they would be accounted for twice, which clearly is not justified. However, if competition is admitted, it is unadvisable for the regulator to

385 Cf. the overview of empirical investigations of this issue in section 4.2.3.

386 Cf. also Oftel (1992, 11): „[T]he value of the [market-to-book] ratio cannot necessarily be taken as implying anything about monopoly power and profits, as it will depend on other accounting issues such as treatment of R&D, advertising and goodwill."

387 For possible reasons, see section 5.2.

pass through these investments completely as OPEX to regulated rates in the period in which they are incurred. As these investments are relevant for the market entry decision of potential competitors, competition will be distorted if the incumbent regulated firm receives immediate compensation for these investments when they are incurred. Therefore, if the regulator aims at stimulating competition, these investments should be distributed over the entire period during which they provide a service. For the same reasons that have been discussed in detail in the context of regulatory depreciation schemes,[388] the cost profile over time should reflect the development of replacement costs.

5.2 Explanation of Deviations of Market Values from Book Values in the Case of Rate-Regulated Firms - Rationale for Using Book Values in the Regulatory Rate Base

In most cases of firms that are not rate-regulated, goodwill and synergies exist that drive a wedge between the market value of capital and the book value of assets. Clearly, the theoretically consistent method for determining the cost of capital is multiplying the market value of capital by the rate of cost of capital. However, the relationship between the market value of capital and the book value of assets is a different one for regulated firms.

Regulators use the book value of assets in the regulatory rate base, which prima facie seems to be an innately inconsistent approach for calculating the cost of capital. In a hypothetical system of perfect rate-of-return regulation as described in section 5.1, there would be no deviations between the market value of capital and the book value of assets; therefore, the questions as to whether market values or book values should be used in the regulatory rate base would be of no substantial importance.

In this section, the rather restrictive assumptions of a perfect rate-of-return regulation that excludes goodwill and synergies and establishes a market-to-book-ratio of one are released. The reasons that drive a wedge between the market and book value of rate-regulated firms and their implications for rate-base assessment are discussed. It will be shown that, at closer inspection, there is a clear rationale for using the book value of assets in the regulatory rate base.

[388] See section 5.1.1.

5.2.1 Deviations Due to Characteristics of Real Systems of Rate Regulation

The main problem that arises when using market values for the regulatory rate base is that the market value of a regulated utility's capital is not given independently from the regulatory regime, but depends circularly on it.[389] The circularity problem is produced by the very fact that the regulator sets rates and that these rates determine the expected future cash flows and thereby the market value of the regulated utility. In addition, rate regulation suffers from a possible time-consistency problem.[390] Moreover, the regulator does not have the necessary cost and demand information to realize a perfectly buffering regulatory system, even if he would strive for it.[391] Rate adjustment is not carried out continuously, but only can be made in certain intervals and with a lag. Finally, rate regulation does not necessarily cover all business activities during a firm's entire life.

Cost Assessment Errors Made by the Regulator

If the regulator strictly applied market values to the regulatory rate base, errors in the assessment of cost of capital (or other cost elements) would be reinforced.[392] Assuming that the regulator overestimates the true cost of capital and, as a consequence, calculates too high an interest on current market value and sets rates too high, so that the regulated utility earns supernormal profits, the market value of the utility would increase until the return on the market value equals the true risk-adjusted cost of capital. This effect is illustrated by the simple numerical example in Table 5.7.

---

389 Cf. in this spirit also Bromwich/Vass (2002, 1682) who note: „Generally, asset valuation must be based on some type of accounting values ... This is because the stock market valuation of the enterprise incorporates the market's view as to the effect of future regulation on the enterprise's cash flows." See also Myers (1972, 85); Greenwald (1980, 359); Bonbright/Danielsen/Kamerschen (1988, 216f.).

390 For the circularity and time-inconsistency of rate regulation, see section 3.2.

391 As discussed in section 3.3.1, issues of regulatory governance provide good reasons why the regulator should refrain from even aiming at such a system.

392 Along a similar line of argument, Kahn (1988, 49/If.) argues in favor of using book values for the regulatory rate base, on the grounds that it is due to an allowed rate of return set above the cost of capital, when market value increases above book value. This reasoning seems too narrow, as there are other causes that might drive a wedge between market and book value; they are discussed throughout section 5.2.

Table 5.7. Effect of assessment errors on the regulated firm's market value (true cost of capital 8%, cost of capital estimated by the regulator 10%)

Iteration	Book value [€]	Market value if cost of capital is applied to book value [€]	Market value if cost of capital is applied to market value [€]
0	100	100	100
1	100	125	125
2	100	125	156
3	100	125	195
4	100	125	244
...	...	...	...

It is assumed that the regulated firm's cost of capital is 8%, and that the regulator uses an overestimated cost of capital of 10% to calculate costs and rates. At the outset, book value is € 100 and by assumption equals market value. The regulator sets rates, so that the regulated firm earns a return of € 10. In this situation, market value will increase until these € 10 correspond to 8% of the market value, i.e. € 125. If the overestimated cost of capital is applied to book values, the adjustment process here comes to an end. If, however, the regulator continues applying the overestimated cost of capital of 10% to the higher market value, i.e. 10% of € 125 = € 12.5, market value increases to € 156 in the next iteration. This upward spiral of rates results from the circularity of rate regulation, and inevitably leads to instability. In theory, the regulator could avoid this instability by reestimating the cost of capital and readjusting regulated rates as part of an iterative process until the market value was kept constant at € 100. However, this is not practically feasible for several reasons. Firstly, such an iterative process would be time-consuming and would affect real transactions. Secondly, the impact of a rate setting decision cannot be isolated from other simultaneous influences. As a consequence, reestimating the adequate rates in an iterative process remains a rather academic knife-edge exercise due to the combined problems of circularity and lack of information.

In theory, if the regulator is committed to using market values in the regulatory rate base, and if rational investors receive information that the regulator will overestimate the cost of capital, the market value of the regulated firm would immediately sky-rocket. In reality, this effect would be attenuated by, among other things, the fact that the regulator has the discretionary power to deviate from an announced regulatory policy. In the reversed case of underestimation of true cost of capital, the circularity would cause a downward spiral of rates and market value. This spiral can be broken by using book values in the regulatory rate base.

Imperfect Buffering of Exogenous Shocks by Rate Regulation

Market values of regulated utilities are subject to fluctuations over time due to the impact of exogenous factors, as, in reality, perfect buffering of exogenous shocks by rate regulation is not possible, taking into account inevitable informational problems and time lags alone. The use of market values in the regulatory rate base might even amplify the impact of these fluctuations on market values. If the market value of a regulated firm falls due to the change of some exogenous factor, and if, as a result, a lower valuation of the regulatory rate base and, accordingly, lower rates and lower cash flows are anticipated by capital market participants, the market value will decline even more. This is a reflection of the circularity problem of rate regulation. Instead of buffering the regulated firm against exogenous shocks, as conjectured by the Peltzman-hypothesis, the effects of exogenous shocks, on the contrary, would be reinforced by the use of market values in the regulatory rate base, and the regulated firm would be exposed to a relatively high risk.[393] The use of book values for the regulatory rate base, in contrast, acts as an anchor for regulated rates against the impact of exogenous factors.

Deliberate Use of Costs Different from Actual Costs for Rate Setting

Regulators deliberately deviate from the regulatory policy of reimbursing any actually incurred costs, in order to set incentives for efficient operation and investments as well as in order to set the stage for market entry of competitors. Clearly, the allowed rate of return has to be adjusted accordingly, so that investors of the regulated firm can expect to earn the required return on average. However, in individual cases, the regulated firm will earn a return above or below its cost of capital, and, accordingly, market value will be higher or lower than book value, assuming for simplicity that this is the only reason for deviations between market value and book value. As to the computation of the regulatory rate base, deviations from a one-to-one pass-through of actual costs can be induced by applying a price

[393] The fact that rates are not adjusted continuously, but only in time intervals would moderate this effect.

structure deviating from what actually was paid for regulated assets and/or by a quantity structure deviating from the regulated assets that are actually installed. The effects produced by using values different from acquisition costs in the rate base without consistently adjusting the regulatory depreciation scheme and the interest rate have been discussed already in section 5.1.1;[394] therefore, the following analysis focuses on the quantity structure of the regulatory rate base.

Possible approaches for determining the quantity structure of the regulatory rate base range between two ideal types that are the poles of a spectrum of intermediate forms. One pole is the *actual, path-dependent quantity structure* of the regulated utility, e.g. an actually installed telecommunications or energy network. The development of a network is subject to path dependencies and, in almost all instances, does not lead to the optimal structure from today's point of view. Unexpected developments of demand have numerous possible effects: (1) installed capacity is over- or under-dimensioned, (2) (pipe-)lines are not laid on the optimal routes, or (3) several (pipe-)lines have been built successively in the past, each of which covers part of today's capacity requirements. Due to the cost structures prevailing in (pipe-)line construction involving economies of scale, the same capacity could be provided more efficiently by one (pipe-)line covering the total capacity requirement. Moreover, in many instances technological progress makes it possible to construct more efficiently today the given capacity of a facility installed in the past.

The other pole of the spectrum of possible approaches for determining the quantity structure of the regulatory rate base is the (hypothetical) *structure that is optimal from the today's point of view* and that is likely to deviate considerably from the actual structure for the reasons discussed above. Analytical engineering cost models are used in regulatory practices for the assessment of the optimized structure, e.g. of a utility network.[395] In the extreme case, these models assume that no structure at all is predetermined, i.e. that the network in question can be designed completely anew at the drawing table in a greenfield approach. In doing so, not the assets actually in place, but so-called modern equivalent assets (MEA) are modeled that provide the corresponding service with the newest available tech-

---

[394] For the impact of the determination of the quantity structure of the regulatory rate base on the risk of the regulated firm, see section 4.2.3.

[395] In Germany, for instance, the RegTP uses an analytic cost model of the Wissenschaftliches Institut für Kommunikationsforschung (WIK) for setting rates of DTAG. In the U.S. such models are constructed among others by Telcordia Technologies, Inc. (operating under Bell Communications Research, Inc. (Bellcore) until 1999).

nology. As this approach deals with hypothetical structures, these models by their very nature inevitably open up considerable scope for judgment.

Between these two poles, there is a *continuum of intermediate forms.* For instance, when modeling a hypothetic network, the actual locations of facilities can be used and equipped with modern equivalent assets. This approach is pursued by the German RegTP for the regulation of DTAG on the basis of an analytic cost model developed by the Wissenschaftliches Institut für Kommunikationsforschung (WIK).[396] Alternatively, the concept of *workable efficiency* starts from the incumbent's currently existing network and investigates which efficiency improvements are realizable with future developing.[397]

Which approach for determining the quantity structure is chosen by the regulator depends on the underlying *objectives of rate regulation.* If *profitability* of the incumbent regulated utility and *security of supply* are the predominant objectives, the use of the actual historical structure imposes itself, so that the regulated utility can expect to earn an appropriate return on all its investments and accordingly has incentives for new investments. This corresponds to the basic principle of cost-of-service regulation to compensate a regulated utility for all costs incurred for the provision of a certain service.

If, however, a regulator in the first instance has the aim in mind, to *simulate or stimulate competition*, he will rather orientate rate setting toward the structures deemed optimal from today's point of view, in order to produce price signals for consumers and (potential) competitors reflecting the best technology currently available. Yet even if this is efficient in a static perspective, major objections have to be made. Also, in a market without rate regulation, current prices only reflect at any time the best available technology, in the ideal case of perfect competition. In reality, competition in product markets is not perfect, as any investment is irreversible to a certain degree and, therefore, creates market exit barriers for a firm that already has invested, or market entry barriers for a firm that has not invested yet, respectively. Irreversibility of investment, on the one hand, causes risks and, on the other hand, opens up chances for competitive advantages, i.e. above normal profits. Also, without these chances for (temporary) above normal profits, a non-regulated firm would never be willing to incur the risks associated with irreversible investments, as, otherwise, it would earn its cost of capital in the best case, but there would

[396] Cf. RegTP (2003, 100). For a critical discussion of analytic cost models, in particular of the WIK-model, see Knieps (1998); see also Hohenadel/Reiners (2000, 163).

[397] Cf. Hohenadel/Reiners (2000, 161f.).

also be cases in which it would earn less than its cost of capital, i.e. on average it would expect to earn less than its cost of capital.

This dynamic relationship, in particular, applies to regulated utilities, as the monopolistic bottleneck facilities targeted by regulation are characterized by the very combination of pronounced irreversibility of investment and economies of scale.[398] In the best case, the infrastructure actually in place that has been built by the regulated utility in the past corresponds to the structure deemed optimal by the regulator when setting rates. In almost all instances, however, it will deviate from the structure deemed optimal, taking into account unexpected demand shifts and technological progress alone. If the regulated utility anticipates earning in the best case the cost of capital of its actual investments, but in many instances is only allowed to earn less, *investment incentives* are seriously reduced. Therefore, the asymmetric risk that results from the use of an optimized instead of the actual quantity structure for the regulatory rate base requires adequate compensation. The latter can be accounted for in the allowed rate of return or in an absolute cash flow element and must be high enough so that the regulated utility can expect to earn, on average, its cost of capital.

Furthermore, the regulator can make the determination of the quantity structure of the regulatory rate base contingent on a review of all investments incurred by the regulated utility and disallow according to certain criteria individual investments being included in the rate base.[399] The necessity of *disallowances* is justified on the grounds that under pure cost-of-service regulation without any disallowances, there are no incentives for efficient investment. The review of investments usually is made in the form of a used and useful test or a prudence review.[400] Both methods open up scope for judgment and result in a form of micromanagement of the regulated firm's investment strategy by the regulator. This seems problematic, to say the least, as it can be assumed that, in most instances, the regulated firm has better information about its business than the regulator, and as it has to bear the financial consequences of the investment strategy.[401] The possibility of excluding actually installed investments from the regulatory rate base exposes regulated utility to an asymmetric risk.

The use of a cost structure different from the actual one is also implied by the establishment of *price caps*. The efficiency factor X sets a target for the improvement of cost efficiency during the regulatory review period

---

398 Cf. Knieps (2001, 33).

399 Cf. Averch/Johnson (1962).

400 See section 4.2.3.

401 Cf. with respect to the above discussed analytical cost models also Knieps (1998, 600).

compared to the cost structures actually prevailing at the outset. In almost all instances, the efficiency gains actually realized by the regulated firm will be either above or below this efficiency target. Furthermore, if rates are set for a certain *regulatory review period*, or if rates are adjusted to cost changes with a certain *regulatory lag*, actual costs and revenues from regulated rates usually will differ more or less until the next rate review. If these differences are not compensated *ex post* when setting rates at the next review, the regulated firm will earn above or below normal profits at the bottom line, which will drive a wedge between market value and book value, all other things being equal.[402]

5.2.2 Deviations Due to Future Investment Possibilities After an Anticipated Phasing-Out of Rate Regulation

The market value of a regulated firm is not only determined by investments currently being used (for providing regulated services), but also by prospects of future investment possibilities, provided that these are exclusive to some extent. In principle, this is the case when a firm holds specific assets that grant exclusive access to future investment possibilities. These options do not have any value if it is anticipated that just normal returns equal to the cost of capital will be earned on the future investments, as would be the case especially for a perfect and continuous rate-of-return regulation.[403] If, however, returns above cost of capital are possible, e.g. due to competitive advantages of the firm in the process of further liberalization of the regulated market, these real options incorporate a value and contribute to the current market value of the firm.

It seems unjustified that the current generation of consumers finances the return on this part of the market value by way of higher regulated rates, as future generations will benefit from the investments, provided they will actually be made. This holds true, at least if the regulator applies the principle that a consumer generation should pay only for the investments from which it also benefits. Moreover and a crucial argument *per se*, the value of future investment possibilities increases *ceteris paribus* over time, as they are less discounted due to their approaching in time, so that an additional return on this part of the market value of a regulated firm by way of regulated rates is not required at all.

---

[402] For the impact of price caps as well as of the length of the regulatory review period and the regulatory lag on the risk of the regulated firm, see section 4.1.1 and section 4.1.2.

[403] See section 3.4.2.

5.2.3 Deviations Due to Activities in Non-Regulated Business Divisions

So far, it has been implicitly assumed that the regulated firm consists of a single regulated business, in which its complete capital is invested. Actually, most regulated firms comprise *several divisions* that are differently regulated and/or partially not regulated at all. In this case the market value of the entire firm might be above the book value of its assets, in particular due to the goodwill pertaining to non-regulated business divisions. In addition, synergies between the regulated business and the other divisions might exist, driving the market value of capital even higher above the book value of the assets.

If a regulator, the arguments presented so far notwithstanding, does not refrain from using market values for the regulatory rate base of a regulated division, the additional problem arises of assigning to the individual divisions the market value of the consolidated company that at least can be approximated by readily observable market capitalization in the case of listed firms.[404] This is inextricably related to the issue of the assessment of divisional specific beta factors and cost of capital rates,[405] but goes beyond it. Even if divisional cost of capital can be estimated fairly well on the basis of comparable benchmarks, reliable cash flow forecasts of the individual divisions are needed in addition in order to make an estimate of their respective market values. This inevitably opens up considerable scope for judgment and information asymmetries between the regulator and the regulated firm,[406] not to mention the fact that cash flow forecasts are subject to the circularity problem of rate regulation.

If the company's market value is assigned to the individual divisions proportionally to their respective share of the company's book value, i.e. if a uniform market-to-book ratio across divisions is assumed, the risk arises to make a serious mistake. Assuming a company comprises one rate-regulated and one non-regulated division and, due to competitive advantages, earns above normal returns in the non-regulated business, a significantly higher market-to-book ratio than in the regulated division is likely to result.[407] If, in this situation, the market value of the company is assigned

---

[404] Clearly, this assignment problem does not arise if the divisions are legally autonomous and separately listed companies.

[405] See section 6.2.5.

[406] Cash flow forecasts of independent financial analysts are a possible auxiliary means.

[407] If, as outlined in section 5.1, the regulated division were subject to a regulatory system establishing equality of market value and book value, the entire differ-

proportionally to book values, market value in the regulated division will be overestimated. If, in contrast, the return in the non-regulated division is below the divisional specific cost of capital, market value in the regulated division would be underestimated at the bottom line. Therefore, this simplistic averaging method cannot be given much credit. The assignment of book values to individual divisions is less ambiguous, provided that the assets themselves can be assigned to the divisions.[408] Clearly in the case of synergies due to assets being used by more than one division, these assets cannot be allocated unequivocally to individual divisions.

5.3 Reconciliation of the Use of Book Values in the Regulatory Rate Base with the Return Required by Investors

The issues discussed in section 5.2 clearly show that there are serious problems associated with the use of market values in the regulatory rate base. Due to the circularity problem of rate regulation, the use of market values would reinforce the impact of cost assessment errors made by the regulator and of exogenous shocks. Furthermore, market values might contain elements the return on which seems unjustifiable to be financed by current rate payers, such as investments already accounted for as OPEX and the value of future investment possibilities after an anticipated phasing-out of rate regulation. Book values, in contrast, do not suffer from these problems; therefore, there is a rationale for using them in the regulatory rate base. However, the conflict with the appropriate return on market values required by investors remains to be addressed. This section investigates whether the use of book values for regulatory purposes is compatible with the return required by investors or can be reconciled with it by accompanying measures. In order to analyze this question, several cases are differentiated as depicted in Table 5.8. It is distinguished at the outset whether the regulated firm is public or private property, and, in the latter case, whether new investments or existing investments are subject to rate regulation.

ence between the consolidated company's market value and book value would be attributable to the non-regulated division.

408 For the problem of assigning asset values between regulated and non-regulated businesses in the context of UK privatization, see Newbery (1997, 2).

Table 5.8. Compatibility of book value based regulatory rate base and return required by investors

Present ownership of the firm	Private ownership				Public ownership
Time of investment	New investment / firm	Existing investment / firm			
Previous regulation		Hitherto rate-regulated		Previously not rate-regulated	
Previous rate base		Book values	Market values		
Compatibility of book value based rate base and return required by investors	Book values not problematic, if announced accordingly by the regulator before investment	Book values not problematic, if continuation of previous regulatory policy is to be expected	If book values are used, compensation / lump sum tax required as accompanying measure in order to avoid windfall losses / gains	If book values are used, compensation / lump sum tax required as accompanying measure in order to avoid windfall losses / gains	Book values not problematic, if announced accordingly by the regulator before privatization

5.3.1 New Private Investments

In the case of new private investment, the solution to the conflict is straightforward. Here, the crucial point is that the regulator lays down the regulatory regime to which new investments will be subject before these new investments are made, and actually sticks to this announced regulatory regime after the investments have been made, independently of how this regime is concretely designed. The announcement of the regulator to apply a certain regulatory policy to new investments faces possible time-consistency problems, but this holds true for the announcement of any regulatory policy.[409] Incentives to make a new investment in a certain facility exist, if investors expect to earn an adequate return on the acquisition payment. Therefore, the use of book values is not problematic with respect to investment incentives, and offers the advantage that they do not depend circularly on regulatory policy. The same arguments apply to the incentives to start up a new firm in a rate-regulated industry. If the regulatory rate base, depreciation and interest rate are treated consistently, as discussed in section 5.1.1 for the case of a hypothetical benchmark system of rate regulation, and if there are no synergies, market value should not deviate from book value after new investments have been made. If market value deviates from book value in a real regulatory regime, it will do so for reasons other than the use of book values in the regulatory rate base,[410] at least if the use of book values is credible. In this case, it does not seem justified, that (current) rate payers finance a return on the difference of market value and book value.

5.3.2 Existing Private Investments

If existing private investments are affected by rate regulation, several subcases have to be distinguished. If the rates of the firm already have been *regulated in the past*, the expectations of investors about future regulation determine current market value also in this case. If there are no structural changes of regulation, previous regulatory practice is likely to be a good indicator for these expectations. If the regulator hitherto used *book values* for the regulatory rate base, investors are likely to expect this regulatory procedure to be continued in the future. A surprising switch from book to market values in this scenario would produce windfall gains or losses for

[409] For the problem of time-consistency and ways to mitigate it, see section 3.2.
[410] Possible reasons are discussed in section 5.2.

the existing shareholders and the use of book values is consistent with the objective of allowing capital owners an adequate return.

If, however, the regulator hitherto used *market values* for the determination of the regulatory rate base, and if it can be assumed that capital owners expected this practice to continue in the future, a surprising switch to book values would push market values in the direction of book values and produce windfall losses or gains for the capital owners, unless the market-to-book ratio is one already at the outset.[411] Windfall losses resulting from the unexpected switch of the regulatory regime are incompatible with the property rights of the private owners without appropriate compensation. Alternatively, the regulator could announce with sufficient lead-time the use of book values for new investments only, which is unproblematic, as has been shown in section 5.3.1, and continue to use market values for existing investments. In the case of wasting assets, the use of market values would be phased out continuously with the depreciation of the existing investments.

If the switch to book values came as a complete surprise, and if the impact of this switch on market values could be measured unanimously, the appropriate compensation could be assessed and paid to private capital owners. This could be done either by paying them the complete windfall loss immediately or by creating an allowance equal to the windfall loss and including an adequate return on this allowance as an additional cost element in the calculation of rates from then on. The second approach exposes capital owners to a higher risk, as it is uncertain how the current regulator and future regulators will deal with the allowance at future rate reviews. At the very moment the windfall loss occurs, compensation could be achieved alternatively by converting the rate of return according to the market-to-book ratio[412] prevailing immediately before the unexpected windfall loss.

However, if the rate of return is continuously adjusted according to the currently prevailing market-to-book ratio as a compensation for using book values for the regulatory rate base, this approach is equivalent to using market values for the regulatory rate base with all the problems discussed above. In addition, a switch to a book value-based regulatory rate base together with a completely offsetting adjustment of the rate of return theoretically does not produce a change in market value. The problems associated with the use of market values for the regulatory rate base cannot be

---

[411] Effects other than the employed regulatory rate base that drive a wedge between market and book values are neglected in this argument.

[412] This method is advocated, for example, by Knieps (2003, 1002), see also Busse von Colbe (2002, 15f.).

circumvented by restating the calculation and just shifting the problems to the assessment of the adequate rate of return. Moreover, in section 5.2, it has been shown that market values might contain elements whose financing by (current) rate payers seems unjustified. In this case, the adequate adjustment of the allowed rate of return should not offset completely the difference between market values and book values. Besides, such an adjustment raises serious informational problems of its own.

In reality, problems with the assessment of the appropriate level of compensation arise, because the switch to a new regulatory policy, in most instances, does not come as a complete surprise and its impact cannot be measured unanimously. In order to be able to determine adequate compensation without judgment, the expectations of capital owners regarding future regulation would have to be known, which, of course, are not observable; at best some conclusions can be drawn from capital market reactions to a switch of the regulatory regime.[413] Furthermore, the question is raised, whether the government is willing at all to arrange for compensation. If this is not clearly laid down and ensured in advance, investors are exposed to a considerable regulatory risk. Moreover, this risk is asymmetric if the regulator in the reversed case will claw back windfall gains from the regulated firm, which can be accomplished by way of a lump-sum tax. This has been concretely discussed in the context of privatization discounts in the UK.[414]

Finally, the case of a private firm is investigated, whose prices hitherto were not regulated and that will be subject to rate regulation as from now. As a hypothetical benchmark, it is assumed in the first instance that rate regulation comes as a complete surprise. Changes of the firm's market value triggered by the surprising introduction of rate regulation along the same line of argument as above are windfall losses or gains, respectively, for which the capital owners should receive or pay, respectively, compensation. If, in particular, the market value is reduced by the use of book values for the determination of the regulatory rate base, capital owners should be compensated; otherwise, from the perspective of capital owners, the introduction of rate regulation boils down to expropriation. This holds true independently of current book values. Even if existing assets are already completely written off, i.e. asset life actually is longer than the one used in

[413] Capital market reactions to changes of the regulatory regime have been investigated by a number of event studies, e.g. by Buckland/Fraser (2001); Francis/Grout/Zalewska (2001); Hern/Zalewska (2001); further empirical investigations are cited throughout chapter 3 and 4.

[414] Cf. Grout/Zalewska (2001, 8f.). For the privatization discount in the UK, see section 5.3.3.

the past for the calculation of depreciation, compensation is required, as the assets actually were of value for capital owners before the surprising introduction of rate regulation.

In reality, as outlined above, regulation never comes as a complete surprise, but has been discussed already for a certain while in the run-up to its introduction. Therefore, assessing the changes of market value that are due to the introduction of regulation is practically impossible, not to mention isolating the effect specifically due to the use of book values for the regulatory rate base. However, these information problems also exist when the regulatory rate base is determined on the basis of market values. Here, in particular, the question would arise, at which point in time or within which period of time market value would have to be assessed so that it is not yet affected by the upcoming regulation. When assessing the appropriate level of compensation the entire portfolio of investments made by the firm in the past including failed investments should, in principle, be considered. As the firm expected to earn on average an adequate return on all of its investments, it expected to be compensated for failed investments by a correspondingly higher return on successful investment projects.[415] As discussed in section 5.3.1, an alternative consists in announcing with sufficient lead-time the use of book values for new investments.

5.3.3 Privatization of Public Enterprises

If the regulated firm is a *public enterprise* (listed or not), the use of book values is not problematic with respect to private property rights. Even if the value of the regulated firm is changed by the use of book values, no property rights of private equity owners are concerned. However, redistribution between the state and the consumers of the regulated service might be produced. According to the structure of tax income and the financing measures taken or the public expenditures that cannot be made due to national budget losses, this affects the general public or individual groups of tax payers or beneficiaries of public subsidies.

If the *privatization* of a public enterprise is planned, the selling price is substantially determined by the expectations of the private buyers about future rate regulation.[416] If the regulator clearly communicates before pri-

[415] Along the same line of argument, firms that did not survive should be considered.

[416] See also the related analysis by Ballwieser (2001a, 38ff.), who discusses the relation of fair value [Sachzeitwert] and present value [Ertragswert] in the context that a commune uses its option to buy an existing network from an investor-owned electricity company when the according concession expires. In Ger-

vatization, i.e. before an initial public offering, that he will use a certain type of book value in the regulatory rate base, private investors can take this into account when making their bids.[417] In this case, only the subsequent use of this book value is consistent, as otherwise windfall gains or losses are produced. Consequently, in a hypothetical regime of rate regulation, as outlined in section 5.1, market value after privatization should equal the book value employed in the regulatory rate base. In a real regulatory regime, market value might differ from this book value for the reasons discussed in section 5.2.

It is true, that announcing a certain design of the future regulatory regime is subject to several problems: Firstly, the description of future regulation inevitably remains incomplete, and secondly, the announcement of a certain regulatory behavior is not necessarily time-consistent. However, with respect to the use of book values for the regulatory rate base, at least the first problem obviously is manageable, as it is a fundamental principle of rate setting that can be described relatively easily. The second problem can be attenuated by codifying this principle in laws, executive orders or calculation directives for the regulator. Anyway, these problems also exist if the use of market values for the regulatory rate base is announced.

The circularity problem becomes particularly manifest in the privatization of rate-regulated utilities. Table 5.9 shows market-to-book ratios collected by Grout and Zalewska (2001, 7) of rate-regulated companies in the UK immediately after privatization. Market values are approximated by the sum of debt plus the market capitalization of equity at the end of the first trading day after the initial public offering. Book values are determined according to current cost accounting[418] principles. In the UK, the ratio of market value to the CCA asset value is also referred to as market to assets ratio. The difference between market value and CCA book value is the so-called privatization discount and, with the exception of British Telecom, is not of negligible quantity.[419] In the case of Water & Sewerage Companies, it amounts to more than 95% of the current cost accounting (CCA) book value. Obviously, market participants, in the case of British

many, communes hold a monopoly on rights of way and grant concessions to electricity companies for a limited period of less than twenty years.

417 Against the background of these considerations it is all the more surprising that in the stock exchange prospectuses of DTAG and DPAG relatively little information can be found on the expected design of rate regulation. Even if the concrete design of future rate regulation was not known at that time, its fundamental importance and possible regulatory risks could have been made clearer.

418 For the concept of CCA, see, for example, Whittington (1998).

419 For the issue of privatization discounts in the UK, see also Grout (1995, 405f.); Newbery (1997); Carne/Currie/Siner (1999, 3f.).

Telecom, expected to earn an adequate return on CCA book values. After the experiences with the regulation of British Telecom, market participants obviously did not expect that the respective regulatory commission would allow a risk adequate return on CCA book value of the subsequently privatized companies. The empirical evidence shows that they rather expected regulators to use lower book values in the regulatory rate base, especially in the case of Water & Sewerage, where the acquisition costs of existing assets were almost completely written off at the time of privatization and where the regulator did not use the CCA net asset value for calculating the initial price cap.[420] However, these existing assets still represented an economic value, which is expressed by the higher CCA value.

It would be appropriate, if, immediately after privatization, the capital owners of the companies obtain a return equal to the risk-adjusted cost of capital on the share price they paid.[421] However, profitability of the regulated utility is not the only objective that is relevant for rate regulation. If, in this situation, the regulator would stick to the use of market values for the regulatory rate base, regulated rates would be way below the price level at which a potential competitor could enter the market. The principle of promoting competition is rather incorporated by the concept of CCA, which is orientated towards costs that have to be incurred by a (potential) competitor to provide a certain regulated service.

Here, the regulator faces a serious *dilemma of rate regulation*. If he changes the regulatory regime, changes of market value are triggered. If he sets rates at such a level that the regulated utility earns the adequate risk-adjusted return on a CCA base in order to promote competition, the market value will increase to the level of CCA book value, and windfall gains accrue to current shareholders. To solve this problem, a neutralization of windfall gains with a lump-sum tax has been proposed. However, windfall gains cannot be quantified without a large extent of judgment, as it is not ascertainable, which regulatory regime was expected at the time of the purchase of or subscription for shares, and the effect of changes of the regulatory scheme cannot be isolated unequivocally.

---

[420] Cf. Newbery (1997, 2).

[421] This can be achieved by scaling down CCA interest *and* CCA depreciation of the assets already in place at the time of privatization by the market to assets ratio; cf. Newbery (1997, 4).

Table 5.9. Market-to-book ratios of rate-regulated utilities in the UK immediately after privatization

Year of privatization	Company	Market-to-book ratio
1984	British Telecom	97.3%
1986	British Gas	42.0%
1989	Water & Sewerage Companies	3.6%
1990	Regional Electricity Companies	60.5%
1990	National Grid Company	40.4%
1991	National Power	57.1%
1991	PowerGen	48.9%
1996	Railtrack	68.8%

Adopted with minor extensions from Grout/Zalewska (2001, 7)

This fundamental problem of rate regulation ultimately is caused by any non-anticipated change of the regulatory regime, with the difficulty that, in most instances, it cannot be ascertained, which changes have been anticipated and which not. Clearly, changes of the regulatory regime not only can produce windfall gains but also windfall losses for shareholders. In the latter case, the regulator inevitably comes into conflict with the property rights of shareholders that, in Germany as in many other countries, are protected by constitutional law. This results from the fact that the very objectives of rate regulation are conflicting. Profitability of the regulated utility and (long-run) investment incentives in most instances will be in conflict, at least in the short-run, with the objective of promoting competition.[422]

If the regulator committed to accepting the prevailing market value at a certain moment in time as the adequate value of the regulated utility, and if he aimed to avoid producing windfall gains or losses for the shareholders by his regulatory behavior, he would have to be able to exactly assess the true risk-adjusted cost of capital in order to set the level of rates, so that the market value actually will not be changed by regulation.[423] Moreover, the impact of changes of the regulatory regime on cost of capital would have to be known exactly in order to be able to offset exactly the effect of such

422 Ultimately, this reflects the basic trade-off between static and dynamic efficiency.

423 As discussed in section 5.2.1, reestimating the cost of capital in an iterative process is not a practically feasible approach.

changes on market value by adjusting the allowed rate of return. However, to achieve this end, the regulator would have to know the expectations of capital market participants with regard to his behavior. Even if empirical investigations, e.g. event studies, yield indications of expectations prevailing in the past, it is practically impossible to assess expectations of future regulatory decisions.[424]

Aside from these information problems, by committing to the market value at a certain moment in time the regulator *loses degrees of freedom* in his regulatory decisions, which he might need in order to correct wrong past decisions or to promote competition (in spite of a privatization discount);[425] therefore, the reluctance of regulators to make such a commitment is comprehensible.[426] Due to the circularity problem of rate regulation, an adequate market value only can be the result, not the exclusive starting point of regulatory decisions.[427]

---

[424] Moreover, current capital owners would have no incentive to reveal their true expectations, anticipating that the regulator would set future rates on the basis of the reported expectations.

[425] Cf. Kolbe/Tye/Myers (1993, 109): "Reconsideration of [...] a [regulatory] policy should not be held up by the fact that some investors bought shares before it was reconsidered." After the capital market has incorporated the information on regulatory decisions, the market value adjusts and the appropriate rate of return on this new market value automatically results. Accordingly, the changes of market value produced by regulation are the actual subject of discussion.

[426] Cf. Myers (1972, 85), who comes to the conclusion that "... adopting stock market value as a rate base amounts to a commitment to confirm investors' expectations regardless of what they are based on."

[427] See in this spirit already the decision of the U.S. Supreme Court in the case Federal Power Commission v. Hope Natural Gas 1944: „[F]air value is the end product of the process of rate-making not the starting point ... The heart of the matter is that rates cannot be made to depend upon „fair value" when the value of the ongoing enterprise depends on earnings under whatever rates may be anticipated." 320 U.S. 601. See also the discussion in Robichek (1978, 698f.).

6 Market-Based Assessment of the Cost of Capital for a Rate-Regulated Firm

Cost of capital assessment methods are usually divided into subjective and capital market based approaches.[428] The risk-adjusted cost of capital of a regulated utility is determined by the rate of return expected by its capital owners, whose level, in line with the opportunity cost principle, depends on alternative investment opportunities.[429] Risk averse investors require a premium on the risk-less interest rate as compensation for taking risks. In principle, the subjective risk assessment of investors is relevant for the amount of this risk premium;[430] but in order to quantify the risk premium, the risk utility functions of all capital owners would have to be known, which, to all intents and purposes, is impossible. In addition, inter-subjective verification is not possible; therefore, the subjective approach seems unsuited for the purposes of cost-orientated rate regulation that has to be based on objective evidence, i.e. traceable cost documentation. Capital market oriented approaches, on the other hand, employ capital market data for the assessment of cost of capital. The underlying assumption is that capital market data reflects the risk assessment of all market participants and thereby gives an objectified risk assessment. In regulatory hearings, discounted cash flow methods, in particular the flow to equity ap-

428 Cf. Busse von Colbe (2002, 4ff.); Kempf (2002, 6ff.). This distinction is somewhat misleading as market based approaches, in practice, resort to historical data for estimating the future cost of capital, which *per se* introduces an element of subjectivity in these approaches. The determination of the estimation period, the approximation of the market portfolio that cannot be observed, and the decision for the use of the geometric or the arithmetic mean inevitably involve subjectivity. Furthermore, the CAPM is not free from subjectivism even in theory as it aggregates necessarily subjective expectations and risk preferences of market participants. Cf. Ballwieser (2001b, 23) and (2002, 738).

429 Cf. for example Robichek (1978, 701).

430 Cf. Ballwieser (2001a, 33).

proach with constant dividend growth (the dividend growth model), as well as the CAPM are the most popular approaches.[431]

In spite of its well-known shortcomings,[432] the CAPM is widely used due to its intuitive appeal. In the U.S. regulatory practice, it is used in combination with discounted cash flow techniques in many instances, in order to narrow down a bandwidth within which the true cost of capital is estimated to lie. In the UK, the CAPM is clearly the predominant cost of capital assessment method used across regulatory commissions.[433] Moreover, it is at the center of the current academic debate and subject of recent expert opinions regarding the assessment of the cost of capital for rate-regulated firms in Germany.[434] Therefore, the following analysis focuses on the assessment of the cost of capital with the help of the CAPM.[435]

The chapter is organized as follows. In section 6.1, specifics of rate regulation that are relevant for the method of cost of capital assessment are briefly revised. In section 6.2, methodical issues related to the assessment of the individual input parameters of the cost of debt and the cost of equity of regulated firms are analyzed. In section 6.3, the analysis is extended to methodical issues for the determination of the capital structure and, in particular, their interdependence with the level of the risk-adjusted cost of equity. Income taxes are included in the analysis in section 6.4.

---

431 Beside these methods, the comparable earnings standard has been widely employed in the U.S. utility regulation. This approach is not capital market oriented, as it applies to the book rate of return of companies with comparable risk. For an overview of the most widely used methods of cost of capital assessment for regulated utilities, see Thompson (1991); Morin (1994); Pedell (2004b).

432 For a critical discussion of the assumptions of the CAPM, cf. Schneider (1992, 526ff.); Hachmeister (2000, 178ff.); Ballwieser (2001b, 23f.). For lack of better alternatives, even critics resort to the CAPM when it comes to assessing the cost of capital; see, for example, Schneider (2001, 49).

433 For an overview of the regulatory practice of cost of capital assessment based on the CAPM in the UK, see CAA (2001, 16). For an international overview, see Houston et al. (1999, 20).

434 Cf. Schneider (2001); Busse von Colbe (2001) and (2002); Siegel (2002); Knieps (2003); see also the expert opinions of Kempf (2002) and Gerke (2003).

435 For the CAPM, see the seminal papers of Sharpe (1964), Lintner (1965) and Mossin (1966).

6.1 Identification of Specifics of Cost-Orientated Rate Regulation Relevant for Cost of Capital Assessment

The method for estimating cost of capital of rate-regulated firms based on the CAPM is not fundamentally different from the method used for non-regulated firms.[436] However, some peculiarities exist regarding the assessment of the individual input parameters of the WACC[437] as well as regarding the effects of the cost of capital employed that result from the specific situation of rate regulation. The focus of the analysis is on the following peculiarities.[438]

- Rate setting by the regulator is *circularly* connected with the allowed rate of return.
  - Under a regime of cost-orientated rate regulation, the assessment of cost of capital directly affects the cash flows of the regulated utility by way of imputed interest and depreciation. The cash flows and their expected variability on the other hand influence market value and risk-adjusted cost of capital of the regulated utility, which introduces a specific circularity problem of rate regulation in the cost of capital assessment.
  - Depending on the rules according to which the cost of capital is determined, the risk sharing between the capital owners of the regulated firm and the consumers of the regulated service, e.g. the sharing of interest rate risk, is changed, which feeds back on the cost of capital.

[436] The assessment of cost of capital for non-regulated firms widely found its way in textbooks; see Brealey/Myers (2003); Drukarczyk (2003); Franke/Hax (2004); Grinblatt/Titman (2002). For application to public and partially privatized firms, see the examples in Serfling/Pape (2001). It is not comprehensible why the setting of cost of capital and especially of risk premiums should not be consistent with a market oriented cost assessment, as conjectured by Zimmermann (2003, 49). Even if the setting of rates feeds back on the level of cost of capital, a market oriented assessment of cost of capital in principle still is possible and corresponds to dominant regulatory practice in most countries with highly developed capital markets. For the assessment of the discount rate for public investments see the seminal work of Arrow/Lind (1970) and Lind et al. (1982).

[437] It is assumed that a free cash flow approach is used and that consequently the cost of debt is reduced by corporate taxes in the WACC.

[438] The enumeration of peculiarities focuses on the most substantial issues and does not claim to be exhaustive.

- Regulated utilities can be exposed to a different systematic risk compared to non-regulated firms that, except for regulation, are doing the very same business.[439]
- Rate regulation itself brings about regulatory risks, which can cause an asymmetric distribution of expected cash flows, e.g. if there is the one-sided risk, that part of the actually incurred investments is not accepted in the rate base by the regulator.[440]

- A number of *time-related issues* results from the fact that rates usually are set for a regulatory review period of several years, which is much shorter than the extraordinarily long economic lifetime of many assets in regulated industries.
  - Therefore, not only the currently prevailing cost of capital but also the expected development of cost of capital in the future becomes relevant for rate setting.
  - The economic lifetime of assets usually comprises several regulatory review periods in which the regulator can revise rates. Accordingly, the cash flow time series can be divided theoretically into several subperiods.
  - Depending on whether and in which intervals fluctuations of the input parameters for the cost of capital should be passed through to rates, these input parameters have to be estimated for different periods.

- Finally, there are some peculiarities with respect to the methods employed for the assessment of the *individual input parameters* of the WACC.
  - In Germany, most companies or divisions that are rate-regulated or for whom future rate regulation has been announced are not separately listed. Therefore, assessment of the cost of capital based on accounting data and/or comparable firms is of relatively great importance.
  - Incentives for the regulated firm to change its capital structure possibly result from the specific relation between regulator and regulated utility. On these grounds, some regulatory commissions justify regulation of the capital structure.

---

[439] Peltman's (1976) buffering hypothesis conjectures that systematic risk is decreased by rate regulation. Empirical evidence is not unanimous, but tends to indicate that systematic risk is reduced; see section 3.3.2.

[440] For asymmetric regulatory risk, see section 3.3.3. Disallowances are discussed in detail in section 4.2.2.

– Conversion of a post-tax WACC to a pre-tax cost WACC, in some instances, is complicated by the fact that the regulatory commission uses replacement costs for the regulatory rate base and, accordingly, sets the allowed rate of return on this rate base to the real cost of capital.

6.2 Assessment of the Input Parameters of Cost of Debt and Cost of Equity

6.2.1 Risk-Less Interest Rate

The return of governmental bonds is usually proposed as an approximation of the risk-less interest rate.[441] The return is mostly calculated as yield to maturity, i.e. the expected effective return until the bond matures. The remaining lifetime of the bond, in principle, has to correspond to the capital commitment horizon that, in many instances, is equal to the economic lifetime of the assets in which the capital has been invested.[442] Otherwise capital owners of the regulated utility bear an interest change risk that feeds through to the cost of capital.[443] For a large number of regulated utility investments, above all those in the electricity and natural gas sectors exhibiting extraordinary long capital commitment horizons, 30-year treasury bonds are used. In the U.S., there is the special problem that currently no new 30 year treasury bonds are issued and the government has begun buying back the remaining bonds that are still circulating. Here, regulatory commissions resort to 10 year treasury bonds and make an allowance between 0.2% and 0.3% as a compensation for the shorter lifetime.

The assessed risk-less interest rate should be for a period during which no adjustment of rates by the regulator is expected.[444] Changes of the inter-

441 For the assessment of the risk-less interest rate, see, for example, Ballwieser (2002, 737f.).

442 This view was confirmed by the Australian Competition Tribunal in a recent decision against the Australian Competition and Consumer Commission (ACCC) that had used a bond maturity equivalent to the regulatory review period; see NECG (2003, 1).

443 If an asset is financed with roll-over credits over the capital commitment period, the argument is reversed. Moreover, bonds that are not due to mature for a considerable period of time include a different inflation premium than those due to mature in the near future; cf. Morin (1994, 308).

444 This holds true for all WACC input parameters; see also Oftel (1992), S. 4f. If, however, restrictions are placed on the regulator at subsequent rate reviews, e.g. due to the admission of competition, limiting the rates achievable in the market,

est rate beyond the upcoming regulatory review period are relevant for subsequent regulatory hearings. If, however, the regulator aims at uncoupling rates from fluctuations of the risk-less interest rate over the economic lifetime of the assets that, in many instances, comprises several review periods, he has to assess the risk-less interest rate over the entire lifetime.[445]

Setting the intervals in which rates are adjusted to fluctuations of the interest rate boils down to the question of who should bear the risk of interest rate changes.[446] In the hypothetical benchmark case that rates are adjusted continuously and without any lag to fluctuations of the interest rate, interest rate risk is completely passed through to consumers. In this case, the capital owners of the regulated utility bear no risk in the sense that the regulated utility earns its cost of capital at any moment in time, provided that the other input parameters also are adjusted continuously and without any lag. This means that the residual rate of return of the equity owners equals cost of equity at any moment in time; it does not mean that the rate of return is free from fluctuations, quite the contrary.[447] In other words, market value of equity is immunized against interest rate changes.[448] If, however, there is no adjustment of rates to interest rate changes over a certain period, the risk of interest rate changes lies completely with the capital owners of the regulated utility.

---

he must take into consideration how parameters such as input prices are likely to develop beyond the next regulatory review; cf. section 5.1.1 for a more thorough discussion of this issue in the context of regulatory depreciation schemes.

[445] Gerke (2003, 25) uses the arithmetic mean of the average annual current yield of bonds over the last 40 years for the estimation of the risk-less interest rate. He justifies this approach with the volatility of the interest rate, however he does not refer to the validity period of rates, respectively the regulatory review period. Kempf (2002, 37) uses the currently prevailing yield of 10 year governmental bonds. Mayer/Jenkinson (2000, 16) argue against using the prevailing interest rate on the grounds that the regulator sets rates for an entire review period, usually comprising several years, and that the interest rate tends to revert to its long-term mean. This position is shared by NERA (2003, 14).

[446] Strictly speaking, interest rate changes are not consistent with the standard one-period CAPM. Multi-period applications of the model at least require that market parameters such as the risk-less interest rate develop deterministically; see Fama (1977, 8f.).

[447] The case that actual interest payments on debt already have been committed by contracts in the past and do not fluctuate with the current interest rate is discussed in the subsequent section.

[448] Cf. Haugen/Stroyny/Wichern (1978, 719).

6.2.2 Risk Premium for Debt

Debt owners demand a risk premium on the risk-less interest rate as compensation for the fact that the loss probability of their claims is higher than zero.[449] The expected return on debt, therefore, is below the calculated yield to maturity. One indicator of the risk premium on the debt of a specific firm are the premiums paid in the past by the firm and unequivocally documented by existing debt contracts. However, for the regulation of future rates, ultimately the interest to be paid on debt in the future is relevant, which, in turn, is determined by a multitude of factors.

One of the most important factors determining the debt premium for regulated utilities is the very design of the regulatory system that, in turn, influences a utility's cash flow volatility, depending, for example, on the extent of cost pass-through and the length of rate adjustment lags. Other important regulatory regime variables that have an impact on a utility's risk are universal service obligations and the scope of competition allowed. In telecommunications, the latter involves the issue of interconnection (pricing), which creates new competition-related risks as well as new default risks for interconnection service receivables. If rate regulation is subject to a change process, including structural interruptions, the currently paid risk premium on debt should be used instead of the average over several years in the past. Another important determinant of the debt premium is the capital structure discussed below.

Changes of ratings are a strong indicator of changes of the creditworthiness of a regulated utility and in most instances are translated without considerable delay into higher cost of debt. Moreover, future investments and financing adjustments possibly affect the risk premium for debt. If, for example, major investments exclusively financed with debt are planned for the future, the debt-equity ratio rises. If at the outset the debt-equity ratio is

---

449 If the regulator/government is likely to bail out regulated companies in financial distress, this loss probability is very low. The risk premiums observed during the last few years on European telecommunications companies' bonds, however, tell a different story. In any case, the scope for governmental subsidies is severely restricted by European competition law. In the summer of 2002, the French government issued a guarantee for France Telecom bonds, when rating agencies threatened to downgrade it. This line of action was condemned by the European Commission, and, eventually, France Telecom was ordered in December 2003 to pay back direct subsidies (granted since 1997) amounting to more than one billion Euros, including interest. At the same time the French government was requested to withdraw the bond guarantee; see Frankfurter Allgemeine Zeitung, Nr. 287, 10.12.2003, S. 12; Financial Times Deutschland, 16.12.2003.

already relatively high, the default risk and accordingly the risk premium especially for the new debt (and thereby the average risk premium) are likely to be increased. Clearly, planned investment and financing activities should only be accounted for in assessing cost of capital if documented by detailed and conclusive business plans.

It has to be clarified how to deal with debt financing whose interest rates over the entire life extending into the future already have been fixed by contracts in the past. There is no general answer to this question; the answer depends on the objectives of rate regulation. If rate regulation is orientated towards long run incremental costs with the aim in mind to give signals to potential competitors for efficient investment activities, accordingly incremental cost of debt is relevant, i.e. the cost of additional debt financing form today's perspective.[450] If, however, the regulator aims at actually covering total costs, he will use the interest payments fixed in the past for the future for rate setting purposes. If the first approach is followed, interest payments allowed by the regulator can be above or below actual interest payments partially committed in the past. In this case, capital owners bear an interest change risk that feeds back on cost of capital to the extent that it is correlated with overall market risk.

Risks are usually highly interdependent over divisions in a multi-divisional company comprising other regulated divisions (multi-utility) and/or non-regulated divisions beside the regulated division in question. If debt is raised centrally at a uniform cost, current risk premiums of the individual divisions cannot be observed. If non-diversified utilities are used as comparables, the problem remains that economies or diseconomies of risk[451] cannot be allocated without discretion to the individual divisions even if it can be assumed that the average risk premium of the comparables is a good proxy for the risk premium of the regulated division in question.

6.2.3 Market Equity Risk Premium

The central problem for the assessment of the market risk premium for equity is that the complete market portfolio of all assets cannot be ob-

[450] This view is supported for example by the UK Civil Aviation Authority; see CAA (2001, 23).

[451] The question of whether diversification on the company level is efficient, respectively whether diversification on the investor level is preferable, is not discussed here. For the discussion of diversification discounts or diversification premiums, respectively, see, for example, Berger/Ofek (1995); Rajan/Servaes/Zingales (2000); Graham/Lemmon/Wolf (2002); see also section 6.2.1.

served.[452] It only can be more or less approximated, e.g. using stock price indices or broader indices that also contain real estate assets.[453] The equity premium has to be estimated from historical data, unless the drawbacks inevitably associated with assessing it on the basis of necessarily subjective investor and analyst expectations are accepted. For reasons of consistency, the equity premium should be estimated as a premium on the exact same interest rate as employed by the regulator as the risk-less interest rate.[454]

The average market return over the estimation period can be calculated as the geometric or arithmetic mean. Where rate regulation is concerned, the argument predominantly favors the arithmetic mean, as it is consistent with the CAPM in the case of stationary stochastic processes.[455] If the equity premium is constant both methods yield the same result. The higher the volatility of the equity premium, the more the arithmetic mean lies above the geometric mean. The arithmetic mean estimates the currently prevailing equity premium; however, the equity premium is used to set rates over the entire regulatory review period, particularly for the purposes of rate regulation. Time series analyses find evidence that the equity premium is negatively auto-correlated.[456] This, in turn, is an argument in favor of the geometric mean especially in the case of relatively long review periods.

Empirical evidence has shown that the equity premium is subject to relatively strong fluctuations over time.[457] In this context, the regulator must decide whether to pass through these fluctuations to rates or use a long-run average of the equity premium to smooth out rates. In the second case, it must be ensured that the imputed equity premium is not lowered to the currently prevailing level in times during which it lies below its long-

---

452 Cf. Roll (1977, 136ff.), who shows that testing the CAPM requires the knowledge of the complete market portfolio.

453 Theoretically, a portfolio of the universe of existing assets would have to be constructed.

454 The Australian Competition Tribunal, in a recent decision against the ACCC, stated that the use of different values for the risk-less interest rate and estimation of the market equity premium is not consistent; see NECG (2003, 3).

455 Cf. Kolbe/Read/Hall (1984, 73f.), Cornell/Hirshleifer/James (1997, 17); Brealey/Myers (2003, 156f.). This corresponds to the predominant regulatory practice in the U.S.; see Cooper/Currie (1999, 10).

456 Fama (1996) shows that use of the arithmetic mean can produce false estimations if return is serially negative correlated; see also Damodaran (2002, 161f.) who argues in favor of the geometric mean for just this reason.

457 For the level of the equity premium in Germany, see Stehle/Hartmond (1991, 390); Conen/Väth (1993, 643); Bimberg (1993, 136); Ballwieser (1995, 125); as well as Stehle (1999, 10ff.).

run average, for example because of the exertion of political influence or lobbying. Otherwise, the appropriate rate of return on capital employed is not realized on average. If the average rate of return of the companies currently contained in a certain stock price index weighted with their market values is used as an estimator of the market equity premium, an overestimation can result due to the fact that companies that earned a below average rate of return and dropped out of the index in the past (survival bias) are not accounted for.[458]

Two methodical questions that are the subject of intense debate in relation to rate regulation are (1) how many years and (2) how many companies should be used for estimating the equity premium. The first question boils down to balancing validity and reliability, and is of considerable importance, as equity premiums have been seen to decline over the past few years.[459] Clearly, this decrease has a stronger impact on the estimated cost of equity, if fewer years are included in the estimation. Opinions vary as to the answer. While some experts consider 30 years to be too long, others argue that as many years as possible should be included in the estimation.[460] The crucial factor seems to be that, even with estimation periods of 10 or 20 years, the standard deviation of the equity premium is almost as large or even larger than the equity premium itself.[461] This suggests that estimation periods longer than 20 years should be used.

The second question refers to which stock price index is used and to whether this index is adjusted by excluding some companies where deemed appropriate. For instance, it can be argued against the unadjusted use of the S&P 500 index on the grounds that it contains a relatively large portion of high technology companies, which causes an upward bias of the equity premium compared to the universe of all U.S. companies. Obvious solutions are either to resort to a broader index such as the Wilshire 5000 index or to exclude some high technology companies from the S&P 500

---

[458] For the survival bias, cf. Brown/Goetzmann/Ross (1995); Li/Xu (2002). Cooper/Currie (1999, 10) assess the adjustments of the equity premium appropriate to the survival bias as rather small.

[459] For Germany, see Stehle (1999); for the U.S., see Bernstein (1997), Siegel (1999), Welch (2000), Pettit/Gulic/Park (2001), Arnott/Bernstein (2002).

[460] Cf. Ibbotson Associates (2003). Ibbotson Associates use an estimation period of 50 years in their widely-used Cost of Capital Yearbook. Kempf (2002, 38) uses an estimation period of 20 years. In the case of Germany, Ballwieser (2001a, 35) suggests that estimation periods as long as possible be used, but only after the Second World War and the foundation of the Federal Republic of Germany.

[461] Cf. Damodaran (2002, 161), who supports this with empirical numerical examples.

for the estimation. A broad index that can be used in Europe is the Dow Jones STOXX Total Market Index (TMI) that represents more than 1,100 companies in 17 European countries and approximately 95% of the market capitalization of free floating shares.

6.2.4 Beta Factor

The beta factor reflects the firm-specific systematic risk compared to the overall market risk,[462] with the market portfolio usually approximated using a stock price index. Beta factors can be estimated on the basis of historical daily, weekly, monthly or other returns. Daily returns offer the advantage of more observations in the same period compared to weekly and monthly returns and thereby the standard error of the estimation is reduced. Alternatively the estimation period can be reduced while keeping the standard error constant; this allows the use of comparatively up to date estimation data. If the market for shares is not very liquid, beta factors risk being underestimated by the use of daily returns.[463] In addition, beta factors on the basis of daily returns are subject to particularly wide fluctuations, so that for the purposes of rate regulation monthly returns are predominantly preferred, as rates are set for regulatory review periods comprising several years. The monthly returns usually are collected for a period of five years in order to have a sufficient number of observations for the estimation of the beta factor.[464] The use of historical data for estimation purposes is particularly problematic in the case of the beta factor, as significant structural changes of a regulated utility's risk might result from changes of the regu-

---

[462] The Bundeskartellamt (2003, 23) [German Federal Cartel Office] and Zimmermann (2003, 49) dispute the existence of systematic risk for electricity transmission and distribution companies, and therefore use the risk-less interest rate as the cost of equity. By doing this, they implicitly suggest that the equity owners of these companies are guaranteed a fixed income in the same way as bondholders, and that they, moreover, are not exposed to any default risk. This could only be guaranteed in a hypothetical benchmark case with a perfect rate-of-return regulation, i.e. rates immediately reflected total costs without any lag. In practice, all regulatory systems deviate to some extent from this benchmark and do so on good reason, as such a system would kill any incentive for efficient investment in and operation of the grid. In addition, this is clearly contradictory to empirical findings that the return in the case of electricity companies is actually subject to fluctuation and that beta factors significantly larger than zero can be observed.

[463] For this relation, known as the intervalling effect, see Levhari/Levy (1977); Zimmermann (1997, 99ff.); Gerke (2003, 18f.).

[464] Cf. Cornell/Hirshleifer/James (1997, 14); Cooper/Currie (1999, 25f.).

latory regime.[465] Therefore, estimated beta factors have to be interpreted very carefully and, where necessary, be adjusted especially when the regulatory scheme is modified. The analysis carried out in chapter 3 and chapter 4 provides theoretical and empirical insights into the determinants of regulatory risk that could serve as criteria for such adjustments.

Moreover, the *adjustment of betas* can be justified on several grounds. (1) The shorter the estimation period, i.e. the smaller the sample size, the higher the variance of the estimated beta values. If only very recent data is used in order to avoid misleading estimations due to structural changes in the past, beta values greater than one are overestimated while beta values less than one are underestimated. (2) Furthermore, empirical tests of the CAPM predominantly confirm that return rises linearly with risk. However, the intercept is larger than the risk-less interest rate and the capital market line is flatter than predicted by the CAPM.[466] This implies the necessity to adjust low beta values upwards respectively to adjust high beta values downwards. (3) In addition, it has been shown empirically, that beta values estimated from historical data tend to revert to one.[467] As in many rate-regulated industries beta values of less than one are found, this means that an upward adjustment will be required in many instances. The investment services Bloomberg and Merrill Lynch, for example, use the following pragmatic formula for the adjustment of the beta factor:[468]

$$\beta_{adjusted} = 2/3 \cdot \beta_{unadjusted} + 1/3 \tag{6.1}$$

For example, for a raw beta of 1.2 the adjustment formula yields an adjusted beta of 1.13 and for a raw beta of 0.8 an adjusted beta of 0.87. For a raw beta of 1.0, the adjusted beta is also 1.0. The weight of 2/3 given to the raw unadjusted beta is rather arbitrary. However, some empirical investigations have shown that the adjusted betas used by investment services tend to outperform unadjusted betas in their predictive power.[469] By all means, the criteria for adjustments of beta factors have to be defined clearly and backed up empirically; otherwise they inevitably remain arbi-

---

[465] Cf. section 3.3.2.

[466] For an overview of empirical investigations of the CAPM, see Ross (1978).

[467] In particular for the case of rate-regulated utilities, see Gombola/Kahl (1990, 89ff.) who find that utility betas exhibit a tendency to revert towards their mean, and Buckland/Fraser (2001, 18); for the general issue, see Blume (1975). Further reasons for adjusting beta and the implementation of the empirical CAPM for estimating the necessary adjustment are discussed by Litzenberger/Ramaswamy/Sosin (1980).

[468] Cf. Morin (1994, 68); Grinblatt/Titman (2002, 157).

[469] Cf. Kryzanowski/Jalilvand (1983); Gombola/Kahl (1990).

trary and are not suited to serve as additional evidence in regulatory hearings.

A problem that arises when beta values are used for purposes of rate regulation are their wide fluctuations.[470] Capital market disturbances, as caused by the terrorist attacks in the U.S. on 9/11/2001, drive up the volatility of the overall market and possibly bring about serious distortions in the estimation of the cost of capital of rate-regulated utilities. Moreover, considerable distortions can be produced if the price of a stock is predominantly determined for a certain time by firm or industry specific information and to a lesser extent by the development of the overall market, which results in a temporary decoupling of this stock from the overall market.[471] It is conceivable that, in some cases, the estimated beta factor will decrease in spite of an increase of the systematic risk of the regulated utility in question. If the systematic risk of a firm increases, its cost of capital increases and *ceteris paribus* its stock price declines. If this coincides with a period of overall increasing stock prices, the estimated correlation of the stock price with the market portfolio is downward biased.[472] In the case of rate-regulated firms, firm or industry specific stock price relevant news above all is produced by changes of the regulatory regime itself.

Distortions due to increased volatility of the overall market or due to temporary determination of the stock price by firm or industry specific information are not a specific problem of the estimation of beta factors, but a general statistical problem closely connected with the choice of the data set for the estimation. If the stock price data of the affected periods is excluded from the estimation, it is implicitly assumed that such events never happen, whereas if the stock price data of these periods is included, it is implicitly assumed, that such events will also happen in the future at regular intervals.[473] By choosing the estimation period, it is controlled to which extent such events enter into the averaging, which implicitly gives an assessment of their likelihood in the future.

A method that aims at directly estimating the impact on the beta factor of events such as changes of the regulatory regime is the Kalman filter.[474] With its help beta factors of individual sub-periods and the distorting effect of events can be estimated in principle. Thus, past distortions are ac-

---

[470] For the stability of beta values, see Zimmermann (1997, 209ff.).

[471] Cf. Hern/Zalewska (2001, 4).

[472] Cf. Brigham/Crum (1977, 8ff.)

[473] Cf. Hern/Zalewska (2001, 4.).

[474] The Kalman filter is a method for estimating time-varying coefficients; see Zalweska-Mitura/Hall (1999).

counted for when estimating future beta values, without having to accept the drawbacks of a very long estimation period.[475]

The standard CAPM uses the μ, σ-criterion, which is only consistent with the Bernoulli theory if investors have a quadratic risk utility function with any probability distribution of returns or if returns are normally distributed using any risk utility function. As there is not much support for quadratic utility functions, normally distributed, i.e. symmetric returns are implicitly assumed. However, in particular interventions by the regulator can cause asymmetric distributions. For instance, this might be due to the fact that the regulator does not accept part of the incurred investments in the regulatory rate base and the regulated utility would not receive compensation for these investments without further adjustments. An asymmetric distribution also might be due to the fact, that the regulator uses a hypothetical quantity structure when assessing the regulatory rate base, that constitutes an improvement compared to the actual, path-dependent quantity structure.[476] The asymmetric risk has to be compensated somehow by the regulator in order to avoid drastically reduced investment incentives. This can be done by way of a higher allowed rate of return or by way of a separate cost element in the calculation of rates. It has been suggested using an extended version of the CAPM capturing the first three moments of the return distribution for the assessment of the cost of equity for rate-regulated firms exposed to asymmetric regulatory risk.[477]

The beta factor obtained from stock price data refers to the equity of a firm. Based on this equity beta, an *asset beta* (unlevered betas) is calculated as the sum of debt beta and equity beta weighted with the respective market values of debt and equity (delevering). Assuming by approximation

---

[475] For applications of the Kalman filter on the assessment of beta factors for regulated utilities, see Buckland/Fraser (2001); Francis/Grout/Zalewska (2001); Hern/Zalewska (2001).

[476] For these examples in the context of the determination of the regulatory rate base, see section 4.2.2. For asymmetric effects of regulation on utilities' distribution of returns, see section 3.3.3.

[477] For the assessment of cost of equity of utilities with such an extended CAPM, see Conine/Tamarkin (1985). Another extension of the CAPM shows that the return of an individual asset not only depends on its systematic risk but also on its liquidity; see the theoretical work of Amihud/Mendelson (1986) and Jacoby/Fowler/ Gottesman (2000), who derive a positive relation between the liquidity measured by the bid-ask spread and the expected return on an asset. The liquidity effect was confirmed empirically by Brennan/Subrahmanyam (1996) und Datar/Naik/Radcliffe (1998). See also Gerke (2003, 22) who employs the ratio of zero daily returns over all daily returns as a measure of liquidity.

that the debt beta is zero,[478] the following formula is used to calculate the asset beta in a Modigliani/Miller-world with uniform conditions for raising debt, without transaction costs and without bankruptcy risk:[479]

$$\beta_{\mathrm{A}} = \frac{\beta_{\mathrm{EK}}}{1+(1-\mathrm{s})\dfrac{\mathrm{FK}}{\mathrm{EK}}} \tag{6.2}$$

where s denotes the corporate tax rate. Asset betas are applied for several reasons:

- If it is assumed that a rate-regulated utility will operate with a different capital structure in the future, the corresponding expected future equity beta is calculated from the asset beta and the planned or forecasted capital structure (relevering).[480] However, it is contentious if this capital structure adjustment is justified, in particular, if the debt-equity ratio is low at the outset.[481]
- If the aim is to avoid basing the risk estimation exclusively on the individual regulated utility in question, and if gathering a broader risk estimation by using a group of comparable companies is preferred, the average of asset betas weighted with the respective firm values is computed, and, subsequently, the individual equity betas are calculated by relevering the average asset beta with the individual capital structures.[482] This approach is also applicable when a rate-regulated utility is not listed.

6.2.5 Beta Factors for Non-Listed Rate-Regulated Firms or Divisions

If the shares of a regulated utility are not listed, the beta factor cannot be estimated directly from readily available capital market data. In this case,

[478] For the practical implications of deviations from this assumption, see Aders/Wagner (2004, 33ff.).

[479] Cf. Hamada (1969, 20); Rudolph (1986, 894), Callahan/Mohr (1989, 161); Modigliani/Miller (1958); Ballwieser (2004, 129).

[480] For the starting point of the discussion of the relation between capital structure and cost of capital of rate-regulated utilities, see Miller/Modigliani (1966); Elton/Gruber (1971).

[481] Cf. CAA (2001, 22).

[482] For this approach, see Cornell/Hirshleifer/James (1997, 14f.).

the regulator can resort to betas of comparable companies that are listed as an approximation.[483] However, this involves a number of problems:

The selected reference companies have to be actually comparable with regard to their business risk. For instance, many non-listed utilities in Germany have activities exclusively in the electricity or natural gas sector, whereas potential candidates for listed comparables such as E.ON or RWE promote diversification into several utility sectors, in other words, they embark on a so-called multi-utility strategy. Some utility sectors exhibit considerable differences that are reflected in a different business risk.[484] Therefore, a criterion for comparableness between different multi-utilities is a similar utility-mix. Using foreign utilities with a similar structure of business activities as comparable gives rise to the problem that, possibly, in other countries a completely different regulatory regime is prevailing, which ultimately makes risk incomparable in spite of similar business activities.

Moreover, the companies have to be comparable with respect to the financing risk resulting from their capital structure, as, in particular, the cost of equity varies systematically with the debt-equity ratio. Therefore, directly comparing the cost of equity of companies that have similar business risk but different capital structures makes no sense.[485] The latter can be accounted for by firstly calculating the asset beta of a comparable company (delevering) and subsequently relevering the asset beta with the capital structure of the regulated utility in question. However, this conversion is not unproblematic from the regulated utility's point of view, as, according to experience, regulatory commissions tend to object to any adjustment of parameters used for rate setting purposes.

Instead of using beta values of individual companies for the comparison, the beta factor of an entire sectoral index estimated from its correlation

---

[483] These are the so-called pure-play betas. Besides, accounting betas, earnings betas and fundamental betas could be used among other measures to assess the risk of a non-listed company. For an overview of these and other measures in the context of financing of rate-regulated utilities, see Morin (1994, 343ff.).

[484] Natural gas, for instance, is exposed to competition by other primary energy carriers as heating oil that are substitutes for natural gas. In addition, in many countries, there is competition in natural gas transportation. Both facts contribute to increase the risk in comparison to the electricity market.

[485] On this account alone, the fixing of a uniform cost of equity of 6.5% in real terms in the Verbändevereinbarung II plus for the German electricity sector (BDI et al. 2001, 7) as well as of 7.8% in the Verbändevereinbarung II for the German natural gas sector (BDI et al. 2002, 79) is neither theoretically founded nor reasonable. The Verbändevereinbarung is an association agreement between energy producers and industrial consumers.

with a corresponding index for the overall market could be used. The aim here is to gather more reliable and stable estimations than could be obtained from the use of individual shares.[486] Even if the utilities contained in the sectoral index are exposed to a similar business risk, the effects of differing capital structures on cost of equity are not captured by this approach. Thus, an average capital structure is implicitly assumed for the utility in question. The problem can be circumvented by computing the weighted average of the comparables' asset betas and relevering it with the utility's capital structure. If the beta factor of an international sectoral index such as the Dow Jones Euro Stoxx Utilities is used, the additional problem arises that regulatory schemes possibly exhibit wide differences across countries, which might have a considerable effect on the risk borne by capital owners in the different countries.

These problems also have to be dealt with if a consolidated company is listed, but the rate-regulated individual division for which divisional cost of capital must be assessed is not listed.[487] For instance, in an integrated natural gas company, only the risk of the transportation division is relevant for the setting of rates for access to natural gas transportation facilities and must be strictly separated from the risk of gas trading activities. The same problem arises when separating the different divisions of a multi-utility that, in addition, might be subject to different regulatory regimes. The divisional beta factor will coincide with the company beta only by pure accident; in most instances, the divisional beta will be under- or overestimated if the uniform company beta is used, so that the discussion of comparable betas is triggered once again. If a company consolidates regulated and non-regulated divisions, it cannot be assumed that the risk of the regulated divisions is generally below the risk of the non-regulated divisions. Although rate regulation can smooth cash flow fluctuations, it involves specific regulatory risks that can be of significant importance.[488]

In a recent special report on the development of competition in telecommunications and postal services, the German Monopoly Commission

[486] Cf. Gerke (2003, 28ff.), who estimates beta factors for the Dow Jones Euro Stoxx Utilities and the German CDAX Utilities.

[487] For the issue of divisional cost of capital assessment, see Freygang (1993, 245ff.); Herter (1994, 102ff.); Arbeitskreis Finanzierung (1996, 550ff.). Houston (1996, 8f.) suggests using tracking shares that .."rights to the income from a particular class of business: in this case, the regulated business…", in order to circumvent the problem.

[488] See also Schneider (2001, 49). For the question of whether rate regulation ultimately increases or decreases systematic risk, see Pedell (2003b); the discussion goes back to Peltzman's (1976, 230) hypothesis that regulation acts as a buffer against risks.

argues that risk is higher in non-regulated businesses than in regulated businesses[489], although at the same time it admits that regulatory risks do exist, e.g. due to the use of the regulatory cost concept of efficient service provision.[490] Here, a more careful argumentation is advisable and each individual case should be scrutinized in order to determine whether risk in a regulated division is actually above or below the uniform company risk.

Finally, there might be risk interdependences between divisions that additionally restrict the applicability of the uniform company beta to individual divisions.[491] Risk interdependences between divisions are part of the wider theme of (dis)economies of scope between the individual divisions of a company. Economies of scope can affect all parameters of the cash flow distribution, such as the mean and the standard deviation, and are defined by the fact that these parameters add up non-linearly, i.e. above-linearly in the case of parameters such as the mean and below-linearly in the case of risk parameters such as the standard deviation. On the one hand, in a horizontally diversified company, economies of scope affecting the risk across divisions possibly cause the company beta to lie below the weighted average of divisional betas.[492] Allocation of this effect to the individual divisions inevitably involves an element of arbitrariness. If, nevertheless, a more or less arbitrary allocation is made, this can produce distortions in the concerned rate-regulated industries. Likewise, a vertically

[489] Cf. Monopolkommission (2003, 67, para. 160): „Dann wird man in Rechnung stellen, dass die relevanten Risiken im regulierten Bereich geringer sind als im unregulierten Bereich und dass eine auf das Gesamtunternehmen abstellende Betrachtung die relevante Risikoprämie grundsätzlich überschätzt – mit der Folge, dass der Kapitalkostensatz tendenziell zu hoch angesetzt wird.“

[490] Cf. Monopolkommission (2003, 72, para. 170); the U.S. Federal Communications Commission argues along the same lines, stating that the risk associated with the use of Total Element Long Run Incremental Costs (TELRIC) has to be accounted for in the cost of capital; cf. FCC (2003, 419, para. 680). As a way of reducing this risk, depreciation can be based on economic depreciation, which implies accelerated depreciation in times of decreasing input prices; cf. FCC (2003, 415, para. 671). The use of economic depreciation for regulatory purposes in the case of technological progress has already been proposed by Crew/Kleindorfer (1992). Knieps/Küpper/Langen (2001) suggest that depreciation be based on the difference in used replacement values between different time periods for the same reason. For a detailed discussion of the issues associated with the regulatory rate base, see Pedell (2003a).

[491] See also Schneider (2001, 49).

[492] For the decomposition of the company beta into divisional betas and in particular for the equation with the weighted average of divisional betas when there are no synergies and the principle of value additivity holds, cf. Fuller/Kerr (1981); Callahan/Mohr (1989, 166).

integrated utility might have lower cost of capital than the weighted average of the individual links of the supply chain due to risk reducing interdependences.[493] These might result, for example from the reduction of contracts with suppliers and customers, which remain necessarily incomplete, or from better chances of deterring (potential) competitors.

On the other hand, a number of empirical investigations showed that diversified companies are traded rather at a diversification discount than at a diversification premium; obviously diseconomies of scope between the divisions dominate.[494] This could be due to the fact that diversification of risks possibly is carried more efficiently by the company's capital owners diversifying on the capital market than by the company internally diversifying and could mean that the cost of capital of the consolidated company lies above the weighted average of the divisions' cost of capital. Diseconomies of scope, just as economies of scope, by their very definition cannot be allocated without discretion to the individual companies; at best they can be distributed according to more or less plausible criteria.[495]

6.3 Weighting of the Cost of Equity and the Cost of Debt with the Capital Structure

6.3.1 Components of the Capital Structure

After adjusting for flotation costs that reduce the net capital available to the firm from capital issues,[496] cost of equity and cost of debt are weighted with the capital structure to compute the overall cost of capital. It is widely accepted that market values, not book values, should be used as weights, as market values adequately reflect the opportunities of capital owners, i.e.

---

493 By separating the supply chain, additional risks are added on both sides of the newly created market relation; cf. Wilson (2002, 1329f.).

494 For empirical support of the diversification or conglomerate discount, see Berger/Ofek (1995); Lins/Servaes (1999); Rajan/Servaes/Zingales (2000); Graham/Lemmon/Wolf (2002); Burch/Nanda (2003).

495 The individual risks are not reduced by economies of scope affecting the company risk as argued by Gerke (2003, 33f.).

496 In the case of equity, flotation costs comprise a direct component, the underwriter fees, and an indirect component, the market pressure on the stock price caused by new equity issues. For the flotation cost adjustment, see Arzac/Marcus (1981), (1983) and (1984); Patterson (1983); Howe (1984); Beranek/Howe (1990); Howe/Beranek (1992). For an overview of the discussion, see Brigham/Tapley (1986, 16.29ff.); Morin (1994, 161ff.); Pedell (2004b, 84ff.).

the return they expect.[497] If debt is not traded on capital markets in the same way as bonds, book values can be used for debt as approximations of market values, as the deviations between market and book value of debt are usually not very large. In most instances, market capitalization will be used as an approximation of the market value of equity, as it is readily observable.[498]

In the hypothetical case that a regulated firm earns exactly its cost of capital on the capital employed at every moment, market value would theoretically equal book value all the time.[499] In this case, the share price should be independent of the capital structure. Tax advantages due to debt financing would exist also in this case, but they would benefit exclusively the rate payers not the capital owners.[500] In reality, neither the regulatory rate base permanently equals book value, nor does the expected rate of return on book values[501] permanently equal the cost of capital; alone for these reasons, market values and book values diverge.

The German RegTP uses book values to weight the cost of equity and the cost of debt, and justifies this approach on the grounds that market values are too volatile for the purposes of rate regulation.[502] The Monopoly Commission, in a review of the conflict between the RegTP and DTAG, rightly objects that market values are the correct weights from a financial theory perspective, and argues that the issue of smoothing rates should not be mixed up with the issue of capital weights valuation but instead should be dealt with separately.[503] The latter problem can be solved by adopting some form of averaging over time.

Interest-free debt, in principle, has to be accounted for with an interest rate of zero in computing the weighted average cost of capital. As an alter-

[497] Cf. for example Modigliani/Miller (1958, 267ff.); Miller/Modigliani (1961; 412ff.); Robichek (1978, 701); Oftel (1992, 5); Ballwieser (1998, 85); Ickenroth (1998, 4); Busse von Colbe (2002); Küpper (2002, 27); Kempf (2002, 27); Knieps (2003, 994).

[498] Market capitalization is only an approximation of the market value of equity due to possible premiums and discounts for blockholdings alone. For a thorough discussion of the relation between market capitalization and market value, see Ballwieser (2003, 19ff.).

[499] This implies that there are no synergies and no goodwill. For synergies in the context of valuation, see Ballwieser (2004, 201).

[500] Cf. Brigham/Tapley (1986, 16.33).

[501] The expected rate of return can diverge significantly from the allowed rate of return on the regulatory rate base, e.g. when asymmetric regulatory risk is present; see section 3.3.3.

[502] Cf. RegTP (2003, 62).

[503] Cf. Monopolkommission (2003, 69, para. 164).

native, it can be deducted from the capital base. Debt with hidden interest payments has to be accounted for with the hidden interest rate. For instance, fiscal accruals for pensions have to be increased annually by 6% if the headcount does not change; suppliers are likely to take into account hidden interest if they grant time for payment.[504] The level of an unused cash discount is an indicator for the hidden interest rate. However, debt with hidden interest only may be included with the hidden interest rate in the capital base if the corresponding hidden interest payments are not yet included in the cash flows. For example, it is not acceptable that allocations to accruals for pension are included in the cash flows if at the same time accruals for pension funds are contained in the capital base with the hidden interest rate.[505]

In addition, a hidden leverage on the risk of equity owners is exerted by long-term payment obligations, as they result for example from lease contracts that cannot be cancelled unilaterally, where it is irrelevant if the leased assets are on the balance sheet of the lessee or the lessor. Another example are long-term contracts with independent power producers, who finance their investments with these contractual commitments.[506] Such obligations usually increase the risk of equity owners. However, in the case of rate-regulated utilities this does not necessarily hold true if the costs resulting from this are passed-through one-to-one to rates. In this case, consumers bear the risks associated with long-term payment obligations.

6.3.2 Actual Versus Optimized Capital Structure

Regulatory practice varies as to whether the actual capital structure or an alternative structure deemed more appropriate by the regulator is used.[507] From a financial theory perspective, a utility's cost of capital clearly is determined by its actual capital structure. This does not necessarily imply that the currently prevailing capital structure should be used for calculating rates, as the latter are set not only for the moment but for a certain period in the future.[508] Until now, no comprehensive theory has been developed for the objective determination of the optimal capital structure. Therefore,

---

504 Cf. Schneider (2001, 47).

505 Cf. Richter/Simon-Keuenhof (1996, 707). Hidden interest on supplier credits is already contained in purchases, cf. Schneider (2001, 47).

506 Cf. Myers (1992), S. 17f.; McMullen (1993, 62f.); Kahn/Stoft/Belden (1995, 3f.).

507 See the overview of regulatory practice in the UK in Pedell (2004b, 74ff.). See also McMullen (1993, 17ff.).

508 For the temporal dimension of the capital structure, see section 6.3.3.

the regulated utility itself should decide on its capital structure, as it has to bear the residual financial consequences of this decision, unless the financing effects are passed through to regulated rates on a one-to-one basis without any frictions, which obviously is not possible taking into account inevitable informational problems and time lags alone. This argument notwithstanding, some regulators set a certain debt-equity ratio for the weighting of cost of debt and cost of equity, in order to avoid the incentive for the regulated utility to finance its investments with more equity as would be the case without rate regulation.[509] The assessment of an optimized imputed debt-equity ratio necessarily involves a certain degree of discretion and does not guarantee an adequate return on capital employed.

Furthermore, as the cost of debt and the cost of equity vary with the financing structure, they have to be adjusted consistently, at least when a hypothetical capital structure deviating from the actual one is employed for rate setting purposes. For the assessment of the cost of equity, it is assumed for simplicity in the first place that debt has no default risk and that accordingly a higher debt-equity ratio does not change the cost of debt. Under this assumption a higher debt-equity ratio means that the same business risk has to be borne by less equity and that fluctuations of the overall return are translated into correspondingly wider fluctuations of the rate of return on equity, for which equity owners demand an adequate increase in the allowed rate of return.[510] If a higher debt-equity ratio increases the default probability of debt, the average cost of debt also is driven up. However, making an objective and adequate adjustment of the cost of debt for the higher default risk resulting from a higher debt-equity ratio is impossible.[511] On the other hand, the tax deductibility of interest payments on debt reduces the cost of capital if a free cash flow-approach is used and, consequently, the cost of debt is reduced by corporate taxes in the WACC.[512]

If a regulatory commission, these is objections notwithstanding, sets unilaterally a capital structure deviating from the actual capital structure, this should be done with sufficient lead time so that the regulated utility has a chance to adjust its actual capital structure to the imputed one. Otherwise, it has to be accepted that risk and, accordingly, the adequate allowed rate of return are increased. For example, the German Monopoly

[509] For the incentive to use more equity due to rate regulation, see the seminal work of Averch/Johnson (1962).

[510] Applied to rate regulation and supported by numerical examples cf. Myers (1992, 13ff.).

[511] See also Myers (1992, 19).

[512] Tax deductibility is only partially fulfilled under the current regime of trade income tax in Germany; see section 6.4.2.

Commission extends the concept of efficient service provision cost to financing measures, and argues that the capital structure should be adapted to achieve the lowest possible financing costs.[513] The question of *how* this capital structure is to be identified is not addressed by the Monopoly Commission.

6.3.3 Temporal Dimension of the Capital Structure

The period specific target capital structure weighted at market values is relevant for the computation of weighted average cost of capital.[514] Future changes of the capital structure have to be documented by investment and financing plans, for the purposes of rate regulation. If no changes of the capital structure are planned, the currently prevailing one should be used.[515] There is a circularity problem inherent in the planning of the capital structure insofar as the choice of capital structure depends on operational risks as well as on the possibilities of internal financing that, in turn, depend on the design of the regulatory system and level of allowed rates. If changes of the capital structure are anticipated, this feeds back on risk, i.e. where necessary the beta factor and the risk premium for debt have to be adjusted consistently,[516] which inevitably opens scope for discretion.

As the capital structure usually is not changed abruptly, but only gradually, the problem of assessing a future capital structure becomes relevant above all if rates are set for a long regulatory review period. Therefore, the issue is intensely discussed for example in the UK and Canada, where the regulatory review period for the majority of rates comprises five years, whereas it is less important in the U.S. where regulatory review periods are significantly shorter. The validity period of rates set by the German RegTP ranges in between. For instance, rates for interconnection in the past have been set for a period of about two years.

[513] Cf. Monopolkommission (2003, 75, para. 177, and 81, para. 194).

[514] See, for example, Arbeitskreis Finanzierung (1996, 562).

[515] Kempf (2002, 28) suggests employing principally the currently prevailing capital structure, in order to avoid the circularity problem inherent in the assessment of the target capital structure. However, he makes an exception for financing measures that already have been publicly announced (p. 30, fn. 38).

[516] For the adjustment of the beta factor, see Cooper/Currie (1999, 5f.).

6.4 Accounting for Income Taxes in the Cost of Capital

6.4.1 Narrowing down the Object of Investigation to Definitive Corporate Income Taxes

Income taxes reduce the revenues available for meeting the demands of capital owners. That revenues of a rate-regulated utility on top of investments and operating expenses have to cover tax payments is undisputed. This holds true regardless of whether taxes are classified as costs or part of profits,[517] which is immaterial from a decision-theoretic point of view.[518] The crucial point is whether a regulated utility can expect that its tax payments are completely covered by revenues. While for the investment behavior the marginal tax rate is relevant, for the purposes of cost-orientated rate regulation total tax payments have to be covered, which is achieved by using the average tax rate for the calculation of rates.[519]

If the regulator differentiates between existing investments and new investments in order to control the investment behavior of the regulated utility, he should use the marginal tax rate[520] for the new investments. However, the investment behavior of regulated utilities only can be influenced by taxes if the latter are not passed through one-to-one to rates and if deviations between expected tax payments used for rate setting and actual tax payments are not completely compensated *ex post*. If the regulated utility knows for certain that it will receive exact compensation for its tax payments, investment decisions cannot be influenced by taxes.[521] Taxes only have an incentive effect if the regulated utility does not get back all taxes and therefore bears itself the economic consequences of marginal investment decisions on tax payments. This is no contradiction to the fact that a regulated utility might *expect* in advance that its tax payments are covered on *average*.

---

[517] It is noteworthy that the U.S. Supreme Court decided already back in 1922 in the context of rate regulation that taxes are to be treated as costs; cf. Houston et al. (1999, 14).

[518] Cf. Schweitzer/Küpper (2003, 177ff.).

[519] Also in the case of non-regulated companies depending on the accounting purpose the marginal tax rate, e.g. for investment decisions, respectively the average tax rate, e.g. for performance measurement, is applied.

[520] Strictly speaking, from the point of view of cost-orientated rate regulation the incremental tax rate of the non-infinitesimal profit change due to the increment of new investments is relevant.

[521] Cf. also Rothwell/Gomez (2003, 102) who state that the net present value is not changed, if the regulated utility receives exact compensation for its tax payments.

Capital providers compare the effects of alternative investments on their consumption possibilities, i.e. after corporate and personal taxes. Personal taxes must be accounted for explicitly in the calculation of cost-orientated regulated rates, if the return on the investment in the regulated utility is treated differently with respect to personal taxes than the return on alternative investments. In this case, the differential of personal taxes should be included as a separate element in the calculation of regulated rates; otherwise the return on the investment in the regulated firm after corporate and personal taxes differs systematically from the return on alternative investments. In an efficient capital market, such differences will be compensated immediately by share price movement. For the assessment of cost of capital of regulated utilities it is usually assumed for simplicity that the return on all investments is equally treated with respect to personal taxes of the investor.[522] In this case, personal taxes are not accounted for explicitly when setting rates, and it is sufficient to assess the adequate risk-adjusted return after definitive corporate taxes and before personal taxes of the investors.[523] Above all, in most instances, the necessary information about all investors as well as their treatment for tax purposes is not available and the effects resulting from personal taxes cannot be assessed. In this case, the attempt to account for personal income taxes in the cost of capital inevitably would be discretionary.

Accounting for corporate taxes in the cost of capital (described in more detail under current German tax law in section 6.4.2) raises a number of methodic questions in its practical application: It has to be decided, whether a post-tax or a pre-tax rate of cost of capital is used in the calculation of regulated rates. If a post-tax rate is used, only the cost of capital after taxes is expressed as a percentage, and absolute tax payments directly enter the calculation of rates. If a pre-tax rate is used, the post-tax rate has to be converted into a pre-tax percentage rate that covers taxes and post-tax claims of capital providers. In this case, absolute tax payments are not considered separately. Both methods are equivalent, if applied consistently; however, they raise different methodic problems in the practical implementation (section 6.4.3). Furthermore, if taxes are accounted for, serious differences in the cost of capital calculation exist, conditional on whether the real interest rate combined with replacement cost depreciation

522 For a discussion of the premises for the irrelevance of personal taxes in the CAPM under German tax law, see Wiese (2003); Richter (2004).

523 However, the problem remains that it is not clear which returns are actually observable at the market; cf. Richter (2003, 326); Wiese (2004, 20).

or the nominal interest combined with either acquisition cost depreciation or used replacement cost depreciation is used.[524]

6.4.2 Accounting for Definitive Corporate Income Taxes Under Current German Tax Law

In the following it is briefly analyzed, how taxes are to be accounted for in the weighted average cost of capital under current German tax law. Definitive corporate income taxes are relevant for the calculation of the post-tax rate of cost of capital, as interest payments on debt reduce the base on which definitive corporate income taxes have to be paid, i.e. they establish a tax shield in the WACC when a free cash flow-approach is used.[525]

$$WACC\,(\text{post - tax}) = \frac{E}{E+D} \cdot r_E + \frac{D}{E+D} \cdot r_D \cdot (1-t) \qquad (6.3)$$

where E and D denote the market value of equity and debt respectively, r_E and r_D denote the cost of equity before personal taxes and the cost of debt before personal taxes respectively and t is the definitive corporate tax rate. It is assumed that the effective tax rate equals the statutory tax rate.

In Germany, a definitive tax on the corporate level is the trade income tax. One thing to take into consideration is that half of the interest payments on durable debt is added to the trade income tax calculation base, and, accordingly, only half of the effective trade income tax rate t_{TI} is to be applied to durable debt. In addition, under the so-called 'Halbeinkünfteverfahren' that came into effect in 2001, the corporate income tax amounting to 25% plus the solidarity surcharge on the corporate income tax amounting to 5.5% together yield a definitive tax burden on corporate income t_{CI} of 26.375%, regardless of whether profits are retained or distributed.[526] If all debt is durable, the post-tax WACC is calculated as follows:[527]

---

[524] For consistent combinations of regulatory rate base, regulatory depreciation scheme and interest rate, see section 5.1.1 and, in particular, Table 5.5.

[525] Alternatively, the tax shield can be accounted for in the cash flows, i.e. in the numerator of discounted cash flows. The denotation as tax shield is somewhat misleading in the case of rate-regulated utilities, at least from the point of view of equity owners, because, assuming a corresponding adjustment of rates to costs, ultimately, rate paying consumers benefit from the tax savings resulting from an increased debt-equity ratio. For the practical implications of uncertain tax shields, see Aders/Wagner (2004, 36ff.).

[526] Accounting for taxes in the WACC under the German Halbeinkünfteverfahren is discussed, among others, by Auge-Dickhut/Moser/Widmann (2000, 366f.);

$$WACC\,(\text{post - tax}) = \frac{E}{E+D} \cdot r_E + \frac{D}{E+D} \cdot r_D \cdot (1-0{,}5 \cdot t_{TI}) \cdot (1-t_{CI}) \qquad (6.4)$$

Thus, the pre-tax WACC yielding the adequate post-tax WACC can be computed:

$$WACC\,(\text{pre-tax}) = \frac{1}{(1-t_{TI}) \cdot (1-t_{CI})} \cdot WACC\,(\text{post-tax}) \qquad (6.5)$$

The pre-tax WACC is the minimum return required by debt and equity owners, plus definitive corporate income taxes. For the purposes of rate regulation, the pre-tax WACC is relevant, as tax payments have to be covered by regulated revenues.[528]

A clear alternative would be to use the post-tax WACC and include absolute tax payments in the calculation of regulated rates, which will be argued for in the next section.

6.4.3 Critical Discussion of the Formula-Based Conversion of a Post-Tax into a Pre-Tax Rate of Cost of Capital

A simple formula-based conversion of a post-tax into a pre-tax rate of cost of capital as made with equation (9) only yields the correct solution for the pre-tax WACC under the following restrictive premises.[529] Firstly, distributed and retained profits have to be treated equally with respect to taxes. In principle, this is fulfilled in Germany since the reform that became effective in 2001. If this is not fulfilled, however, the simple formula-based conversion only gives the correct solution if complete distribution of profits can be assumed. This assumption could be supported only roughly on the grounds that sooner or later all profits are distributed. Secondly, it has

Ring/Castedello/Schlumberger (2000; 360f.); Schüler (2000, 1534); as well as in the context of rate regulation by Schneider (2001, 50ff.).

527 Cf., for example, Baetge/Niemeyer/Kümmel (2005, 327). If not all debt is durable, it has to be distinguished between durable and non-durable debt in the WACC.

528 Schneider's (2001, 50f.) argument that the WACC-method equates trade income and profit subject to corporate income tax, and therefore causes a loss from financing is not valid, if the WACC-method is applied correctly as formulated in the equations (7), (8) and (9); this is also shown by the numerical example in Pedell (2004b, 71ff.).

529 For the discussion of these premises, see Houston et al. (1999, 7ff.); see also Grout (1995, 395).

to be excluded that tax deductible depreciation is accelerated compared to regulatory depreciation, which would involve the creation of capital reserves. As this would be to the advantage of the regulated utility, the tax wedge between post- and pre-tax rate would be overestimated. Thirdly, the regulated utility must be in a fully tax-paying position. Fourthly, the formula-based conversion implicitly assumes the perpetuity model with a constant stream of identical profits to the regulated utility. If these premises are not fulfilled, an individual tax wedge between post-tax and pre-tax rate of cost of capital has to be determined for the regulated utility.

If cost of capital is computed on the basis of a regulatory rate base valued at current costs combined with the real interest rate, the simple formula-based conversion only gives the correct solution for the pre-tax WACC if, fifthly, there are no price increases, i.e. exactly if there is no difference between CCA and HCA. If the formula is used for the conversion of a real post-tax rate to a real pre-tax rate, an error is made, alone taking into account the fact that taxes are calculated on a nominal, not a real base.[530] If depreciation is calculated on the basis of replacement costs, it is higher than tax deductible depreciation in the case of price increases; the difference is subject to taxation and is no longer completely available to compensate inflation.[531] This even holds true when the same depreciation profile is used. Both effects contribute to underestimating pre-tax cost of equity by the formula-based conversion. If, on the other hand, the tax shield is computed with real cost of debt, it is implicitly assumed that the tax advantage only applies to the real cost of capital; therefore the actual tax deductibility of nominal interest payments on debt is underestimated and, accordingly, the cost of debt is overestimated. The overall error made by using the formula to convert a post-tax into a pre-tax rate in the case of price increases depends on the capital structure.

Even in a system of HCA, deviations between tax deductible depreciation and regulatory depreciation cause frictions of payments over time that *per se* inhibit the exact conversion of a post-tax to a pre-tax rate by any known formula. In a system of CCA, a formula-based conversion is even less suited to capture the tax effects. Therefore, abandoning the advantage

[530] If one uses a real post-tax rate as starting point, it would be the accurate procedure (1) to convert this rate to a nominal post-tax rate by adding the price increase, (2) to convert the nominal post-tax rate to the nominal pre-tax rate with the formula and (3) to deduct the price increase from the nominal pre-tax rate; see Houston et al. (1999, 9, fn. 12).

[531] In Germany, this issue is discussed in the context of concepts of net substance maintenance under the keyword of taxation of sham profits [Scheingewinne]; see. Männel (2003, 72ff); Sieben/Maltry (2002a, 68ff.), and (2002b, 413).

of simplicity of the conversion formula in favor of a correct assessment of the expected tax payments with detailed financing plans should be considered. This alternative implies using the post-tax WACC and directly accounting for tax payments as an absolute cost element in the calculation of rates.[532] To this end, cash flows have to be forecasted until the next regulatory review, which is problematic insofar, as they circularly depend on the assessment of the allowed rate of return and the regulatory rate base by the regulator.

Acceleration of tax depreciation compared to regulatory depreciation, for example, can be due to (1) using the declining balance method of depreciation for tax purposes while using a straight-line regulatory depreciation scheme or (2) employing a shorter asset life for tax purposes than for regulatory purposes. Accelerated tax depreciation brings about that the effective tax rate initially lies below and towards the end of the life of assets lies above the statutory tax rate. Clearly, this effect is significantly attenuated for established regulated utilities by the fact that they have a portfolio of assets that are in different phases of their life. If the effective tax rate is used for rate setting, the period over which it is calculated needs to be clarified.[533] This depends on the degree to which regulated rates follow the path of the effective tax rate over the assets' life.[534]

532 Cf. Houston et al. (1999, 5); Siegel (2002, 265).
533 Cf. Houston et al. (1999, 4).
534 See section 4.2.2 for the issue of tax flow-through versus normalization.

7 Conclusions

The central aim of the analysis is the development of a comprehensive economic *concept explaining the impact of rate regulation on the risk and the cost of capital of regulated firms*. The analysis goes beyond existing research on the assessment of the cost of capital for regulated firms - which, in Germany in particular, is predominantly occupied with methodical issues – insofar as it identifies and scrutinizes the variables of rate regulation that determine regulated firms' risk. The analysis in chapter 2 shows that the cost of capital plays a central role in the setting of rates under any of type of rate regulation, as most regulated industries are very capital intensive and, with a view to long-run investment, rates cannot ignore actual costs; otherwise the regulator runs the risk that investment incentives will be seriously distorted. The assessment of the adequate rate of return is all the more important, as regulated rates not only determine the profitability of marginal investments, but the profitability of all investments.

The fundamental themes underlying the relationship between the regulator and the regulated firm are *circularity*, *time-inconsistency*, and *commitment* (chapter 3). Circularity results from the fact that the cost of capital and the market value of the regulated firm both enter into the calculation of rates and, at the same time, are dependent on the design of the regulatory system and process as well as on their handling by the regulator. Time-inconsistency problems arise as, on the one hand, the regulated firm makes a commitment by irreversibly investing in regulated facilities, and, on the other, the regulator ultimately cannot commit to not expropriating the capital owners of the regulated firm once these investments are made. At best, this problem can only be attenuated, as the government by definition is sovereign and lacks a credible commitment device of the last resort.

Against this background, it comes as no surprise that *regulated firms are not risk-less investments*. The complete elimination of risk for the regulated firm would require a hypothetical regulatory regime that guaranteed the regulated firm earned exactly and continuously its cost of capital. In reality, such a regime cannot exist because of time lags, informational problems, as well as the inability of the regulator to fully commit himself to a predetermined regulatory policy. Moreover, from the regulator's perspective, it would not even be desirable to strive for such a regime, as it would eliminate any incentive for efficient investment and operation on the part of the regulated firm.

As to the question of whether rate regulation exerts a buffering effect on the cash flow distribution of the regulated firm, the answer is not clear *a priori* from a theoretical perspective, as there are effects working in both directions. On the one hand, rate regulation is suited to act as a buffer against external cost and demand shocks, but on the other, rate regulation reduces the flexibility of the regulated firm that could be used to smooth out cash flow fluctuations. Empirical evidence seems to indicate that rate regulation actually has a buffering effect and reduces systematic risk. This effect seems to be stronger the more strictly cost-orientated and the more continuous the rate setting. However, existing empirical investigations unanimously show that rate *regulation does not completely eliminate the systematic risk* of the regulated firm.

Rate regulation not only affects the variance of cash flows, it can also have an asymmetric impact by cutting off the upper and/or the lower tail of the cash flow distribution, e.g. by skimming off above normal profits without compensating for below normal profits. Investors require compensation for such an *asymmetric risk.* The obvious way of granting the necessary compensation is to introduce an additional cash flow element into the calculation of rates. If, however, the allowed rate of return is adjusted to compensate for asymmetric regulatory risk, the degree of adjustment will need to be quite substantial.

The risk to which regulated firms are actually exposed depends crucially on the *design of the regulatory scheme*, which determines the extent to which the implemented system of rate regulation deviates from the hypothetical benchmark system of perfect and continuous rate-of-return regulation. When designing the regulatory scheme, the regulator or legislator must be aware of the effects on the behavior of market participants. Based on the *principle of market orientation*, several *guidelines* can be drawn. Firstly, if a regulated service is to be provided by private capital, an adequate return has to be expected by *capital market* participants from regulated rates, otherwise investment incentives will be distorted downwards. In a protected monopoly, the regulator possesses degrees of freedom concerning the allocation of this adequate return across services and rate payers as well as over time. If, however, the *market for the regulated service* is liberalized and opened up for competition, the regulator loses these degrees of freedom. Cross-subsidization of one service or rate payer by another, e.g. in the context of a universal service obligation, is no longer sustainable, unless competitors are prevented from cream-skimming by accompanying measures. Likewise, the regulator has to take into account the development of *input markets* when setting rates, as, for example, constant regulated rates are no longer sustainable with declining input prices in a state of competition. These guidelines must be reflected in the cost concept employed by the regulator, which at the same time must ensure that the level of rates is sufficiently high so as to yield an adequate expected rate of return, and that the rate structure is sustainable. Presumably, the competitive model of rate regulation and the issues associated with it will continue to gain in importance as further liberalization of markets is promoted, for example, by the European Commission, which supports CCA concepts.

Ultimately, the causes of regulatory risk are the *individual design variables of the regulatory system and process.* In chapter 4, a regulatory control panel is developed featuring numerous design variables that can be divided into three groups: (1) variables that determine the scope of regulated markets, firms and decisions; (2) variables that determine the overall regulatory system; and (3) regulatory accounting directives that concretely determine the procedures according to which costs and rates are calculated. A résumé of the main results of the analysis of these individual regulatory design variables is given below.

As far as the design of the overall regulatory system is concerned, the most important variables are the profit elements that are covered by rate regulation, the length of the regulatory review period and of the regulatory lag, the degree of regulatory discretion, and the bandwidth for the actual rate of return around the allowed rate of return that is admitted by the regulator. Empirical evidence shows that the higher the percentage of profit elements covered by rate regulation, the lower the risk to which the regulated firm is exposed, which, in turn, is consistent with the buffering hypothesis. Put differently, price caps tend to be associated with a higher risk for the regulated firm than rate-of-return regulation. Furthermore, the risk of a regulated firm tends to increase with the length of the review period and of the regulatory lag, as *ceteris paribus* more risks are shifted from rate payers to the regulated firm. However, investment adjustments by the regulated firm might reverse this effect in some instances. Regulatory discretion *per se* increases the risk to which a regulated utility is exposed, however, the effect on the perceived risk ultimately depends on how the regulator handles this discretion. Fluctuations in the value of the regulated firm seem to be larger the wider the bandwidth within which the actual rate of return is allowed to deviate from the allowed rate of return. Moreover, the beta factor seems to systematically vary with the movements of the actual rate of return within this bandwidth as the probability of regulatory intervention changes.

The basic accounting variable to be determined in a regulatory regime is the cost concept employed by the regulator. If the cost concept deviates from historical cost accounting and applies an improved efficiency standard, such as implied by the use of LRIC, an asymmetric risk results for the regulated firm requiring compensation. Based on the overall cost concept, a number of individual accounting directives are analyzed in detail. Automatic cost pass-through clauses tend to reduce risk, while normalization of taxes is preferred by capital owners to tax flow-through, as the latter results in a backloading of revenues in the case of accelerated depreciation for tax purposes. As to the assessment of the allowed rate of return, the methods employed to assess the risk-less interest rate, the market equity premium, the firm specific debt and equity premium, and the capital structure determine whether, to what extent, and in which intervals changes of these input parameters are passed through to the allowed rate of return. This feeds back onto how the risks associated with the development of these input parameters are shared between the regulated firm and its rate payers.

The determination of the regulatory rate base involves a multitude of issues that affect the risks borne by the regulated firm. The use of an optimized quantity structure by the regulator, as well as the possibility of disallowances both expose the regulated firm to an asymmetric downside risk. The same holds true if the possibility exists that investments become stranded due to unforeseeable regulatory changes. The concept that is employed for the inclusion of new investments in the regulatory rate base - CWIP *versus* AFUDC - and the applied regulatory depreciation scheme determine the development of the regulatory rate base over time and, accordingly, the profile of revenues over time. As uncertainty concerning regulatory behavior tends to increase the further ahead it lies, regulatory policies that result in the frontloading of revenues are associated with a lower risk.

Regulatory interventions in investment, financing, and risk mitigation decisions also have an impact on the risk of a regulated firm. If a regulated firm is obligated to invest more or earlier than it would do voluntarily, compensation is required. However, in practice, it will be difficult to assess whether an investment obligation is actually binding or not. If a capital structure is set by the regulator, cost of debt and cost of equity have to be adjusted consistently. The admission of risk mitigation measures, such as long-term contracts and hedging, directly affects the residual risks that remain with the regulated firm. One of the most important risk drivers is the scope of competition admitted, which entails subsequent decisions concerning the regulation of access to essential bottleneck facilities and the symmetry of regulation. The admission of competition limits the possibilities of shifting costs to consumers; more specifically, possible distributions of costs across consumers and over time are restricted. This is relevant, in particular, for the financing of universal service obligations and for the choice of a regulatory depreciation scheme. If this is not accounted for, considerable asymmetric risks will result for the regulated firm. Finally, the scope of regulated markets is relevant for the risk of the regulated firm. In the horizontal perspective, this determines the possibilities of diversification; in the vertical perspective, risks are added at each side of the market via the unbundling of a vertically integrated utility.

The setting of regulatory design variables is inextricably related to methodical issues for the *determination of the regulatory rate base* and for the *assessment of the cost of capital rate*. Regarding the regulatory rate base, the central issue underlying the analysis in chapter 5 is the question of whether book values or market values should be used. On the one hand, capital owners expect an adequate return on market values that reflects their opportunities. On the other, the use of book values is predominant in international regulatory practice. It is analyzed how this conflict can be explained and reconciled. Once more, the starting point of the analysis is a hypothetical benchmark system of perfect and continuous rate-of-return regulation that, in theory, maintains equality of market value and book value. It is shown that, in the case of such a system, more than one consistent combination of regulatory rate base, regulatory depreciation scheme and interest rate exists. However, if competition is admitted, the use of used replacement cost in the regulatory rate base combined with the used replacement cost depreciation scheme and nominal interest rate seems advisable, as it is net present value neutral and sustainable under competition. In reality, market values and book values deviate for numerous reasons.

The rationale for using book values in the regulatory rate base can be justified on a number of grounds, the most important ones being that, due to circularity, the cost assessment errors of the regulator and exogenous shocks would be reinforced by the use of market values, and market values could contain components, the return on which seems unjustifiably to be financed by (current) rate payers. A conflict with the return required by investors only arises in the case of existing investments that were hitherto regulated on the basis of market values or were not rate-regulated at all. In these cases, an unexpected switch to a book value based regime of rate regulation has to be accompanied by adequate compensation, otherwise rate regulation boils down to the expropriation of private investors.

The specifics that arise when assessing the cost of capital for a regulated firm using the CAPM-method are investigated in chapter 6. For instance, the estimation periods of the individual input parameters depend on the frequency with which rates are changed, and on how the regulator wants the risks associated with the changes in these input parameters to be shared between the regulated firm and its rate payers. Depending on the aims that the regulator has in mind, he will use embedded or future cost of debt, which will be reflected in the financing risk of the regulated firm. If the regulator does not use the actual capital structure, but a deviating capital structure deemed optimal in his calculations, cost of debt and cost of equity must be adjusted consistently; otherwise an asymmetric regulatory risk results. Definitive corporate income taxes reduce the revenues that are available for meeting the demands of capital owners; therefore they must be covered by regulated rates. A formula-based conversion of a post-tax WACC to a pre-tax WACC inevitably fails, as the necessary premises are not kept, in particular in a system of CCA. Therefore, it seems preferable to use detailed financing plans to compute the effects of definitive corporate income taxes.

The results of chapter 3 and chapter 4 can be *used for several purposes*. Firstly, a regulator or legislator can draw upon them to predict the impact on the risk of the regulated firm when designing and changing a regulatory scheme. This aids with the assessment of the overall advantageousness of a certain regulatory scheme. Secondly, the results can be used to assess the cost of capital of a regulated firm, in particular, when historical data is of limited use, as, for example, is the case when a regulatory regime undergoes major risk-affecting changes, or when other regulated firms subject to a different regulatory regime are used as comparables. Thirdly, the results provide the conceptual basis for developing testable hypotheses for empirical investigations. This is where the *greatest need for further research* exists. In Europe, in particular, few empirical investigations have been carried out up until now. Based on the analysis of regulatory risk, the results of chapter 5 and chapter 6 give the regulator and the regulated firm concrete advice concerning the methods that are employed for determining the regulatory rate base and assessing the rate of the cost of capital for regulated firms.

References

Aders, Christian / Wagner, Marc (2004): Kapitalkosten in der Bewertungspraxis: Zu hoch für die "New Economy" und zu niedrig für die "Old Economy"?. Finanzbetrieb 6 (2004) 1, 30-42.

Ahn, Chang Mo / Thompson, Howard E. (1989): An Analysis of Some Aspects of Regulatory Risk and the Required Rate of Return for Public Utilities. Journal of Regulatory Economics (1) 1989, 241-257.

Alexander, Ian / Estache, Antonio / Oliveri, Adele (2000): A Few Things Transport Regulators Should Know About Risk and the Cost of Capital. Utilities Policy 9 (2000), 1-13.

Alexander, Ian / Mayer, Colin / Weeds, Helen (1996): Regulatory Structure and Risk and Infrastructure Firms: An International Comparison, Policy Research Working Paper 1698, The World Bank, December 1996.

Amihud, Yakow / Mendelson, Haim (1986): Asset Pricing and the Bid-ask Spread. Journal of Financial Economics 17 (1986) 2, 223-249.

Antoniou, Antonios / Pescetto, Gioia (1997): The Effect of Regulatory Announcements on the Cost of Equity Capital of British Telecom. Journal of Business Finance and Accounting (24) 1997 (1), 1-25.

Appleyard, Tony / McLaren, Josie (1996): The Nature of Regulatory Risk, in: Papers from the seminar on regulatory risk and cost of capital in the utilities, Regulatory Policy Research Centre, Hertford College, July 16 1996.

Arbeitskreis Finanzierung der Schmalenbach-Gesellschaft Deutsche Gesellschaft für Betriebswirtschaft e.V. (1996): Wertorientierte Unternehmenssteuerung mit differenzierten Kapitalkosten. zfbf (48) 1996, 543-578.

Archer, Stephen H. (1981): The Regulatory Effects on Cost of Capital in Electric Utilities. Public Utilities Fortnightly, February 26 1981, 36-39.

Arnott, Robert D. / Bernstein, Peter L. (2002): What Risk Premium Is „Normal"? Financial Analysts Journal 58 (2002) 2, 64-85.

Arrow, Kenneth J. / Lind, Robert C. (1970): Uncertainty and the Evaluation of Public Investment Decisions. American Economic Review 60 (1970), 364-378.

Arzac, Enrique R. / Marcus, Matiyahu (1981): Flotation Cost Allowance in Rate of Return Regulation: A Note. Journal of Finance 36 (1981) 5, 1199-1202.

Arzac, Enrique R. / Marcus, Matiyahu (1983): Flotation Cost Allowance in Rate of Return Regulation: A Reply. Journal of Finance 38 (1983) 4, 1339-1341.

Arzac, Enrique R. / Marcus, Matiyahu (1984): Flotation Cost Allowance for the Regulated Firm: A Reply. Journal of Finance 39 (1984) 1, 293-294.

Auge-Dickhut, Stefanie / Moser, Ulrich / Widmann, Bernd (2000): Die geplante Reform der Unternehmensbesteuerung – Einfluss auf die Berechnung und die Höhe des Werts von Unternehmen. Finanzbetrieb (2) 2000, 362-371.

Averch, Harvey / Johnson, Leland J. (1962): Behavior of the Firm under Regulatory Constraint. American Economic Review (52) 1962 (5), 1052-1069.

Awerbuch, Shimon (1992): Depreciation and Profitability Under Rate of Return Regulation. Journal of Regulatory Economics 4 (1992), 63-70.

Baetge, Jörg / Niemeyer, Kai / Kümmel, Jens (2005): Darstellung der Discounted-Cashflow-Verfahren (DCF-Verfahren) mit Beispiel. In: Praxishandbuch der Unternehmensbewertung, ed. by Volker H. Peemöller, 3rd edn., Herne / Berlin 2005, 265-362.

Ballwieser, Wolfgang (1995): Aktuelle Aspekte der Unternehmensbewertung. Die Wirtschaftsprüfung 48 (1995) 4-5, 119-129.

Ballwieser, Wolfgang (1998): Unternehmensbewertung mit Discounted Cash Flow-Verfahren. Die Wirtschaftsprüfung (51) 1998 (3), 81-92.

Ballwieser, Wolfgang (2001a): Zur Ermittlung des Ertragswertes von örtlichen Stromnetzen, Stuttgart et al. 2001.

Ballwieser, Wolfgang (2001b): Unternehmensbewertung, Marktorientierung und Ertragswertverfahren. In: Zum Erkenntnisstand der Betriebswirtschaftslehre am Beginn des 21. Jahrhunderts, Festschrift für Erich Loitlsberger zum 80. Geburtstag, ed. by Udo Wagner, Berlin 2001, 17-31.

Ballwieser, Wolfgang (2002): Der Kalkulationszinsfuß in der Unternehmensbewertung: Komponenten und Ermittlungsprobleme. Die Wirtschaftsprüfung 55 (2002) 14, 736-743.

Ballwieser, Wolfgang (2003): Unternehmensbewertung durch Rückgriff auf Marktdaten. In: Unternehmen bewerten, ed. by Markus Heintzen and Lutz Kruschwitz, Berlin 2003, 13-30.

Ballwieser, Wolfgang (2004): Unternehmensbewertung – Prozeß, Methoden und Probleme, Stuttgart 2004.

Baron, David P. / De Bondt, Raymond R. (1979): Fuel Adjustment Mechanisms and Economic Efficiency. Journal of Industrial Economics 27 (1979) 3, 243-261.

Baron, David P. / De Bondt, Raymond R. (1981): On the Design of Regulatory Price Adjustment Mechanisms. Journal of Economic Theory 24 (1981), 70-94.

Baron, David P. / De Bondt, Raymond R. (1982): Factor Price Changes, Technical Efficiency, and Revenue Requirements Regulation. European Economic Review 19 (1982), 259-276.

Baron, David P. / Taggart, Robert A. (1977): A Model of Regulation under Uncertainty and a Test of Regulatory Bias. Bell Journal of Economics and Management Science 8 (1977), 151-167.

Baumol, William J. / Sidak, J. Gregory (1994): Toward Competition in Local Telephony, Cambridge/Mass., London, Washington 1994.

BDI / VIK / BGW / VKU (2002): Verändevereinbarung zum Netzzugang bei Erdgas (VV Erdgas II) zwischen den Verbänden Bundesverband der Deutschen Industrie e.V. – BDI, Verband der Industriellen Energie- und Kraftwirtschaft e.V. – VIK, Bundesverband der Deutschen Gas- und Wasserwirtschaft e.V. – BGW und Verband kommunaler Unternehmen e.V. – VKU, 3. Mai 2002.

BDI / VIK / VDEW / VDN / ARE / VKU (2001): Verändevereinbarung über Kriterien zur Bestimmung von Netznutzungsentgelten für elektrische Energie und über Prinzipien der Netznutzung, einschließlich der Ergänzung der Anlage 3 „Preisfindungsprinzipien“ vom 23.04.2002 zwischen den Verbänden Bundesverband der Deutschen Industrie e.V. – BDI, Verband der Industriellen Energie- und Kraftwirtschaft e.V. – VIK, Verband der Elektrizitätswirtschaft e.V. – VDEW, Verband der Netzbetreiber – VDN, Arbeitsgemeinschaft regionaler Energieversorgungs-Unternehmen e.V. – ARE und Verband kommunaler Unternehmen e.V. – VKU, 13. Dezember 2001.

Beranek, William / Howe, Keith M. (1990): The Regulated Firm and the DCF Model: Some Lessons From Financial Theory. Journal of Regulatory Economics 2 (1990), 191-200.

Berger, Philip G. / Ofek, Eli (1995): Diversification's Effect on Firm Value. In: Journal of Financial Economics 37 (1995) 1, 39-65.

Bernstein, Peter L. (1997): What Rate of Return Can You Reasonably Expect… or What Can the Long Run Tell Us about the Short Run? In: Financial Analysts Journal 53 (1997) 2, 20-28.

Besanko, David / Spulber, Daniel F. (1992): Sequential Equilibrium Investment by Regulated Firms. Rand Journal of Economics 23 (1992), 153-170.

Besley, Scott / Bolten, Steven E. (1990): What Factors Are Important in Establishing Mandated Returns? A Survey of Utilities and Regulators. Public Utilities Fortnightly 125, June 7, 1990, 26-30.

Biglaiser, Gary / Ma, Ching-to Albert (1999): Investment Incentives of a Regulated Dominant Firm. Journal of Regulatory Economics 16 (1999), 215-235.

Bimberg, Lothar H. (1993): Langfristige Renditenberechnung zur Ermittlung von Risikoprämien, 2nd edn., Frankfurt am Main et al. 1993.

Binder, John J. / Norton, Seth W. (1999): Regulation, Profit Variability and Beta. Journal of Regulatory Economics (15) 1999, 249-265.

Blacconiere, Walter G. / Johnson, Marilyn F. / Johnson, Mark S. (1997): Stranded Costs and Competitive Forces in the Electric Utility Industry. Journal of Accounting, Auditing and Finance 12 (1997) 3, 199-219.

Blume, Marshall (1975): Betas and Their Regression Tendencies. In: Journal of Finance 30 (1975) 3, 785-795.

Bonbright, James C. / Danielsen, Albert L. / Kamerschen, David R. (1988): Principles of Public Utility Rates, 2nd edn., Arlington/Virginia 1988.

Boyes, William J. (1976): An Empirical Investigation of the Averch-Johnson Effect. Economic Inquiry 14 (1976) 1, 25-35.

Brealey, Richard A. / Myers, Stewart C. (2003): Principles of Corporate Finance, 7th edn., Boston et al. 2003.

Brennan, Michael J. / Schwartz, Eduardo S. (1982a): Consistent Regulatory Policy under Uncertainty. The Bell Journal of Economics (13) 1982 (2), 506-521.

Brennan, Michael J. / Schwartz, Eduardo S. (1982b): Regulation and Corporate Investment Policy. Journal of Finance 37 (1982) 2, 289-300.

Brennan, Michael J. / Subrahmanyam, Avanidhar (1996): Market Microstructure and Asset Pricing: On the Compensation for Illiquidity in Stock Returns. Journal of Financial Economics 41 (1996) 3, 441-464.

Brennan, Timothy J. (1999): Comparing "Stranded Cost" Arguments in Telecommunications and Electricity. In: Regulation under Increasing Competition, ed. by Michael A. Crew, Boston/Dordrecht/London 1999, 79-94.

Brigham, Eugene F. / Crum, Roy L. (1977): On the Use of the CAPM in Public Utility Rate Cases. Financial Management 6 (1977), 7-15.

Brigham, Eugene F. / Tapley, T. Craig (1986): Public Utility Finance. In: Handbook of Corporate Finance, ed. by Edward I. Altman und Mary Jane McKinney, New York et al. 1986, 16.1-16.45.

Bromwich, Michael / Vass, Peter (2002): Regulation and Accounting. In: Handwörterbuch Unternehmensrechnung und Controlling, ed. by Hans-Ulrich Küpper and Alfred Wagenhofer, 4th edn., Stuttgart 2002, 1677-1685.

Brown, Stephen J. / Goetzmann, William N. / Ross, Stephen A. (1995): Survival. Journal of Finance 50 (1995) 3, 853-873.

Buckland, Roger / Fraser, Patricia (2001): Political and Regulatory Risk: Beta Sensitivity in U.K. Electricity Distribution. Journal of Regulatory Economics 19 (2001) 1, 5-25.

Bundeskartellamt (2003): Beschluss der 11. Beschlussabteilung des Bundeskartellamts vom 14.02.2003 in dem Verwaltungsverfahren TEAG Thüringer Energie AG wegen der missbräuchlichen Ausnutzung einer marktbeherrschenden Stellung und unbilligen Behinderung von Stromanbietern durch das Fordern überhöhter Netznutzungsentgelte.

Burch, Timothy R. / Nanda, Vikram (2003): Divisional Diversity and the Conglomerate Discount: Evidence from Spinoffs. Journal of Financial Economics 70 (2003) 1, 69-98.

Burness, H Stuart / Patrick, Robert H. (1992): Optimal Depreciation, Payments to Capital, and Natural Monopoly Regulation. Journal of Regulatory Economics 4 (1992), 35-50.

Burns, Phil / Estache, Antonio (1999): Infrastructure Concessions, Information Flows, and Regulatory Risk. Public Policy for the Private Sector Note No. 203, The World Bank Group, December 1999.

Busse von Colbe, Walther (2001): Kostenorientierte Entgeltregulierung von Telekommunikationsdienstleistungen bei sinkenden Beschaffungspreisen für Investitionen. In: Zum Erkenntnisstand der Betriebswirtschaftslehre am Beginn des 21. Jahrhunderts, Festschrift für Erich Loitlsberger zum 80. Geburtstag, ed. by Udo Wagner, Berlin 2001, 47-59.

Busse von Colbe, Walther (2002): Zur Ermittlung der Kapitalkosten als Bestandteil regulierter Entgelte für Telekommunikationsdienstleistungen. zfbf-Sonderheft 48 (2002), 1-25.

CAA (2001): Economic Regulation and the Cost of Capital. Heathrow, Gatwick, Stansted and Manchester Airports' price caps 2003-2008, CAA preliminary Proposals, London, November 2001 (Annex).

Callahan, Carolyn M. / Mohr, Rosanne M. (1989): The Determinants of Systematic Risk: A Synthesis. The Financial Review 24 (1989) 2, 157-181.

Carleton, Willard T. / Chambers, Donald R. / Lakonishok, Josef (1983): Inflation Risk and Regulatory Lag. Journal of Finance 38 (1983) 2, 419-431.

Carne, Simon / Currie, David / Siner, Martin (1999): The Competition and Policy Implications of Regulatory Depreciation and the Asset Base. Regulation Initiative Discussion Paper Series No. 25, London Business School, February 1999.

Chandrasekaran, P.R. / Dukes, William P. (1981): Risk Variables Affecting Rate of Return of Public Utilities. Public Utilities Fortnightly, February 26, 1981, 32-35.

Chao, Hung-po (2002): Risk Management in Electricity Market Design. Presentation at Conference on Wholesale Markets for Electricity, Toulouse, November 22-23, 2002.

Clarke, Roger G. (1980): The Effect of Fuel Adjustment Clauses on the Systematic Risk and Market Values of Electric Utilities. Journal of Finance 35 (1980) 2, 347-358.

Conen, Ralf / Väth, Hubertus (1993): Risikoprämien am deutschen Kapitalmarkt. Die Bank 1993 (11), 642-647.

Conine, Thomas E. / Tamarkin, Maurry (1985): Implications of Skewness in Returns for Utilities' Cost of Equity Capital. Financial Management 14 (1985), 66-71.

Cooper, Ian / Currie, David (1999): The Cost of Capital for the UK Water Sector. Regulation Initiative Discussion Paper Series No. 28, London Business School 1999.

Cornell, Bradford (1992): Regulation, The Cost of Capital and Utility Capital Budgeting - Some New Issues. Discussion Paper, University of California, Los Angeles 1992.

Cornell, Bradford / Hirshleifer, John I. / James, Elisabeth P. (1997): Estimating the Cost of Equity Capital. Contemporary Finance Digest 1 (1997) 1, 5-26.

Courville, Léon (1974): Regulation and Efficiency in the Electric Utility Industry. Bell Journal of Economics and Management Science 5 (1974), 53-74.

Crespo, Joseph G. / Giacchino, Leonardo (2003): Improving Market Power Mitigation Rules for Peaking Units. The Electricity Journal 16 (2003) October, 47-60.

Crew, Michael A. / Kleindorfer, Paul (1985): Governance Costs of Rate-of-Return Regulation. Zeitschrift für die gesamte Staatswissenschaft 141 (1985) 1, 104-123.

Crew, Michael A. / Kleindorfer, Paul R. (1986): The Economics of Public Utility Regulation. Cambridge/Mass. 1986.

Crew, Michael A. / Kleindorfer, Paul (1992a): Economic Depreciation and the Regulated Firm under Competition and Technological Change. Journal of Regulatory Economics 4 (1992) 1, 51-61.

Crew, Michael A. / Kleindorfer, Paul R. (1992b): Incentive Regulation, Capital Recovery and Technological Change in Public Utilities. In: Economic Innovations in Public Utility Regulation, ed. by Michael A. Crew, Boston/ Dordrecht/London 1992, 57-79.

Crew, Michael A. / Kleindorfer, Paul R. (1998): Efficient Entry, Monopoly, and the Universal Service Obligation in Postal Service. Journal of Regulatory Economics (14) 1998 (2), 103-125.

Crew, Michael A. / Kleindorfer, Paul R. (1999): Stranded Assets in Network Industries in Transition. In: Regulation under Increasing Competition, ed. by Michael A. Crew, Boston/Dordrecht/London 1999, 63-78.

Crew, Michael A. / Kleindorfer, Paul R. (2001a): Whither the USO under Competitive Entry: A Microstructure Approach. In: Future Directions in Postal Reform, ed. by Michael A. Crew and Paul R. Kleindorfer, Boston/Dordrecht/London 2001, 117-140.

Crew, Michael A. / Kleindorfer, Paul R. (2001b): A Critique of the Theory of Incentive Regulation: Implications for the Design of Performance Based Regulations for Postal Service. In: Future Directions in Postal Reform, ed. by Michael A. Crew und Paul R. Kleindorfer, Boston/Dordrecht/London 2001, 37-65.

Crew, Michael A. / Kleindorfer, Paul R. (2001c): Deregulation and the Default Service Obligation: Putty-Putty, Putty-Clay or Humpty-Dumpty, Working Paper 01-36-PK, Risk Management and Decision Processes Center, Wharton School, University of Pennsylvania.

Crew, Michael A. / Kleindorfer, Paul R. (2002): Regulatory Economics: Twenty Years of Progress? Journal of Regulatory Economics 21 (2002) 1, 5-22.

Crew, Michael A. / Kleindorfer, Paul R. / Schlenger, Donald L. (1987): Governance Costs of Regulation for Water Supply. Regulating Utilities in an Era of Deregulation, ed. by Michael Crew, Houndsmills/London 1987, 43-62.

D'Almeida, Jaime / Tardiff, Timothy / Taylor, William / Zarkadas, Charles (2000): An Economic Evaluation of Network Cost Models. NERA, August 7, 2000 (Appendix A).

Damodaran, Aswath (2002): Investment Valuation. 2nd edn., New York 2002.

Dasgupta, Sudipto / Nanda, Vikram (1993): Bargaining and Brinkmanship: Capital Structure Choice by Regulated Firms. International Journal of Industrial Organization 11 (1993) 475-497.

Datar, Vinay T. / Naik, Narayan Y. / Radcliffe, Robert (1998): Liquidity and Stock Returns: An Alternative Test. Journal of Financial Markets 1 (1998) 2, 203-219.

Davidson, Wallace N. / Chandy, P.R. / Walker, Mike (1985): The Stock Market Effects of Trucking Deregulation. Akron Business and Economic Review 16 (1985) 4, 44-50.

Davidson, Wallace N. / Rangan, Nanda / Rosenstein, Stuart (1997): Regulation and Systematic Risk in the Electric Utility Industry: A Test of the Buffering Hypothesis. The Financial Review 32 (1997) 1, 163-184.

Diedrich, Ralf (2004): Gutachten zur Bestimmung und zur Höhe des kalkulatorischen Eigenkapitalkostensatzes von Netzbetreibern in der Gaswirtschaft. By order of Bundesverband der deutschen Gas- und Wasserwirtschaft e. V. and Verband kommunaler Unternehmen e. V., Leipzig, June 2004.

Dixit, Avinash K. / Pindyck, Robert S. (1994): Investment under Uncertainty. Princeton NJ 1994.

Drukarczyk, Jochen (2003): Unternehmensbewertung. 4th edn., Munich 2003.
Dubin, Jeffrey A. / Navarro, Peter (1982): Regulatory Climate and the Cost of Capital. In: Regulatory Reform and Public Utilities, ed. by Michael A. Crew, Boston/Dordrecht/London 1982, 141-166.
Economides, Nicholas (1999): Real Options and the Costs of the Local Telecommunications Network. In: The New Investment Theory of Real Options and its Implications for Telecommunications Economics, ed. by James Alleman and Eli Noam, Boston/Dordrecht/London 1999, 207-213.
Ehrmann, Thomas / Mellewigt, Thomas (1997): Die Kostenrechnung des marktbeherrschenden Anbieters als Kernproblem einer effizienten Regulierung im Telekommunikationssektor. zfbf 49 (1997), 255-263.
Elton, Edwin J. / Gruber, Martin J. (1971): Valuation and the Cost of Capital for Regulated Industries. Journal of Finance 26 (1971), 661-670.
Elton, Edwin J. / Gruber, Martin J. (1977): Optimal Investment and Financing Patterns for a Firm Subject to Regulation with a Lag. Journal of Finance 32 (1977) 5, 1485-1500.
Elton, Edwin J. / Gruber, Martin J. / Lieber, Zvi (1975): Valuation, Optimum Investment and Financing for the Firm Subject to Regulation. Journal of Finance 30 (1975) 2, 401-425.
Ergas, Henry / Hornby, James / Little, Iain / Small, John (2001): Regulatory Risk. Paper prepared for the ACCC Regulation and Investment Conference, Manly, March 26-27, 2001.
Fama, Eugene F. (1977): Risk-adjusted Discount Rates and Capital Budgeting under Uncertainty. Journal of Financial Economics 5 (1977) 1, 3-24.
Fama, Eugene F. (1996): Discounting Under Uncertainty. Journal of Business 69 (1996) 4, 415-428.
FCC (2003): Triennial Review Order. Federal Communications Commission (FCC 03-36), Report and Order and Order on Remand and Further Notice of Proposed Rulemaking, Washington, released August 21, 2003.
Financial Times Deutschland, various editions.
Fitzpatrick, Dennis B. / Stitzel, Thomas E. (1978): Capitalizing an Allowance for Funds Used during Construction: The Impact on Earnings Qualtiy. Public Utilities Fortnightly, January 19, 1978, 18-22.
Francis, Nic /Grout, Paul / Zalewska, Anna (2001): The Impact on the Stock Market of Changes in Regulation of Companies. mimeo Leverhulme Center for Market and Public Organisation, University of Bristol, June 2001.
Franke, Günter / Hax, Herbert (2004): Finanzwirtschaft des Unternehmens und Kapitalmarkt. 5th edn., Berlin et al. 2004.
Frankfurter Allgemeine Zeitung, various editions.
Freygang, Winfried (1993): Kapitalallokation in diversifizierten Unternehmen: Ermittlung divisionaler Eigenkapitalkosten. Wiesbaden 1993.
Friedl, Gunther (2003): Abschreibungsermittlung, Preisregulierung und Investitionsanreize, Working Paper, Institute of Production Management and Management Acounting, Ludwig Maximilian University of Munich, 2003.

Fuller, Russell J. / Kerr, Halbert S. (1981): Estimating the Divisional Cost of Capital: An Analysis of the Pure-Play Technique. Journal of Finance 36 (1981) 5, 997-1009.

Gandolfi / Jenkinson / Mayer (1996): Regulation and the Cost of Capital. Working Paper, School of Management Studies, University of Oxford, 1996.

Geddes, Rick / Vinod, Hrsihikesh D. (2002): CEO Tenure, Board Composition, and Regulation. Journal of Regulatory Economics 21 (2002) 2, 217-235.

Gerke, Wolfgang (2003): Gutachten zur risikoadjustierten Bestimmung des Kalkulationszinssatzes in der Stromnetzkalkulation. Friedrich Alexander University of Erlangen-Nürnberg, February 2003.

Gilbert, Richard J. / Newberry, David M. (1994): The Dynamic Efficiency of Regulatory Constitutions. Rand Journal of Economics (25) 1994 (4), 538-554.

Golec, Joseph (1990): The Financial Effects of Fuel Adjustment Clauses on Electric Utilities. Journal of Business 63 (1990) 2, 165-186.

Gombola, Michael J. / Kahl, Douglas R. (1990): Time-Series Processes of Utility Betas: Implications for Forecasting Systematic Risk. Financial Management 19 (1990) 3, 84-93.

Gordon, Myron J. (1977): Comparison of Historical Cost and General Price Level Adjusted Cost Rate Base Regulation. Journal of Finance 32 (1977) 5, 1501-1512.

Graham, John R. / Lemmon, Michael L. / Wolf, Jack G. (2002): Does Corporate Diversification Destroy Value? Journal of Finance 57 (2002) 2, 695-720.

Grayburn, James / Hern, Richard /Lay, Helen (2002): A Report for the National Audit Office on Regulatory Risk by NERA. Published in "Pipes and Wires", National Audit Office, 10 April 2002.

Greenwald, Bruce C. (1980): Admissible Rate Bases, Fair Rates of Return and the Structure of Regulation. Journal of Finance 35 (1980) 2, 359-368.

Greenwald, Bruce C. (1984): Rate Base Selection and the Structure of Regulation. Rand Journal of Economics 15 (1984) 1, 85-95.

Grinblatt, Mark / Titman, Sheridan (2002): Financial Markets and Corporate Strategy. 2nd edn., Boston/Mass. et al. 2002.

Grout, Paul (1995): The Cost of Capital in Regulated Industries. In: The Regulatory Challenge, ed. by M. Bishop, J. Kay und C. Mayer, Oxford 1995, 386-407.

Grout, Paul A. / Zalewska, Anna (2001): Circularity and the Undervaluation of Privatised Companies. CMPO Working Paper Series No. 01/39, University of Bristol, August 2001.

Gunn, Calum (2003): On Intertemporal Subsidy-free Prices and Economic Depreciation: Constrained Market Pricing Revisited. Journal of Regulatory Economics 24 (2003) 2, 135-159.

Gupta, Pankaj / Lamech, Ranjit / Mazhar, Farida / Wright, Joseph (2002): Mitigating Regulatory Risk for Distribution Privatization – The World Bank Partial Risk Guarantee. Energy & Mining Sector Board Discussion Paper Series, Paper No. 5, World Bank, November 2002.

Hachmeister, Dirk (2000): Der Discounted Cash Flow als Maß der Unternehmenswertsteigerung. 4th edn., Frankfurt am Main et al. 2000.

Hagerman, Robert L. / Ratchford, Brian T. (1978): Some Determinants of Allowed Rates of Return on Equity to Electric Utilities. The Bell Journal of Economics 9 (1978) 1, 46-55.

Hamada, Robert S. (1969): Portfolio Analysis, Market Equilibrium and Corporation Finance. Journal of Finance 24 (1969) 1, 13-31.

Haugen, R.A. / Stroyny, A.L. / Wichern, D.W. (1978): Rate Regulation, Capital Structure, and the Sharing of Interest Rate Risk in the Electric Utility Industry. Journal of Finance 33 (1978) 3, 707-721.

Hausman, Jerry A. (1997): Valuing the Effect of Regulation on New Services in Telecommunications. Brookings Papers on Economic Activity: Microeconomics, 1-38.

Hausman, Jerry A. (1999): The Effect of Sunk Costs in Telecommunications Regulation. In: The New Investment Theory of Real Options and its Implications for Telecommunications Economics, ed. by James Alleman and Eli Noam, Boston/Dordrecht/London 1999, 191-204.

Hausman, Jerry / Myers, Stewart (2002): Regulating the United States Railroads: The Effects of Sunk Costs and Asymmetric Risk. Journal of Regulatory Economics 22 (2002) 3, 287-310.

Hax, Herbert (1998): Finanzierung. In: Vahlens Kompendium der Betriebswirtschaftslehre, ed. by Michael Bitz, Klaus Dellmann, Michel Domsch and Franz W. Wagner, Vol. 1, 4th ed., Munich 1998, 175-233.

Hern, Richard / Zalewska, Ania (2001): Recent Evidence on Beta and the Cost of Capital for UK Electricity Companies. NERA Topics 25, London, October 2001.

Herter, Ronald N. (1994): Unternehmenswertorientiertes Management: Strategische Erfolgsbeurteilung von dezentralen Organisationseinheiten auf der Basis der Wertsteigerungsanalyse. Munich 1994.

Hofmann, Christian (2002): Relative Performancebewertung in regulierten und nicht-regulierten Märkten. zfbf-Sonderheft 48 (2002), 57-91.

Hohenadel, Werner / Reiners, Frank (2000): Das Kalkulationssystem INTRA der Deutschen Telekom AG. Kostenrechnungspraxis 44 (2000) 3, 159-170.

Holburn, Guy L.F. / Spiller, Pablo T. (2002): Interest Group Representation in Administrative Institutions: The Impact of Consumer Advocates and Elected Commissioners on Regulatory Policy in the United States. Working Paper, University of California, October 2002.

Houston, Graham (1996): Regulatory Tobin's Q, Tracking Shares and All That. NERA Topics 18-1996.

Houston, Greg / Makholm, Jeff / Hern, Richard / Whitfield, Ann (1999): Taxation and the Cost of Capital: A Review of Overseas Experience. Final Report for ACCC. Prepared by NERA, Sydney, April 1999.

Howe, Keith M. (1984): Flotation Cost Allowance for the Regulated Firm: A Comment. Journal of Finance 39 (1984) 1, 289-291.

Howe, Keith M. / Beranek, William (1992): Issue Costs and Regulated Returns: A General Approach. Journal of Regulatory Economics 4 (1992), 365-378.

Ibbotson Associates (2003): Stocks, Bonds, Bills, and Inflation 2003 Yearbook. Chicago 2003.

Ickenroth, Bernd (1998): Ein integrativer Ansatz zur Bestimmung der Kapitalkosten von Telekommunikationsunternehmen. WIK-Newsletter 1998 (33), 3-6.

Jacoby, Gady / Fowler, David, J. / Gottesman, Aron A. (2000): The Capital Asset Pricing Model and the Liquidity Effect: A Theoretical Approach. Journal of Financial Markets 3 (2000) 1, 69-81.

Johanning, Lutz / Ruhle, Ernst-Olav (2004): Assessment of Major Regulatory Decisions in France: An Event Study for France Télécom. In: Regulation and Capital Market Evaluation in Telecommunications, ed. by Hermann-Josef Piepenbrock, Fabian Schuster and Ernst-Olav Ruhle, Lohmar – Cologne 2004, 143-164.

John, Kose / Saunders, Anthony (1983): Asymmetry of Information, Regulatory Lags and Optimal Incentive Contracts: Theory and Evidence. Journal of Finance 38 (1983) 2, 391-404.

Joskow, Paul L. (1972): The Determination of the Allowed Rate of Return in a Formal Regulatory Hearing. Bell Journal of Economics and Management Science 3 (1972) 2, 632-644.

Kahn, Alfred E. (1988): The Economics of Regulation – Principles and Institutions. Cambridge/Mass. et al. 1988.

Kahn, Alfred E. (2002): The Deregulatory Tar Baby: The Precarious Balance Between Regulation and Deregulation, 1970-2000 and Henceforward. Journal of Regulatory Economics 21 (2002) 1, 35-56.

Kahn, Alfred E. / Stoft, Steven / Belden, Timothy (1995): Impact of Power Purchases from Non-Utilities on the Utility Cost of Capital. Utilities Policy 5 (1995) 1, 3-11.

Karl, Hans-Dieter (2003): Allgemeine Elektrizitätswirtschaft: Stabilisierung der Investitionen. ifo-Schnelldienst 56 (2003) 1, 38-44.

Kempf, Alexander (2002): Sachverständigengutachten gemäß Beschluß der 1. Kammer des Verwaltungsgerichts Köln vom 21.06.2001 in dem verwaltungsgerichtlichen Verfahren 1 K 8003/98 Deutsche Telekom AG gegen Bundesrepublik Deutschland. Köln, 18. September 2002.

Knieps, Günter (1998): Der Irrweg analytischer Kostenmodelle als regulatorischer Schattenrechnungen: Kritische Analyse der Stellungnahmen zum WIK-Kostenmodell. MultiMedia und Recht (MMR) 1 (1998) 11, 598-602.

Knieps, Günter (2001): Wettbewerbsökonomie, Berlin et al. 2001.

Knieps, Günter (2002): Entscheidungsorientierte Ermittlung der Kapitalkosten in liberalisierten Netzindustrien, Working Paper, Albert Ludwig University of Freiburg 2002.

Knieps, Günter (2003): Entscheidungsorientierte Ermittlung der Kapitalkosten in liberalisierten Netzindustrien. ZfB 73 (2003) 9, 989-1006.

Knieps, Günter / Küpper, Hans-Ulrich / Langen, René (2001): Abschreibungen bei fallenden Wiederbeschaffungspreisen in stationären und nicht-stationären Märkten. zfbf 53 (2001) 8, 759-776.

Kolb, Robert W. / Morin, Roger A. / Gay, Gerald D. (1983): Regulation, Regulatory Lag, and the Use of Futures Markets. Journal of Finance 38 (1983) 2, 405-418.

Kolbe, A. Lawrence / Borucki, (1998): The Impact of Stranded-Cost Risk on Required Rates of Return for Electric Utilities: Theory and an Example. Journal of Regulatory Economics (13) 1998, 255-275.

Kolbe, A. Lawrence / Read, James A. / Hall, George R. (1984): The Cost of Capital – Estimating the Rate of Return for Public Utilities. Cambridge/Mass. / London 1984.

Kolbe, A. Lawrence / Tye, William B. / Myers, Stewart C. (1993): Regulatory Risk: Economic Principles and Applications to Natural Gas Pipelines and Other Industries. Boston / Dordrecht / London 1993.

Kole, Stacey R. / Lehn, Kenneth M. (1999): Deregulation and the Adaptation of Governance Structures: The Case of the U.S. Airline Industry. Journal of Financial Economics 52 (1999), 79-117.

Kryzanowski, Lawrence / Jalilvand, Abolhassan (1983): Statistical Tests of the Accuracy of Alternative Forecasts: Some Results for U.S. Utility Betas. The Financial Review 19 (1983) 3, 319-335.

Küpper, Hans-Ulrich (1985): Investitionstheoretische Fundierung der Kostenrechnung. zfbf 37 (1985), 26-46.

Küpper, Hans-Ulrich (1995): Unternehmensplanung und –steuerung mit pagatorischen oder kalkulatorischen Erfolgsrechnungen.. zfbf-Sonderheft 34 (1995), 19-50.

Küpper, Hans-Ulrich (2005): Controlling: Konzeption, Aufgaben und Instrumente. 4th edn., Stuttgart 2005.

Küpper, Hans-Ulrich (2002): Kostenorientierte Preisbestimmung für regulierte Märkte. zfbf-Sonderheft 48 (2002), 27-55.

Küpper, Hans-Ulrich / Pedell, Burkhard (2005a): Gutachten zum Entwurf der Verordnung über die Entgelte für den Zugang zu Gasversorgungsnetzen (Gasnetzentgeltverordnung – GasNEV) vom 13. April 2005, insbesondere zur Saldierung von Abschreibungen und Reinvestitionen, Munich, April 2005.

Küpper, Hans-Ulrich / Pedell, Burkhard (2005b): Gutachten zum Entwurf der Verordnung über die Entgelte für den Zugang zu Gasversorgungsnetzen (Gasnetzentgeltverordnung – GasNEV) vom 16. Juni 2005, insbesondere zur kalkulatorischen Eigenkapitalverzinsung, Munich, forthcoming.

Laffont, Jean-Jacques / Tirole, Jean (1993): A Theory of Incentives in Procurement and Regulation. Cambridge/Mass. / London 1993.

LaGattuta, Daniel A. / Stein, Jeremy C. / Tennican, Michael L. / Usher, Stephen E. / Youngen, Jeff (2000): Cashflow-at-Risk and Financial Policy for Electricity Companies in the New World Order. The Electricity Journal 2000, 15-20.

Lehn, Kenneth M. (2002): Corporate Governance in the Deregulated Telecommunications Industry: Lessons from the Airline Industry. Telecommunications Policy 26 (2002), 225-242.

Lesser, Jonathan A. / Ainspan, Malcolm (1996): Using Markets to Value Stranded Costs. The Electricity Journal 9 (1996) October, 66-74.

Levhari, David / Levy, Haim (1977): The Capital Asset Pricing Model and the Investment Horizon. Review of Economic Studies 59 (1977) 1, 92-104.

Lewellen, Wilbur G. / Mauer, David C. (1993): Public Utility Valuation and Risk under Incentive Regulation. Journal of Regulatory Economics 5 (1993), 263-287.

Li, Haitao / Xu, Yuewu (2002): Survival Bias and the Equity Premium Puzzle. Journal of Finance 57 (2002) 5, 1981-1995.

Lind, Robert C. / Arrow, Kenneth J. / Corey, Gordon R. / Dasgupta, Partha / Sen, Amartya K. / Stauffer, Thomas / Stiglitz, Joseph E. / Stockfisch, J.A. / Wilson, Robert (1982): Discounting for Time and Risk in Energy Policy. Washington D.C. 1982.

Lins, Karl / Servaes, Henri (1999): International Evidence on the Value of Corporate Diversification. Journal of Finance 54 (1999) 6, 2215-2239.

Lintner, John (1965): The Valuation of Risk Assets and the Selection of Risky Investments in Stock Portfolios and Capital Budgets. Review of Economics and Statistics 47 (1965), 13-37.

Litzenberger, Robert / Ramaswamy, Krishna / Sosin, Howard (1980): On the CAPM Approach to the Estimation of A Public Utility's Cost of Equity Capital. Journal of Finance 35 (1980) 2, 369-383.

Loudder, Martha L. / Khurana, Inder K. / Boatsman, James R. (1996): Market Valuation of Regulatory Assets in Public Utility Firms. The Accounting Review 71 (1996) 3, 357-373.

Loxley, Colin J. (1999): An Economic Analysis of the Stranded Cost Issue Facing Electric Utilities and Policymakers Today. In: Regulation under Increasing Competition, ed. by Michael A. Crew, Boston/Dordrecht/London 1999, 95-104.

Lücke, Wolfgang (1955): Investitionsrechnungen auf der Grundlage von Ausgaben oder Kosten. zfbf (7) 1955, 310-324.

MacKerron, Gordon / Lieb-Doczy, Enese (2003): Balancing Security and Liberalization. Power in Europe, Issue 408, September 1st, 2003, 9-11.

Männel, Wolfgang (2003): Gutachten zu den Preisfindungsprinzipien der Verbändevereinbarung VV II plus vom 13.12.2001 und 23.04.2002, Nürnberg and Lauf an der Pegnitz, March 14, 2003.

Maloney, Michael T. / McCormick, Robert E. / Sauer, Raymond D. (1997): On Stranded Cost Recovery in the Deregulation of the U.S. Electric Power Industry. Natural Resources Journal 37 (1997) 1, 59-123.

Mandy, David M. (2000): Killing the Goose That May Have Laid the Golden Egg: Only the Data Know Whether Sabotage Pays. Journal of Regulatory Economics 17 (2000) 2, 157-172.

Marshall, William (1980): The Effect of Fuel Adjustment Clauses on the Systematic Risk and Market Values of Electric Utilities: Discussion. Journal of Finance 35 (1980) 2, 385-387.

Mayer, Colins / Jenkinson, Tim (2000): Regulatory Short-termism Revisited. The Utilities Journal, January 16, 2000.b

McMullen, Starr B. (1993): Profits and the Cost of Capital to the U.S. Trunk Airline Industry Under CAB Regulation, New York / London 1993.

Miller, Merton H. / Modigliani, Franco (1961): Dividend Policy, Growth, and the Valuation of Shares. The Journal of Business 34 (1961) 4, 411-433.

Miller, Merton H. / Modigliani, Franco (1966): Some Estimates of the Cost of Capital to the Electric Utility Industry, 1954-1957. American Economic Review 56 (1966), 333-391.

Modigliani, Franco / Miller, Merton H. (1958): The Cost of Capital, Corporation Finance, and the Theory of Investment. American Economic Review 48 (1958) 3, 261-297.

Monopolkommission (2003): Telekommunikation und Post 2003: Wettbewerbsintensivierung in der Telekommunikation – Zementierung des Postmonopols. Sondergutachten der Monopolkommission gemäß § 81 Abs. 3 Telekommunikationsgesetz und § 44 Postgesetz, Bonn 2003.

Morana, Claudio / Sawkins, John W. (2000): Regulatory Uncertainty and Share Price Volatility: the English and Welsh Water Industry's Periodic Price Review. Journal of Regulatory Economics (17) 2000 (1), 87-100.

Morin, Roger A. (1994): Regulatory Finance: Utilities' Cost of Capital. Arlington/Virginia 1994.

Mossin, Jan (1966): Equilibrium in a Capital Asset Market. Econometrica 34 (1966), 768-783.

Myers, Stewart C. (1972): The Application of Finance Theory to Public Utility Rate Cases. Bell Journal of Economics and Management Science 3 (1972) 1, 58-97.

Myers, Stewart C. (1992): Capital Structure and the Cost of Capital for Regulated Companies. Prepared for: The New York Energy Utilities Collaborative, The Brattle Group, Cambridge/Mass., December 4, 1992.

Navarro, Peter (1982): Public Utility Commission Regulation: Performance, Determinants, and Energy Policy Impacts. The Energy Journal 3 (1982) 2, 119-139.

NECG (2003): Australian Competition Tribunal Condemns ACCC Approach to Setting Allowed Returns for Regulated Firms. Network Economics Consulting Group, Canberra 2003.

NERA (2003): Evidence on the Cost of Capital for UK Water. A Summary Paper, National Economic Research Associates (NERA), London, August 2003.

Newbery, David M. (1997): Determining the Regulatory Asset Base for Utility Price Regulation. Utilities Policy 6 (1997) 1, 1-8.

Norton, Seth W. (1985): Regulation and Systematic Risk: The Case of Electric Utilities. Journal of Law and Economics 28 (1985), 671-686.

Nwaeze, Emeka T. (1997): Economics Determinants of ROE Adjustments in the Electric Utility Industry. Advances in Financial Planning and Forecasting 7 (1997), 35-50.

Nwaeze, Emeka T. (2000a): Positive and Negative Earnings Surprises, Regulatory Climate, and Stock Returns. Contemporary Accounting Research 17 (2000) 1, 107-134.

Nwaeze, Emeka T. (2000b): Deregulation of the Electric Power Industry: The Earnings, Risk, and Return Effects. Journal of Regulatory Economics (17) 2000 (1), 49-67.

Oftel (1992): BT's Cost of Capital: A Consultative Document issued by the Director General of Telecommunications. London, January 1992.

Patterson, Cleveland S. (1983): Flotation Cost Allowance in Rate of Return Regulation: Comment. Journal of Finance 38 (1983) 4, 1335-1338.

Pedell, Burkhard (2000): Commitment als Wettbewerbsstrategie, Berlin 2000.

Pedell, Burkhard (2003a): Festlegung der Kapitalkostenbasis für Zwecke der Entgeltregulierung, Working Paper, Institute of Production Management and Management Accounting, Ludwig Maximilian University of Munich, 2003.

Pedell, Burkhard (2003b): Regulatory Risk and the Cost of Capital for Regulated Utilities, Working Paper, Institute of Production Management and Management Accounting, Ludwig Maximilian University of Munich, 2003.

Pedell, Burkhard (2004a): Kapitalmarktbasierte Ermittlung des Kapitalkostensatzes entgeltregulierter Unternehmungen, Working Paper, Institute of Production Management and Management Accounting, Ludwig Maximilian University of Munich, 2004.

Pedell, Burkhard (2004b): Cost of Capital Assessment for Rate Regulated Utilities - A Critical Overview of Methods Used in Regulatory Hearings. In: Regulation and Capital Market Evaluation in Telecommunications, ed. by Hermann-Josef Piepenbrock, Fabian Schuster and Ernst-Olav Ruhle, Lohmar – Cologne 2004, 51-99.

Pedell, Burkhard (2005): Regulierung von TIME-Märkten und ihre Implikationen für die Kostenrechnung regulierter Unternehmen, in: Zeitschrift für Controlling & Management 49 (2005), Sonderheft 2, Controlling in TIME-Unternehmen, ed. by Thomas Hess, 4-14.

Peltzman, Sam (1976): Towards a More General Theory of Regulation. Journal of Law and Economics (19) 1976, 211-40.

Petersen, H. Craig (1975): An Empirical Test of Regulatory Effects. Bell Journal of Economics 6 (1975) 1, 111-126.

Pettit, Justin / Gulic, Ivan / Park, April (2001): The Equity Risk Measurement Handbook. EVAluation 3 (2001) 3, Stern Stewart Research, New York.

Picot, Arnold / Burr, Wolfgang (1996): Regulierung der Deregulierung im Telekommunikationssektor. zfbf 48 (1996) 2, 173-200.

Picot, Arnold / Burr, Wolfgang (1997): Zur Leistungsfähigkeit von Regulierungsinstrumenten und Regulierungsinstanzen. zfbf 49 (1997) 3, 264-272.

Posner, Richard A. (1974): Theories of Economic Regulation. Bell Journal of Economics and Management Science 5 (1974) 2, 335-358.

Posner, Richard A. (1975): The Social Costs of Monopoly and Regulation. Journal of Political Economy 83 (1975) 4, 807-828.

Prager, Robin A. (1989): The Effects of Regulatory Policies on the Cost of Debt for Electric Utilities: An Empirical Investigation. Journal of Business 62 (1989) 1, 33-53.

Preinreich, Gabriel A.D. (1937): Valuation and Amortization. The Accounting Review 12 (1937), 209-226.

Rajan, Raghuram / Servaes, Henri / Zingales, Luigi (2000): The Cost of Diversity: The Diversification Discount and Inefficient Investment. Journal of Finance 55 (2000) 1, 35-80.

Rao, Ramesh / Moyer, Charles R. (1994): Regulatory Climate and Electric Utility Capital Structure Decisions. The Financial Review 29 (1994) 1, 97-124.

RegTP (1999): Tätigkeitsbericht 1998/1999 der Regulierungsbehörde für Telekommunikation und Post nach § 81 Abs. 1 Telekommunikationsgesetz und § 47 Abs. 1 Postgesetz. Bonn 1999.

RegTP (2003): Tätigkeitsbericht 2002/2003 der Regulierungsbehörde für Telekommunikation und Post nach § 81 Abs. 1 Telekommunikationsgesetz und § 47 Abs. 1 Postgesetz. Bonn, December 2003.

Reichelstein, Stefan (1997): Investment Decisions and Managerial Performance Evaluation. Review of Accounting Studies 39 (1997) 2, 157-180.

Reiners, Frank (2000): Bemessung kalkulatorischer Abschreibungen, Zinsen und Gewinne vor dem Hintergrund des Unternehmenserhaltungsziels – Eine Analyse unter Berücksichtigung der Rahmenbedingungen verschiedener Wirtschaftszweige. Frankfurt am Main et al. 2000.

Richter, Frank (2003): Relativer Unternehmenswert und Einkommensteuer oder: Was ist paradox am Steuerparadoxon? In: Kapitalgeberansprüche, Marktwertorientierung und Unternehmenswert, Festschrift für Jochen Drukarczyk zum 65. Geburtstag, ed. by Frank Richter, Andreas Schüler and Bernhard Schwetzler, Munich 2003, 307-329.

Richter, Frank (2004): Valuation With or Without Personal Income Taxes? Schmalenbach Business Review 56 (2004) 1, 20-45.

Richter, Frank / Simon-Keuenhof, Kai (1996): Bestimmung durchschnittlicher Kapitalkostensätze deutscher Industrieunternehmen – Eine empirische Untersuchung. BFuP 48 (1996) 6, 698-708.

Riddick, Leigh A. (1992): The Effects of Regulation on Stochastic Systematic Risk. Journal of Regulatory Economics 4 (1992), 139-157.

Riechmann, Christoph / Schulz, Walter (1996): Rahmenbedingungen der Preisreglementierung aus volkswirtschaftlicher Sicht. BFuP 48 (1996) 4, 382-403.

Ring, Stephan / Castedello, Marc / Schlumberger, Erik (2000): Auswirkungen des Steuersenkungsgesetzes auf die Unternehmensbewertung. Finanzbetrieb (2) 2000, 356-361.

Robichek, Alexander A. (1978): Regulation and Modern Finance Theory. Journal of Finance 33 (1978) 3, 693-705.

Robinson T.A. / Taylor, Mark P. (1998a): The Effects of Regulation and Regulatory Risk in the UK Electricity Distribution Industry. Annals of Public and Cooperative Economics (69) 1998 (3), 331-346.

Robinson T.A. / Taylor, Mark P. (1998b): Regulatory Uncertainty and the Volatility of Regional Electricity Company Share Prices: The Economic Consequences of Professor Littlechild. Bulletin of Economic Research (50) 1998 (1), 37-46.

Rogerson, William P. (1992): Optimal Depreciation Schedules for Regulated Utilities. Journal of Regulatory Economics 4 (1992), 5-33.

Rogerson, William P. (1997): Intertemporal Cost Allocation and Managerial Investment Incentives: A Theory Explaining the Use of Economic Value Added as a Performance Measure. Journal of Political Economy 105 (1997) 4, 770-795.

Roll, Richard (1977): A Critique of the Asset Pricing Theory's Tests – Part I: On Past and Potential Testability of the Theory. Journal of Financial Economics 4 (1977) 2, 129-176.

Rose, Nancy L. (1985): The Incidence of Regulatory Rents in the Motor Carrier Industry. Rand Journal of Economics 16 (1985) 3, 299-318.

Ross, Stephen A. (1978): The Current Status of the Capital Asset Pricing Model. Journal of Finance 33 (1978) 3, 885-901.

Rothwell, Geoffrey S. / Gómez, Tomás (2003): Electricity Economics: Regulation and Deregulation. New York et al. 2003.

Rudolph, Bernd (1986): Neuere Kapitalkostenkonzepte auf der Grundlage der Kapitalmarkttheorie. zfbf 38 (1986) 10, 892-898.

Rudolph, Bernd / Johanning, Lutz (2004): Untersuchung der Aktienkursentwicklung der Deutschen Telekom AG. In: Regulation and Capital Market Evaluation in Telecommunications, ed. by Hermann-Josef Piepenbrock, Fabian Schuster and Ernst-Olav Ruhle, Lohmar – Cologne 2004, 1-50.

Sawkins, John W. (1996): Balancing Multiple Interests in Regulation: An Event Study of the English and Welsh Water Industry. Journal of Regulatory Economics (9) 1996, 249-268.

Schildbach, Thomas (1993): Kapital- und Substanzerhaltung. In: Handwörterbuch der Betriebswirtschaft, ed. by Waldemar Wittman et al., Stuttgart 1993, 2088-2101.

Schmalensee, Richard (1989): An Expository Note on Depreciation and Profitability Under Rate-of-Return Regulation. Journal of Regulatory Economics 1 (1989) 3, 293-298.

Schneider, Dieter (1992): Investition, Finanzierung und Besteuerung. 7th edn., Wiesbaden 1992.

Schneider, Dieter (2001): Substanzerhaltung bei Preisregulierungen: Ermittlung der "Kosten der effizienten Leistungsbereitstellung" durch Wiederbeschaffungsabschreibungen und WACC-Salbereien mit Steuern? In: Neuere Ansätze der Betriebswirtschaftslehre – in memoriam Karl Hax, zfbf-Sonderheft 47-01, ed. by Gert Laßmann, Düsseldorf / Frankfurt 2001, 37-59.

Schüler, Andreas (2000): Unternehmensbewertung und Halbeinkünfteverfahren. DStR (38) 2000, 1531-1536.

Schweitzer, Marcell / Küpper, Hans-Ulrich (2003): Systeme der Kosten- und Erlösrechnung. 8th edn., Munich 2003.

Serfling, Klaus / Pape, Ulrich (2001): Risikoadjustierte Eigenkapitalkosten öffentlicher Unternehmen. Zeitschrift für öffentliche und gemeinwirtschaftliche Unternehmen 24 (2001) 3, 308-325.

Sharpe, William F. (1964): Capital Asset Prices: A Theory of Market Equilibrium under Conditions of Risk. Journal of Finance 19 (1964) 3, 425-442.

Shuttleworth, Graham / MacKerron, Gordan (2002): Guidance and Commitment: Persuading the Private Sector to Meet the Aims of Energy Policy. A Report for Powergen plc by NERA, December 17, 2002.

Sieben, Günter (1974): Kritische Würdigung der externen Rechnungslegung unter besonderer Berücksichtigung von Scheingewinnen. zfbf 26 (1974), 153-168.

Sieben, Günter / Diedrich, Ralf / Price Waterhouse (1996): Kosten und Erlöse in der Stromversorgung. Gutachten zur Bestimmung der kalkulatorischen Kosten unter besonderer Beachtung der Unternehmenserhaltung. By order of Verlags- und Wirtschaftsgesellschaft der Elektrizitätswerke m.b.H. – VWEW, Frankfurt am Main, Köln / Berlin, April 1996.

Sieben, Günter / Maltry, Helmut (2002a): Netznutzungsentgelte für elektrische Energie: Gutachten zu den Grundsätzen der Bestimmug von Netznutzungsentgelten für elektrische Energie auf der Basis einer Kostenermittlung unter besonderer Beachtung der Unternehmenserhaltung. Frankfurt am Main 2002.

Sieben, Günter / Maltry, Helmut (2002b): Zur Bemessung kalkulatorischer Abschreibungen und kalkulatorischer Zinsen bei der kostenbasierten Preisermittlung von Unternehmen der öffentlichen Energieversorgung. BFuP 54 (2002) 4, 402-418.

Sieben, Günter / Schildbach, Thomas (1973): Substanzerhaltung und anteilige Fremdfinanzierung: Ein Beitrag zur Behandlung des Schuldenproblems in Jahresabschlüssen bei Geldentwertung. In: BFuP 25 (1973) 10, 577-592.

Siegel, Jeremy J. (1999): The Shrinking Equity Premium: Historical Facts and Future Forecasts. Journal of Portfolio Management 26 (1999) 1, 10-17.

Siegel, Theodor (2002): Kosten der effizienten Leistungserstellung im Falle von Preisregulierungen. In: Aktuelle Aspekte des Controllings, Festschrift für Hans-Jörg Hoitsch, ed. by Volker Lingnau und Hans Schmitz, Heidelberg 2002, 243-266.

Spann, Robert M. (1974): Rate of Return Regulation and Efficiency in Production: An Empirical Test of the Averch-Johnson Thesis. Bell Journal of Economics 5 (1974) 1, 38-52.

Spiegel, Yossef (1994): The Capital Structure and Investment of Regulated Firms under Alternative Regulatory Regimes. Journal of Regulatory Economics 6 (1994), 297-319.

Spiegel, Yossef (1996): The Choice of Technology and Capital Structure under Rate Regulation. International Journal of Industrial Organization 15 (1996) 2, 191-216.

Spiegel, Yossef / Spulber, Daniel F. (1994): The Capital Structure of a Regulated Firm. Rand Journal of Economics 25 (1994) 3, 424-440.

Spiegel, Yossef / Spulber, Daniel F. (1997): Capital Structure with Countervailing Incentives. Rand Journal of Economics 28 (1997) 1, 1-24.

Spiegel, Yossef / Wilkie, Simon (1996): Investment in a New Technology as a Signal of Firm Value under Regulatory Opportunism. Journal of Economics & Management Strategy 5 (1996) 2, 251-276.

Spulber, Daniel F. (1989): Regulation and Markets. Cambridge/Mass. 1989.

Stehle, Richard (1999): Renditevergleich von Aktien und festverzinslichen Wertpapieren auf Basis des DAX und des REXP, Working Paper, Institut für Bank-, Börsen- und Versicherungswesen, Humboldt University of Berlin 1999.

Stehle, Richard / Hartmond, Anette (1991): Durchschnittsrenditen deutscher Aktien 1954-1988. Kredit und Kapital 1991 (3), 371-411.

Studness, Charles M. (1995): The Flawed Case for Stranded Cost Recovery. Public Utilities Fortnightly, February 1, 1995, 38-40.

Subrahmanyam, Marti G. / Thomadakis, Stavros B. (1980): Systematic Risk and the Theory of the Firm. Quarterly Journal of Economics 94 (1980) 3, 437-451.

Sullivan, Timothy G. (1977): A Note on Market Power and Return to Stockholders. Review of Economics and Statistics 59 (1977) February, 108-113.

Swoboda, Peter (1973): Die Kostenbewertung in Kostenrechnungen, die der betrieblichen Preispolitik oder der staatlichen Preisfestsetzung dienen. zfbf 25 (1973), 353-367.

Swoboda, Peter (1996): Zur Anschaffungswertorientierung administrierter Preise (speziell in der Elektrizitätswirtschaft). BFuP 48 (1996) 4, 364-381.

Taggart, Robert A. Jr. (1981): Rate-of-Return Regulation and Utility Capital Structure Decisions. Journal of Finance 36 (1981) 2, 383-393.

Taggart, Robert A., Jr. (1985): Effects of Regulation on Utility Financing: Theory and Evidence. Journal of Industrial Economics 33 (1985) 3, 257-276.

Teets, Walter (1992): The Association between Stock Market Responses to Earnings Announcements and Regulation of Electric Utilities. Journal of Accounting Research 30 (1992) 2, 274-285.

Teisberg, Elizabeth Olmsted (1994): An Option Valuation Analysis of Investment Choices by a Regulated Firm. Management Science (40) 1994 (4), 535-548.

The Economist, various editions.

Thomadakis, Stavros B. (1976): A Model of Market Power, Valuation and the Firm's Return. Bell Journal of Economics and Management Science 7 (1976) Spring, 150-162.

Thompson, Howard E. (1991): Regulatory Finance – Financial Foundations of Rate of Return Regulation. Boston/Dordrecht/London 1991.

Trigeorgis, Lenos (1993): Real Options and Interactions with Financial Flexibility. Financial Management 22 (1993), 202–224.

Trigeorgis, Lenos (1996): Real Options: Managerial Flexibility and Strategic Resource Allocation. Cambridge/Mass. / London 1996.

Trout, Robert R. (1979): The Regulatory Factor and Electric Utility Common Stock Investment Values. Public Utilities Fortnightly, November 22 1979, 28-31.

UCTE – Union for the Co-ordination of Transmission of Electricity (2002): UCTE Systems Adequacy Forecast 2003 – 2005. December 2002.

utilityregulation.com (2003): Costing definitions and concepts. http://www.utilityregulation.com/essays/et1.htm.

Valletti, Tommaso M. / Hoernig, Steffen / Barros, Pedro P. (2001): Universal Service and Entry: The Role of Uniform Pricing and Coverage Constraints. Journal of Regulatory Economics 21 (2001) 2, 169-190.

VDN – Verband der Netzbetreiber VDN e.V. beim VDEW (2002): Leistungsbilanz der allgemeinen Stromversorgung in Deutschland: Vorschau 2003 bis 2005. Berlin, November 2002.

Vogelsang, Ingo (2002): Incentive Regulation and Competition in Public Utility Markets: A 20-Year Perspective. Journal of Regulatory Economics 22 (2002) 1, 5-27.

Weisman, Dennis L. / Kang, Jaesung (2001): Incentives for Discrimination when Upstream Monopolists Participate in Downstream Markets. Journal of Regulatory Economics 20 (2001) 2, 125-139.

Welch, Ivo (2000): Views of Financial Economists on the Equity Premium and on Professional Controversies. Journal of Business 73 (2000) 4, 501-537.

Whittington, Geoffrey (1998): The Role of Current (Replacement) Cost Accounting for Regulated Businesses. In: Proceedings 23, The Financial Methodology of "Incentive" Regulation: Reconciling Accounting and Economics, Proceedings 23, ed. by Peter Vass, Centre for the Study of Regulated Industries, University of Bath, 1998, 41-61.

Wiese, Jörg (2003): Bedingungen für die Irrelevanz persönlicher Steuern im Capital Asset Pricing Model mit deutschem Steuersystem. Working Paper 2003-03, Munich School of Management, Ludwig Maximilian University of Munich, May 2003.

Wiese, Jörg (2004): Unternehmensbewertung mit dem Nachsteuer-CAPM? Working Paper 2004-01, Munich School of Management, Ludwig Maximilian University of Munich, February 2004.

Wilson, Robert (2002): Architecture of Power Markets. Econometrica 70 (2002) 4, 1299-1340.

Witte, Eberhard (2002): Telekommunikation: Vom Staatsmonopol zum privaten Wettbewerbsmarkt. ZfB-Ergänzungsheft 3/2002, 1-49.

Yard, Stefan (2004): Costing Fixed Assets in Swedish Municipalities: Effects of Changing Calculation Methods. International Journal of Production Economics 87 (2004), 1-15.

Zalewska-Mitura, Anna / Hall, Stephen G. (1999): Examining the First Stages of Market Performance: A Test for Evolving Market Efficiency. Economics Letters 64 (1999) 1, 1-12.

Zimmermann, Gebhard (1998): Kalkulation von Zinskosten in nach Substanzerhaltung strebenden Betrieben. Kostenrechnungspraxis 42 (1998) 2, 101-102.

Zimmermann, Gebhard (2003): Die kalkulatorischen Kosten bei der Kalkulation von Netznutzungsentgelten, Gutachten im Auftrag des Bundeskartellamts, Oldenburg, October 15, 2003.

Zimmermann, Peter (1997): Schätzung und Prognose von Betawerten: Eine Untersuchung am deutschen Aktienmarkt. Bad Soden/Ts. 1997.

Index

CPSIA information can be obtained
at www.ICGtesting.com
Printed in the USA
LVHW081252110220
646562LV00007B/60

9 783540 308010

Pico-solar Electric Systems

This book provides a comprehensive overview of the technology behind the pico-solar revolution and offers guidance on how to test and choose quality products. The book also discusses how pioneering companies and initiatives are overcoming challenges to reach scale in the marketplace, from innovative distribution strategies to reach customers in rural India and Tanzania, to product development in Cambodia, product assembly in Mozambique and the introduction of 'pay as you go' technology in Kenya.

Pico-solar is a new category of solar electric system which has the potential to transform the lives of over 1.6 billion people who live without access to electricity. Pico-solar systems are smaller and more affordable than traditional solar systems and have the power to provide useful amounts of electricity to charge the increasing number of low power consuming appliances from mobile phones, e-readers and parking meters, to LED lights which have the power to light up millions of homes in the same way the mobile phone has connected and empowered communities across the planet.

The book explains the important role pico-solar has in reducing reliance on fossil fuels while at the same time tackling world poverty and includes useful recommendations for entrepreneurs, charities and governments who want to participate in developing this exciting and rapidly expanding market.

John Keane is Managing Director and a founding member of SunnyMoney, the largest distributor of pico-solar lighting products in Africa. Previously, he was Head of Programmes for SolarAid, the international NGO that set up and owns SunnyMoney. He became acutely aware of the pressing need for affordable, renewable energy in off-grid communities from living in the village of Uhomini in rural Tanzania as a volunteer in 2000. He has since spent more than a decade leading and developing solar projects across east and west Africa and has played an instrumental role in building both SolarAid and SunnyMoney into respected international organisations.

Earthscan Expert Series
Series editor Frank Jackson

Solar:

Grid-Connected Solar Electric Systems
Geoff Stapleton and Susan Neill

Pico-solar Electric Systems
John Keane

Solar Domestic Water Heating
Chris Laughton

Solar Technology
David Thorpe

Stand-alone Solar Electric Systems
Mark Hankins

Home Refurbishment:

Sustainable Home Refurbishment
David Thorpe

Wood Heating:

Wood Pellet Heating Systems
Dilwyn Jenkins

Renewable Power:

Renewable Energy Systems
Dilwyn Jenkins

Energy Management:

Energy Management in Buildings
David Thorpe

Energy Management in Industry
David Thorpe